Leading and Managing in Silicon Valley

Thomas Hempel
Marilson Campos
Leo Dagum
Sam Hahn
Ed Komo
Byron S. Lee
Mike Moody
Jacob A. Taylor

Leading and Managing in Silicon Valley

ISBN: 978-0-615-28365-4
Library of Congress Control Number: 2009902712
Revision: 1.0

All persons or entities named in this work are fictitious. Any resemblance to real entities or persons, living or dead, is purely coincidental. This book is intended as a general guide, but the advice given cannot be applied literally to your situation without proper adjustment to your particular circumstances.

If you would like to give us any feedback or suggestions, you can contact us by email at info@leadingmanagingsiliconvalley.com. Also visit us on the web at www.leadingmanagingsiliconvalley.com for the latest updates.

Acknowledgments

Special thanks to Stephen McHenry for organizing VPE/CTO Community of Practice (COP) and for motivating us to write the book, and to everyone in the VPE/CTO COP for all their advice. We also want to thank a couple of folks who contributed shorter parts of the book. Ron Park made valuable contributions to the chapter on Open Source. George Chitouras, Graham Golder, Dave McClaren, and Bob Quinn also contributed to the early evolution of the text. Thanks also go to Mark Wegman and Frieda Naaijer from WCC for their comprehensive review and comments on the draft. We would also like to thank Kimberly Wiefling for her advice on publishing.

We would not have finished the book without our trusty editor Kristine Magadia who worked ever so hard cleaning up our convoluted drafts.

Last but not least we need to thank our families for putting up with our Tuesday phone calls all these many months.

Table of Contents

Preface

The Intersection of Management and Technology

In any technology-oriented company, there is a mass of talented engineers skilled in technical matters but generally not too versed in management and business. In turn, a team of executives with a clear understanding of the market opportunity, customers, and financial situation oversees the organization. Often though, these executives do not understand the technical implications of their efforts. In every organization, there is some level of management that has to bridge this gap, understanding how to manage the engineering focused parts of the organization while using their engineering knowledge to act as an interface between the business and the product sides of the organization. In a small company, this role is filled by the vice-president of Engineering (VPE) or the chief technology officer (CTO). In big companies, on the other hand, directors or even senior managers find themselves in this role.

These jobs are immensely hard to perform because they require understanding an enormous range of topics and marrying different ways of thinking and personality traits— from finance, to marketing and the details of different development techniques. It is also a difficult job to learn because in our compartmentalized and specialized world, there is little instruction in such a thing. You can find many books on how to become a good engineer or a good manager, but where can you learn how to do both? Also, you often find yourself as the only person doing this job in your company or division. Thus, there are not many people to turn to with whom you can exchange ideas.

If you find yourself on this frontier between management and technology, then this book is for you. We have tried to write a practical guide to the myriad disciplines involved in modern engineering leadership. We are not advancing any particular point of view, rather, we want to give you a very down-to-earth orientation as to how to cope with all the major skills required to succeed as a hi-tech leader. We have tried hard to capture what works from our own experience and to provide overviews and specific advice that you can directly apply.

Who are we?

This book was written by a number of Silicon Valley Engineering directors, VPEs, and CTOs. Our combined experiences span a diverse set of companies, from startups to Fortune 500. While most of these companies are engaged in software development, ranging from open source to embedded systems, some are also in the hardware field.

Our recognition that our jobs are a quite unique combination of management, technical, and business skills led us to form the VPE/CTO COP. This organization allows us to get together monthly to exchange ideas and learn from expert speakers. The great thing about this club, other than the excellent dinners associated with the meetings, is the realization that we are not alone. We share similar problems. Since most of us have few people at work whom we can discuss our jobs with, this group provides an excellent source of support, learning, and discovery.

Why a Book?

During our meetings, we had an idea to share our knowledge with all the people doing this kind of work who are not so lucky to belong to our august society. We've also never really seen a book specifically about our line of work; most of us have simply learned on the job. Thus, we decided to author a book of best practices and lessons learned so the engineering managers and others associated with the practice of software engineering can benefit from the combined experiences of the VPE/CTO COP members.

Our Target Audience

- Current vice-presidents and directors of Engineering, as well as the occasional CTO

- Aspiring engineering managers
- Software engineers considering moving into management
- Software engineers trying to better understand their work environment
- Colleagues of software engineering VPs/management

Other Interested Parties

- Non-engineering managers
- Chief Executive Officers (CEOs) and other C-level peers to learn more about the VPE role
- Business schools or Master of Computer Science (MSCS) programs

Lessons from the Book

- Responsibilities of an engineering leader
- Characteristics of a good engineering leader
- What do engineering leaders and managers do?
- How do engineering leaders think?
- What are the problems engineering leaders solve?
- Common mistakes made by engineering leaders

Being hi-tech folks, we decided to collaboratively write the book as a Wiki, and then later extract the resulting pages to create a book. This turned out to be a very productive way of working since it allowed us to closely collaborate almost sentence-by-sentence. Unlike in a traditional compendium of this kind where different people would write different chapters, this book is entirely our collective effort, although the reader will surely find in these pages the different viewpoints we cooperatively bring to the table. Since we come from a range of companies— from small startups to very big ones— we often cover topics from multiple angles, reflecting how these topics change as a company matures. We also include some fun stories about our adventures along the way. We tried to include both examples of how to do things right as well as how to do things wrong, although the latter are often infinitely more entertaining.

While the Wiki was a good idea, our hectic schedules as senior managers became a challenge to us. It was very easy to get distracted from the arduous work of creating prose. To address this issue, we arranged a sequence of weekly teleconferences to discuss the progress of the project. Since no one wanted to admit on the phone to being unproductive, these phone calls worked wonders at getting the book done.

Little did we realize when we started that this would turn into a two-year project, but here we are, so enjoy reading this book! We hope you will learn something valuable.

Find Us Online

If having read this book you want to learn more, please visit our web site at www.leadingmanagingsiliconvalley.com. There you will find the latest updates and discussion of the material. You can also email us at info@leadingmanagingsiliconvalley.com.

1. Role of the Engineering Leader

This book will discuss the various functional, technical, and people-related tasks that Engineering directors and vice-presidents should accomplish. But before we go there, we should define first what the job is, what makes it special, and what it takes to get, keep, and succeed at this role. Since nothing lasts very long in Silicon Valley, we should also discuss when it is time to leave!

1.1 Engineering Leader Defined

What Job is this?

In discussing engineering leadership, we are looking at individuals with a vice-president or director title. Viewed organizationally, this person is simply the titular head of Engineering for an organization, and both runs that organization and represents it to the other functions of the company. A little more interesting is to look at the job functionally. Here, we see a plethora of tasks and responsibilities to be mastered. These are:

- Working with Product Management to define a Product Roadmap
- Providing engineering leadership to execute on that roadmap
- Hiring, managing, motivating and growing the people in an engineering organization
- Figuring out how and where to find those people
- Interacting with the company's senior management team and often the board of directors.
- Interacting with all the other organizations in the company
- Worrying about budgets, patents, security, and host of other issues.

That is a mouthful and we will tackle these in detail later in the book. However, none of these answers the questions as to what personal characteristics and skills one must have to succeed at this job.

Important Skills

Because of the breadth of the job as well as its variation from one company to another, the VPE/CTO COP did a survey on its members, a group of approximately 25 VPEs and a few CTOs, to discover the most important skill set for an engineering leader. Each participant distributed 100 points among a set of skills that was derived from an open discussion.

Here is the resulting list together with the points our members assigned to each:

Skill	Definition	Score
Execution	Ability to work with the entire company to accomplish business goals	100
Build and manage the team	Hire good people, coach, and develop existing team members, and transition out poor performers	96
Lead with integrity and principles	Act with integrity and establish a culture of honesty, credibility, and reliability	75
Manage well upwards and sideways and represent the Engineering view	Work effectively with CEO and board of directors as well as executive peers	65
Understand the business goals and strategy	Be able to communicate company goals in a way that makes sense to Engineering	58
Ability to work with ambiguous or incomplete information	Steer a clear course with best information available	30
Strong technical background	Sets company technical direction in all areas— Development, IT, Sales, and Marketing	30
Balance delegation and detailed management	Know how much leeway to give and when to drill down in details	30
Build relationships and develop consensus throughout the company	Work with other groups such as Sales and Marketing to help drive toward a united goal	30
Communicate and inspire with the company vision	Communicate strategy and vision into actionable principles for your teams	20
Customer understanding	Ability to work closely with customers and understand their worlds	12

Grace under fire	Act as a calming influence during crisis, boosting morale, and increasing confidence	6
Adapting your management style for different situations	Able to move away from your comfort zone to use most appropriate methods	5
Risk management	Able to balance risk and reward and communicate this with the company	5
Deep understanding of what is really happening in the company	Listens well and talks with people at all different levels and departments	5

Analysis of Skill Survey Results

While the results offer us some insight into what experienced managers feel are the most important skills for their job, one has to be careful not to draw too strong conclusions from this sort of data. People have different interpretations and experiences that influence what they read into the traits listed above. Some managers felt that many of the skills listed were nearly identical, while others sought an even more subtle distinction between points.

However, there are some general conclusions that are safe to draw. First, the participants agree that most important skills have to do with getting the job done: executing, building, and managing the team. The second most important group of skills was leading with integrity, managing upwards and sideways, and understanding the business.

Also, it is interesting that none of the more technically oriented skills were at the top of the list. While this is probably partly due to the fact we assumed that the leader has technical skills, it is still interesting how low these results were. This is an important reminder that this is an executive management job. No matter how good their technical skills are, the successful vice-president/director is still a leader, communicator, and organizer.

One of the highly ranked skills is different from the others— and that is leading with integrity. While the other skills are pragmatic skills of being an effective manager, leading with integrity is more of a value and an approach to the job. In a discussion, the VPE/CTO COP group felt that the leader is often called upon to be the voice of reason and the sometimes to be forced to deliver the unpleasant truths. While it is fairly common for Marketing and Sales departments to lead with optimism, even when unfounded, it is the actual job of the engineering leader to keep the company tied to reality. A number of us said they would leave a job that forces them to compromise on their integrity, and several of us have. Others have pointed out that while there may be gray areas around integrity, companies that operate too close or too long in this area are ultimately headed for disaster. Executives often have to operate with unknowns and partial information and leading with integrity is one of the principles that can guide you through this.

1.2 Becoming an Engineering Leader

Your Career Development

Your career development is your responsibility. If you are lucky, you can find a mentor or a professional organization from whom you can get valuable help but the ultimate responsibility is still going to be yours. At each stage of your career, you must learn the skills for your current position and start discovering the background needed for your next position.

One of the most valuable things is simply having an understanding of the roles of other positions. Nothing could be worse than fighting to get to a job you dislike. In a perfect world, you have a close role model for your next "target" position. You can observe that person in action; learn the rewards, roles, responsibilities, and challenges before making a commitment. At each position, there will be more than one way you can proceed and it is important that you explicitly choose the direction you want. One of the most fundamental career choices is to stay technical or choose the management path. It is presumed that you have selected to read this book because you have already chosen the management route or simply because you want to understand what make a senior engineering manager tick.

Reviewing your resume is one way to evaluate how your efforts are aligned with your goals. A resume should tell a story. If the story that your resume represents does not match your goals, you should try to identify the missing points typical in positions for which you want to be hired.

Advancing your Career

The pace at which you develop your career depends on a several factors including:

- **Prior experience**

  Have you built a solid foundation for the next career change?

- **Is the career change in a new industry?**

  If you have been a software manager and are considering a Director of Systems position (hardware, software, and ASICS, among others), ask yourself, "Am I technically prepared for the new challenges?"

- **State of the industry**

  It is generally easier to take risks when times are booming. Hiring companies are a little more forgiving when the talent pool is tight. Likewise, in difficult times (after the bubble), your risks are greater because you are signing up for more responsibility in a time when business success is more difficult and your backup plans are more limited.

You also need to examine your personal risk tolerance:

- You need to consider the cash flow needed for you to operate as a person or family. Career advancement means taking more risks. If you do not have any financial protection against unplanned situations, it is going to be very difficult for you to be focused.
- Are you making a risky career change in order to gain valuable experience? Is the risk worth it?
- How much of a stretch is this position for you? You can gauge this by mapping your "experience/skill" history against the detailed job description (make sure you get one for any position you interview). As an example, one of us has not even considered interviewing for several high profile promotion positions. This is simply because of a few lines in the job description that at that time would require traveling extensively, being an industry evangelist, or becoming active in a standards committee that requires a degree of political skill beyond their comfort level.
- Are you willing to live outside your comfort level for the next one to two years or more for the potential monetary rewards and personal recognition?

- What are the downsides? Can you predict or tolerate the potential impact to your well-being, relocation, and valuable family time?
- Do you have a backup plan if this fails? (Maintain your networking contacts)
- Have you discussed the pros and cons with your family?
- Is there an easier way to get to your goals? If your goal is to get to a senior management position quickly, it may take longer at a larger company. Thus, you may consider going to a startup if timing is important to you.

Becoming a Senior Engineering Leader

There are many different paths one can take to get into senior management. Before we cover these paths, let us look first at what makes someone qualified (in order):

1) Strong interpersonal skills
2) Solid leadership abilities
3) Good organization skills
4) Decent technical background

Note that technical skill is a requirement but not a strong one. Also, one can imagine these four items as ingredients for a position and try to identify the ones that need improvement and work on these. A good rule of thumb is to reevaluate your situation every two months. Review your progress in improving in the areas required to position yourself into the next level and seek advice from a trusted peer(s) who can give you an honest assessment of your strengths and weaknesses in these four areas.

Now how does one get there? There is no formula. But the following outline summarizes a typical progression. Note that many of the skills discussed are precisely the things this book will teach you about, so you have found the right place!

Desire

First, you should have the desire to become an engineering leader. A big part of assessing that is your understanding what the role is about. It has a variety of different challenges and demands, as you will discover from reading this book. It is not for everyone, so be sure you understand what it means before deciding you want it.

Start as a Real Engineer

More than most other disciplines, having experience being an engineer helps one to effectively lead an engineering organization. You need to have worked on real projects from start to finish and learned all aspects of the job. You need real experience with the many different ways things can go wrong and the many different ways things can be made right. Learn from your peers on how to be a good engineer, how to build things that meet requirements as well as customer expectations, and how to estimate the time required for a task. Watch and learn from your managers and their managers and think how you would handle the many challenging decisions they make. Listen to the vice-president that you work for. What information do they present? How do they present it?

Your First Management Job

At some point, you will lead a team and/or manage a group. This is when you discover that you can no longer spend 100 percent of your time on pure engineering tasks (i.e. individual contributor). Success will come from delivering projects on time and within the budget. The proper way to accomplish this is by getting the most out of your team by keeping them focused, clearing potential roadblocks early, and making the right decisions along the way. The wrong way to do this is by jumping in as an individual contributor and by trying to rescue the project when things go wrong. The "hero" approach does not scale and will not work when you are managing managers.

Managing Managers

From your first management jobs, you should have learned how to get things done by assigning tasks to people. A big part of your job now is getting things done through a layer of indirection. Just like in your first management job where you learned not to act as individual contributor, you should resist the urge to act as a first line manager in your first mid-management job. Success here will come from helping your managers make the right decisions and not from doing their work for them. At this point, you will also find that your peer interactions most often will be outside of Engineering, most commonly in Product Management and Sales. These interactions are important for advancing your career, so give them the attention they deserve since you will also find yourself interacting more with "upper management". You have to learn how to communicate with them effectively. This means providing directed and actionable answers with no more detail than what is necessary. Learn to admit mistakes but provide remedies so they will not occur again. Learn to assess risk and call it out early so there are no surprises.

Once you have successfully managed managers, you are ready to take on a more senior role, assuming you are at a small to medium-sized company. That may happen through a promotion with your current employer or it may require changing jobs. Almost certainly, it will require someone who knows you well enough to place that confidence in you. So make sure that along the path of your career, you have made the effort to stay connected with your colleagues and bosses who would be willing to trust you with that responsibility.

Our Gigs and What We Learned

First Story

I started working at Acme Corp in 1980. What I learned from Acme Corp. was to spend approximately 10 percent of my professional time (which is different than 10 percent of my working time), making sure I was staying current. If I were to concentrate solely on doing the job and none on maintaining technical currency,

I would eventually lose technical edge, currency, credibility, and relevance. That piece of advice from a senior engineer was very valuable to me. Another one which I felt was very appropriate and valuable was that of all the skills I could be acquiring, the most useful one was to get good at estimating the size of a task. That also has held me in good stead over two decades.

I moved to Acme2 Corp. in 1982. What I learned there was that your first job pegs you as a junior engineer. One almost has to switch jobs to shake off the title "Junior Engineer". While at Acme2, I eventually moved to a position where I had responsibility for people (Department Manager), customer (Marketing/Sales), and budget (Project Manager). In retrospect, this was perfect, as I could operate as a mini-company supported by the infrastructure of a very large company. I learned in this gig the value of "intrapreneuring"— making something happen in a new business area but inside a large company.

I started my first company in 1993 with a friend of mine. The lessons I learned here were many. One was to understand that venture capitalists are more interested in managing their portfolio rather than making a specific company successful.

I joined Acme3 in 1997. Acme3 was a challenge. I learned there how a top-down organization stifles innovation and creativity bubbling up from the ranks. This can work in the short term, but not long-term.

Second Story

I started as an engineer out of college and was quickly promoted to be a director of a software engineering position. Unfortunately, I had not learned the basics of management at that point and was ineffective at it. Feeling frustrated, I started a consulting company with some friends. That was the time when I learned the basics of running a business. When the dotcom boom happened, I left the consulting firm to work for one of our customers to get real stock. At that company, I bounced around in various management jobs until I formed a good connection with a boss who was kind enough to promote me to VPE. The key to my breakthrough was to learn how to build the right kind of relationships with others in the company, and make myself successful even in a relatively politicized environment. Once I had grown into that new role, it was easy finding an appropriate similar job at a much bigger company, taking advantage of a mutually known recruiter. More than ever, I have become convinced of the importance of building and maintaining strong networks of support inside and outside the organization, both to succeed at a job and to find the next one.

Third Story

I guess I am in a somewhat similar situation to story #1. My last position was as a VPE for four and a half years and I am now juggling the possibilities.

VPE at startups

There seems to be more money now than a few years ago so there are more startups. But I think there has been a change in the climate for VPEs. Of course, this is a small sampling but I have run into quite a few positions where the business types are not sure they need a VPE and are considering getting by with a Director level or a just someone in Product Management to manage outsourcing. Another trend I have seen is companies with a CTO seemingly looking for a VPE to "make the trains run on time". You can almost read their complaints about the CTO in the job description! There is also the return of the undergraduate taking a leave of absence from school and somehow getting venture capital funding to start a company. I had thought that went away with the dotcom bust, but I am seeing it again.

Starting a company

I am working with some friends to investigate doing a startup. The positive side is the excitement and the ability to influence things from early on. Of course, there is always the struggle for funding or revenue. I will say you learn a lot about people when you work together with them this way. I have already had one potential startup blow up before there was even any money involved. It is interesting to see how egos and personalities can be an issue even when there is no investment or revenue and people are just getting started.

Going to a larger company for the experience

Another thing I am considering is going back to larger companies after having spent nearly 10 years in startups as a way of learning new skills. I have found that there is so much scrambling in early stage startups that you often do not get to concentrate on any one topic for very long. It tends to give a very broad but not so deep experience, unless you are in a very technology-driven startup. I can see how working at a different capacity at a larger company could give me a chance to focus on new skills. However, it would have to be the right company.

Consulting

I am doing consulting as it comes up but I do not think I have the network to do enough of this to make it full time. I have found it a good experience because it changes your perspective to be a "hired gun", rather than management or an employee.

Fourth Story

I started working with computers early in my life. I had good experience working with different projects and getting a feeling for what computers could and could not do easily. When I graduated from college, I took my first full-time position. I was quite surprised to see a global name-brand product that was worked on by an engineering team that could literally all go to lunch in one car. School did not prepare me for this reality. My initial onramp into the organization consisted of a mentoring period and a simple project. The simple project and the mentoring were both done within the first two weeks. My second project was to rewrite the installation for this program from scratch. While this was a very successful project, it pigeonholed me and the company kept reaching out to me when installations were in trouble anywhere in the organization. I finally ended up asking a VPE if I had to leave the company to get out of installs. He responded affirmatively. I updated my resume and was gone in weeks. Let this be a lesson for all the aspiring VPEs. Sometimes, you are best served by using someone other than your best at solving a particular problem. If you do not rotate who you call on, you can quickly alienate top talent.

In my first company, I gained some valuable technical and business experience and a lot of credibility. I also managed to earn a master's degree while working full-time. I then joined a dotcom company and quickly became a technical expert and started to grow. By gaining an excellent mentor who was on the VPE track, I quickly gained key skills and started to grow an organization by having a track record of consistent quality deliveries.

I decided then to leave and go found another company when I was on the verge of getting on the VPE track. Now I have proven delivery at a company where I was clearly leading all of Engineering. Sometimes, going to a startup entails less money and resources but far more control. Startups also have less existing product to move along and adapt to new technologies and techniques.

As a warning to those looking to rise up in the ranks, it is very important to learn to manage and work well with others. A BS degree and an MS in Computer Science and Engineering did not teach me to project plan, manage down, manage up, or collaborate with peers.

Conclusion

Back to the topic of Career Development, there are many different experiences that could help a person become an Engineering vice-president or director. You need to manage your career by choosing the best option at each junction and then making the best of the opportunities you have. During the dotcom boom many individuals rose quickly to high management positions without spending any significant time as a line manager or even as a senior developer. For a time, they were rising stars but the bust left them without a firm foundation to get another executive position and their job title made potential employers concerned about their dedication to a more modest position. The lesson here is that the vice-president title is not a goal in itself; you must also want to develop the skills and the experience to manage the people and the technology at a company.

1.3 Finding your Engineering Leader Job

To VPE or Not to VPE

The first part of a job hunt is to understand what you want from a job and how well your background fits your ideal job. There are many good career books that can help you examine your background and think about how you want to develop your career. For our purposes, we will assume that you have decided to become an Engineering vice-president or director or continue in that role in your next job. However, understanding what you like and dislike about the work is a good idea because the same job title can mean different things at different companies. In particular, the VPE job at a small company often approximates to a director role at a much larger company.

Startups and some small companies tend to expect the VPE to be very hands on. In the extreme the VPE may be the only developer before funding. If you have no executive experience and you enjoy being very hands on, this can be a way to get your first VPE experience. However, it is important to distinguish between companies that want hands on executives before funding from companies that do not understand what a VPE job is. Some companies that are not primarily focused on technology do not understand the executive and strategic roles of a VPE and expect the VPEs will spend most of their time doing hands on work. These companies might be highly dependent on technology but they may still consider it a sort of implementation detail.

Careful reading of job descriptions can help reveal this corporate philosophy. If you see a job title that combines individual contributor skills with the VPE title, then you might expect they are hoping the VPE title will attract candidates who will then do the work of multiple staff. Be wary of job descriptions such as "VPE, Senior Developer, and QA", "VPE/Developer", or even "VPE/Office Manager"! These jobs can still be good ways to get your first VPE position, so long as you understand what you are getting into. When a company with a very hands on VPE role grows larger, you may be holding the company back unless you have quickly grown your management and leadership skills, or are willing to step aside to a different (possibly CTO) or smaller (possibly, director) role. Your exit strategy is important to consider if you are joining a company as a very hands on VPE without solid VPE skills.

If you have no executive experience and are looking to become an executive with your next job, you will often have to go to a smaller company to get an executive position. In the other direction, you might well find that your executive experience at a small company will mostly qualify you for a director or senior manager position at a much larger company. The same kinds of factors are involved when changing industries or company types. Every individual has to make up their own mind what combination of company size, industry, type, and job titles make sense to pursue.

It is very difficult to get hired into a new level, especially at a new company. People prefer to hire applicants who already have the right experience. So once you have been a VPE, it is easier to get another VPE position. Otherwise, it is hard to break in. Generally, jumping into a new industry or a new level of position is easier if you know people the right people. If someone already trusts you, they may well give you a chance. If you are hired by strangers, they will more likely demand an exact match to their requirements.

In addition, with so much variety in job duties, titles, and industries, it is important not to make the VPE title the only criteria. A good title in a small underperforming startup is not necessarily as good for your career as a lesser title in an established and well-respected company. It is important to look at the company, the people you would be working with, and the nature of that specific job. Keep this in mind as we describe the different ways to find and evaluate these positions.

Where to Get Opportunities

Finding a job can be likened to finding love— it is easiest when you are not looking for it. Success has a lot to do with your degree of preparedness. Good executive positions are hard to find. Unless you randomly stumble into something wonderful out of the blue, you should expect to spend time on the job search. In many cases, the process can take up to a year, so be patient! A good approach is to always think about the next position— build your resume and keep the connections going so when the right time comes, there may already be good opportunities available.

Connections

The best way to find any job is through connections. The people who know you and your abilities are always the easiest and fastest way of finding any job. Knowing the executives hiring for the position and having a common and trusted acquaintance is a huge advantage. Having connections is a double advantage because they can make you aware of opportunities that you did not know existed. Often, this can be quite indirect. One of the authors of this book frequently used a certain recruiter to find engineers and one day asked him if he had any ideas for him. Sure enough, he said he knew one of his other clients had an opening and because both the author and the other client trusted this recruiter, a connection was made! Even though that recruiter knew about the position, he had never been formally engaged for it. This illustrates the power of random connections and maintaining networks of trusted friends and colleagues. There are many good books on networking and building connections. The key thing is that building networks is a habit that needs to be formed early and continually nurtured. Bear in mind also that connections are best made when you are not looking for anything from another person and ideally and when you have something to offer the other person— be it friendship, help, or advice. So plant the seeds early and keep working on it! The more people you know, the better off you will be.

Reputation

Your reputation is closely related to your connections. The hi-tech world is a surprisingly small place. Once you have had a couple of high level positions, people will know what is good and bad about you. When your name comes up for a position, it will be easy to find people who will say, "Oh, I know her, she is really smart!" or, "What a flake!" This explains why it is important to leave jobs gracefully and in general, to avoid burning bridges. In addition to the tight network of people you trust, there is a larger network of people who have opinions about you and you should make sure that that opinion stays positive.

Recruiters

Most large companies and well-funded startups will use recruiters to help find executive candidates. Recruiters come in three main flavors: retained, internal, and contingency. Retained recruiters are consultants hired to fill a position. Internal recruiters are like retained recruiters, but are employees of the hiring company. Finally, contingency recruiters only get paid if one of their candidates gets hired and stays for a while. They usually get 20 to 30 percent of the annual salary.

Retained recruiters typically look for candidates who are currently employed and successful and try to pry them loose for their client. They work a lot through their networks and are very aware of the candidates' reputations. Always remember that the employer pays them so they are emphatically not motivated to help you in your job search and always expect them to side with the employer. Some of the authors have had the experience with recruiters telling them when their staff has submitted their resume to that firm. That could happen to the VPE too! But retained recruiters are also very aware of the need to protect their own reputation and so they tend to very careful in terms of which candidates they present.

While retained recruiters have the advantage of being closer to the hiring company, in some of our experience, this leads to their being more mechanical about comparing resumes to job requirements, rather than looking more creatively to see if there is a match. Because of this, some feel that retained recruiters work best for very specialized technical areas where filtering for specific background is very important.

Contingency recruiters, for their part, are another matter. Many of them handle many lower level positions as well and you need to make sure that they are trustworthy before engaging with them, lest your resume get published all over the internet.

A key danger with all kinds of recruiters is that if your resume is already on file with a company, even if the resume was never seriously considered by the hiring executives, then the recruiter cannot get paid for that resume and hence, they will never present you to the client. Therefore, you need to be very careful to have your resume sent only to a company when they are in a position to look at it properly. The best way to protect yourself against this is not to work with recruiters you do not know and trust. Having good working relationships over a period of time with a group of recruiters is a very useful kind of networking.

Typically, when working on a new opening, recruiters begin by finding as many qualified candidates as they can and narrow those down to a list they can present to the CEO. The recruiter will interview you first and based on their judgment and understanding of the CEO's requirements will decide if you are suitable for presenting to the CEO. The next step will then be a meeting with the CEO. If that goes well, then there will be meetings with the rest of the executive team and possibly with board members as well. These meetings may take many weeks to complete because of the usual scheduling difficulties and the likelihood that other candidates are being scheduled for interviews with these people. However, once a recruiter has candidates into that phase, they are most definitely not going to present any other candidates to the CEO. The recruiter's main goal is to close the deal as quickly as possible and thus, bringing in new faces at this stage will only delay the process. Therefore, it is important to get into the process early. Although you may see an opening going unfilled for months, the only real chance you have of getting in is within the first few weeks of it having posted.

A number of recruiters are pretending that they are doing retained search when they are not. You have to ask point blank if they are retained or they will leave you the impression they are when they are not. A retained recruiter will almost always say it immediately and directly because it is beneficial for them. There is no reason for them to be coy about it. Being submitted by a recruiter can cause you problems because once they refer you as a candidate, they can claim the fee, even if you subsequently apply independently or through another recruiter. Thus, you need to be careful when you allow this to happen. You should not allow recruiters to indiscriminately submit your resume.

Job Postings

Smaller companies or early stage startups may not use recruiters and instead rely on the Internet. Examples of useful websites are Craigslist.org, which is popular in California, as well as LinkedIn. Both websites carry job postings. LinkedIn deserves a special mention because it is a powerful tool for advertising yourself on an ongoing basis so recruiters can find information about who you are and what you do (finding a job when you are not looking for it). LinkedIn can also be used to research on other companies to find out whom you know at those companies.

Executive jobs that do not use a recruiter and are simply posted like non-executive jobs are viewed by some people as a bad sign about the companies' attitude. However, many large Silicon Valley companies with internal recruiters such as Yahoo! routinely fill high level positions in this way. Sometimes, companies will post first and then resort to recruiters only if they are convinced they cannot get qualified candidates from the Internet. Also bear in mind that many job advertisements are posted by recruiters trolling around for resumes. Unless they are brand new, the job postings at retained recruiting companies are rarely useful except as a way to get into the recruiters' files.

As mentioned above, the lead generation cycle for recruiters is the first few weeks after a new job posting. So if you are answering job postings as part of your search, it is very important to stay current with them because after a couple weeks, you will be late to the party.

Checking out a Job

Once you have found out about a job opportunity, it pays to carefully investigate the company and the position to understand if this is something you truly want and if you are someone the company truly needs. You can avoid a lot of frustration and wasted time in a job search by making sure that you are in fact a good match for the job. You should never apply for a job you do not want and for which you would not want to hire yourself. If after reading this book you think this is a perfect job for you and you feel you are a great candidate, then you can start thinking about how to sell yourself to a prospective employer.

Are You Right for the Job?

You should not bother to apply for a job if you have not even decided for yourself that you are right for it. While some people say applying for jobs you do not want is a good practice, it is difficult to give the proper effort and sell yourself with the right attitude if you do not care. This does not mean you have to believe you are a perfect fit or that there is no one else in the world as qualified as you. You simply have to believe that you can do the job and you can be valuable to the company. You should also feel that it would be a good opportunity for you.

Once you have given these factors enough thought, you will be better able to present yourself to your potential employers. Your cover letter as well as your answers in a job interview should explain why you are a good match and what strengths you can bring to the job. Everyone has weaknesses so you should be prepared to discuss how you would work around these. The more you have thought this out, the better your answers will be.

Due Diligence - Is this the Company for You?

Make sure you understand the company and that working for that company is something you want.

- What is the most important aspect for you? Is it the market, investor, salary, stock, people, technology, or title? Do all of these appeal to you?
- What is the level of VC/investor influence?
- What are the key milestones for investment?
- Talk to customers
- Talk to employees and ask what needs to be done
- Talk to ex-employees and ask why they left
- Check out competitors and see if this company is in a good place
- Why did the last guy leave?
- Where is the last guy now?

- Can you trust these people? Can you live with them day in and day out?

Financial Due Diligence on a Prospective Employer

If you are considering joining a company, do some homework first on the company's financials if possible. The key questions you want to ask for privately held or VC-backed companies include:

- **What is the current and projected net profit or burn rate?**
  If a non-profitable company is burning money, then the burn rate and the current cash balance per month will tell you how long before the company will need another round of funding or debt. This is important since each round of financing implies additional dilution from a stock incentive plan.

- **What stage of funding is the company at?**
  Is it Round A? If so, stock options at earlier rounds of funding are generally more valuable than future rounds. In some cases before vesting, the strike price is usually low enough that the employee may buy their shares outright. However, you should be careful in weighing the risks. During the technology bust in 2000, many hi-tech workers were caught by unforeseen Alternative Minimum Tax (AMT) liabilities when they exercised their options and held them at a loss instead of executing a same-day sale or exercised their options before they could sell them. You can talk to your financial and tax advisers regarding all stock option transactions.

- **How many total shares are outstanding?**
  More importantly, if you are offered a job at a startup, what percentage of the total outstanding shares does that represent? It is typical for a VPE to be offered between 1.5 and two percent of outstanding shares at a Round A startup. The percentages drop significantly as the company matures and the risks of longer term success decrease.

- **What is the growth rate?**

    Assuming expenses are contained, the faster the company is growing revenue, the more valuable your options will be over time.

Considering and Negotiating the Offer

Once a job offer is imminent, you need to negotiate terms. You should make sure you understand your worth in the market place. There are a couple of sources of information that can help you:

- Salary.com
- Radford surveys
- VPE/CTO COP compensation data (another benefit of our club)

Negotiation is a skill with specific strategies and techniques. However, there are a few things different about negotiating job compensation. First, the candidate is usually asked early on their current salary and their salary expectation. While some references insist you should refuse to answer this question, it can be a rough way to start the interview process. The safest course is to use the salary references mentioned above to discuss a total compensation that is within the normal range for the geographical region, industry, and company size. While startups will often have compensation packages that are heavier in equity than in salary, established companies will generally be heavier in salary than in compensation. Both types of companies will use a bonus package tied to both candidate and company performance.

While theoretically everything can be negotiated, there are often things that companies are inflexible on. If you are feeling brave, you can try to negotiate in some of the following areas. However, only a few of us have had particular success in the following:

- Accelerated vesting terms (stock or bonuses)
- Change of control or Merger and Acquisition terms
- Severance terms

There are some things that might be negotiable besides compensation that can sometimes help close the deal. Startups can be more flexible with job titles than established companies so there are times when you can get a more desirable title or an additional title. Established companies, for their part, tend to be less flexible with titles. However, they may have more range to negotiate on salary.

The most important thing to remember when negotiating for job compensation is that you are starting a relationship with the company. Some kinds of negotiation such as buying a car can be done without much concern for the future. But with job negotiations, both sides expect to work closely together after a successful conclusion. Keep this in mind when you are negotiating.

Starting Your New Job

Congratulations! You have found your new job. Getting a good start on your new job is critical. Where do you begin? How will you make a good impression? The general concept is to spend the first period of time carefully watching and listening to everything. All the while you will want to act confident and at least pretend to know what is going on. The right mixture of apparent competence and humility will come in handy. It can be a tricky balance.

Initial Investigations

You need to understand the risks and liabilities of the job. You should:

- Find out what your boss wants. What is his vision and what are the deliverables? Check this constantly since he is your first customer!
- Assess the team, understand their strengths and weaknesses, see if people are unhappy, and check for retention issues
- Study the history of the company's products. Will a one-time cleanup leave underlying issues?
- Find out what problems your predecessor left behind

As you investigate, you will get a better sense of the role of Engineering in the company. In companies whose products and services are technology-driven, Engineering is often viewed as critical in creating the value in the company. Companies with products and services that are a mixture of technology and business often view Engineering as more of a support function or—in extreme cases—simply as a cost center. Even if a company is strongly dependent on technology, the CEO and other executive may still not view Engineering as a strategic asset. It is important to understand the role of Engineering in your company and then to lead and manage your team within that context. Keep in mind that not all best practices will be appropriate for any specific situation.

One of your tasks here is to take control of the organization. This requires finding those people you can trust and those you cannot. Here are some of the things you should consider:

- Do you have all directors as direct reports? As an example, one of the authors has been the VPE for three different companies. The strengths, skills, and experience levels of his direct reports at the three companies have been very different. In his first VP role, he managed a team of approximately 60, including five directors and two managers. In the second one, he managed a startup of 12 engineers, one Quality Assurance (QA) engineer, one technical writer, and two college interns directly. At his current company, he manages three directors, a QA manager, a junior IT admin, and a technical writer, each with different motivators and management styles. As a result, the way he supervises the organization depends on several factors: size of organization, attributes of direct reports (most importantly seniority), and company culture.
- Where do you want your organization to be (in six or 12 months, etc.)? Well, it depends.
- What is the company growth or decline curve?
- Can your direct reports scale with the organization? More importantly, can you scale with the organization? Where would you like to end up if the company outgrows you?
- Have you done a stack ranking of your entire organization and distinguish the stars from the weak players?
- What is the seniority of my direct report? The resume will tell a lot in most cases. But if you inherit a new team at a new company, be VERY careful, especially if the direct report is also new at the company. You should fault on the side of "over managing/tracking" of

such direct reports until you understand their predictability and ability to be managed without frequent direction. Also, when you first start at a company, it is a great opportunity to reveal their strengths and especially their weaknesses to your boss. This often makes your honeymoon period "longer" and gives you an opportunity to reset aggressive delivery dates or feature sets you inherited from your predecessor.

• Have you built up a track record with this direct report? If you can trust them, they get a bigger sandbox and are rewarded with little to no micro-management.

Establishing Yourself

If there are serious and urgent problems, you need to go for some quick wins to get credibility and buy time. If you can see some obvious organizational or process inefficiency that can be remedied through management action which requires no extensive technological effort, then go for it! Showing people you know enough to make some tangible improvements will make them more patient as you undertake more ambitious projects. However, you must be careful not to act too rashly. If you act without understanding the company's operation and history, you risk loosing credibility or being seen as an outsider.

After your initial investigations, you begin the learning phase where you discover the company's products and history as well as what your predecessors or peers have done. The larger the company, the longer you might be viewed as a "new person" and be given some benefit of doubt. But in today's fast-moving economy, it is unlikely you can count on more than two to three months of transition before you need to be established and be able to move forward. During this time, you need to figure out what your boss, peers, and staff expect of you and these three groups may well not want the same things. In a large and well-established company with moderate growth, you might be expected to maintain consistency and to "stay the course" rather than make major changes. This kind of role would emphasize following process and protocols so that everyone stays in their comfort level. On the other hand, in a small and high growth startup, you are more likely to be expected to grow the team and mentor staff members to reach their full potential and pull together the team to sprint toward product releases. Some positions are "recovery" operations where the team has been dysfunctional or the previous management has left things in shambles. Here you might be expected to stabilize the situation and then determine which staff is a part of the future and which is a part of the problem. To establish yourself, you have to determine the requirements of your position and begin to make enough moves in the right direction to reassure observers that you understand the situation and you respond accordingly.

The willingness to listen to everyone to get the full story is also important. The more neutral and impartial you can be in the beginning, the more likely people will feel you are giving their opinion a fair hearing. What is especially difficult for new managers is avoiding the tendency to play favorites as well as spending more time with the group you are comfortable with. It is human nature to have more affinity with some people or feel more comfortable with certain groups within your organization. If you came from the software development department, it would be natural to feel more at ease with the software developers than with the QA group or with Tech Pubs. However, if you overdo that, other departments will feel like you do not have their best interests at heart. Thus, you will lose some influence over them. Always remember that your influence is heavily based on your credibility with the team. Management often requires being careful with the instincts you follow and with the circumstances when to let your analytical side balance your natural tendencies.

1.4 Leaving your Job

Reasons for Leaving

The era of staying at one job for your entire career is over. Most people are going to find themselves changing jobs a number of times— sometimes voluntarily and sometimes initiated by their company. While the reasons for both kinds of transition vary, there are many similarities in what you should do and how you should behave. The ultimate goal is to make the transition as smooth as possible to avoid burning bridges or making enemies and, if possible, to create possibilities for the future.

From time to time, it is important to ask yourself, "If I were interviewing for the company that I am at today, would the CEO have hired me? If not, why? What kind of engineering leader would they be looking for?" If it does not look like your profile, you have two options: Try to adapt and fill the gaps or prepare your exit to the next job. Also, you should realize that sometimes the business environment can improve significantly after the biggest obstacles are surpassed. Trying to preserve the relationships with the CEO and the board can help make a better transition in the long run.

When To Leave A Company

Indicators

There are many factors that might influence you to leave. These in-clude:

- You are invited to join a super-hot new opportunity.
- You have this great idea.
- The business has deteriorated or never took off.
- The business model changed (e.g. more consulting/services over product or a hardware business becomes more of a software busi-ness).

- You have lost faith in the rest of the management team and board of directors.
- You believe that you are on the way out.
- You are not empowered to build the product/s to a sufficient level of quality.
- You do not like the area that the product line has moved into.
- You are being asked to compromise your integrity in some way.
- Your ability to run your organization has been or is being compromised.
- The company has outgrown your abilities (yes, it is hard to admit that).
- The company culture has changed and does not suit your work style or personality.
- Personality clashes with other key executives become irreparable.

The Value of Patience - When leaving is Premature

The term "grass is greener" does often apply to searching for new employment. If you are disenchanted with one or more aspects of your employment, you can do some soul-searching. Which of these issues can be corrected? Which of these may likely go away within a reasonable timeframe? Every senior management position has its unique challenges and it always looks better on your resume if you can demonstrate perseverance and stick out in a challenging situation and thrive well enough to contribute to the company's success.

So think hard about any of the above reasons for leaving and make sure it is compelling. You have to make sure that a change will be a change for the better.

Being Asked to Leave

Then again, rather than you wanting to leave, you might be asked to leave. Do not worry because it happens to most of us!

Reasons for Being Asked to Leave a Company

There is a wide range of reasons you might be asked to leave. This includes:

- Incompetence
- Insubordination
- Change in management (new CEO)
- Change in investors (new board)
- Business has deteriorated or never took off
- Business model changed (e.g. more consulting services over product or a hardware business becomes more of a software business)
- Lack of consistent product delivery

Recourse You Might Take if You Feel This was Unwarranted

The most obvious difference between leaving on your own and being fired is the natural desire to reverse the decision. No one likes being fired even from a job they might have been trying to leave. One of the authors has actually been fired two days before he was going to give notice and it is amazing how the same feelings of rejection occur and made him want to fight to keep the job even though he was already leaving. While it is natural to argue and prove the firing was unwarranted and unfair, it is difficult to be satisfied. There are two basic situations where the termination can be reversed: getting the decision over ruled by a higher authority or taking legal action.

The Engineering vice-president or director generally reports to the CEO or to the president of a company and thus, there are only few management levels to appeal to. While you can plea to higher ups, in general, they would have discussed this, especially for executives. While in principle the board of directors or a major investor can have influence on corporate management, they will rarely get involved in these decisions.

Employment law varies by state but generally, many states do not require cause for termination, and a company can always create a case for cause. Larger corporations often have internal Human Resource (HR) department rules that require a specified process to be followed when terminating an employee. However, these HR processes are primarily designed to reduce the risk of wrongful termination suits. These processes may very well not have been followed in your case, but that does not mean you were wrongfully terminated in the eyes of the law. Nonetheless if you believe you have been wrongfully terminated, you should seek legal advice, just be aware that wrongful termination is generally a difficult thing to prove. A VP level position negotiating for an employment contract is very rare. However, there are specific clauses that can be negotiated, specifically those regarding diminishment of responsibilities, diminishment of title, right to annual reviews, and a few others.

Even if one was able to reverse a firing decision, it is unusual that the job will be worth having. CEO's can make the head of Engineering's job very difficult in the normal course of events. Imagine what it would be like if they were trying to drive someone to quit after being forced to take them back. The only situation that would work would be if the firing manager and all their supporters were all gone. While a pleasant thought for the fired employee, this is an almost impossible situation. By the time a situation has reached this stage, it is time to make the best of things and move forward with your career. Most executive firings involve a severance package contingent on the employee leaving quietly. This can smoothen the transition. It is important to retain legal review of your severance package, especially since most companies require you to sign a release clause, making it difficult for you to take legal recourse at a later date. With the exception of cases where there is legal recourse, taking a severance package and managing the transition is the best strategy. Along with passing of the era of staying at one company for your whole career is the passing of the stigma of being fired. At the very least, there was a serious mismatch and it is time to look towards finding a better situation. This starts with making the best transition possible.

Story

One thing to keep in mind is that it is possible to negotiate your release of liability while leaving the company. I watched the VP of Sales do this at the company I was with. He did not sign the release, and actually managed to negotiate a better severance package and then signed. When it came time for me to leave, I took this lesson to heart and modified some of the terms of the release that I did not like. Even though they stick a piece of paper in front of you, you do not have to sign it. It is in their best interest to get you to sign and to keep things amicable. If there are some non-favorable terms, use this to your advantage and have them modified.

Leaving Gracefully

How you leave on the best terms possible is the same whether you initiated the transition or the company did. In fact, it is fairly common that the company announces the transition ambiguously so it is not clear who initiated the action. It is expected that the transition will feel different to the person doing it. When leaving for a new and promising opportunity, certain situations such as having the patience to leave things in a clean state and avoiding boasting about the new job and how much better it is than the old job can be difficult. When being fired, it is difficult to avoid bitterness or to hope that some things fail in order to "teach them a lesson". Both of these reactions are emotional and counterproductive. The goal of the transition is to leave your peers, CEO (if possible), team, co-workers and any partners, and investors or board members feeling you did things in a mature professional manner. It is a small world and you will be running into these people again. These people can be an important part of your network that you will need someday. In addition, it is likely that you hold stock options in the company and thus have a vested interest (no pun intended) in making a smooth transition, as difficult as it may be.

1.5 Engineering Management Dashboard

Introduction

We have already discussed topics such as how to rise to the level of a senior engineering management position and how to get appropriate positions. But how do you do the job itself? This is what we will tackle for the rest of the book. As engineers, we will talk first about what we are doing (Products, Engineering) and then look at both the people and organizational issues involved. We asked ourselves, "What is the best way to give an overview of the engineering leader's position?" We decided to approach the problem by looking at the metrics we use to understand our world. Metrics are the basis of successful management because we cannot definitively assess, control, or improve what we are not measuring.

Thus, this chapter focuses on a basic sample set of metrics any engineering leader would want to monitor. Since every business is different, everyone in real life will want to modify these and add more that are specific to their own business. Not all of these metrics are equivalent in nature since there will be some that you will want to monitor weekly, daily, monthly, or quarterly and still others on an as needed, periodic basis. Nonetheless between them, they capture many variables that needed to be tracked in a healthy organization. These metrics can be compiled using simple spreadsheets in many cases. In large organizations, you will want many of these to be reports that are automatically generated from various databases. Many Silicon Valley companies turn to vendors like Prognostics for certain variables that are harder to measure and for more strategic factors such as customer satisfaction (For up to date information on tools and tool vendors, check out the website for this book).

Roadmaps

Preset a roadmap indicating key deliverables of all products for the planning period. This might also include levels of investment and revenue targets over the same time period. This will give you an overview of where your investments are going and what you are getting in return.

Resources

Make a map showing assignment to projects of all past, present, and known future hires— historically, presently, and for n months into the future. This will tell you what your people are working on. This tends to become more useful as the number of engineers goes beyond a hundred or so. Beyond that size, the nature of who is doing what tends to become opaque to the managers without further instrumentation.

Development

While there are many ways of displaying the data, you want one that provides you a concise overview for each project. Consider the following:

- What are the upcoming milestones? What are the committed dates as well as the current best guess for each date?
- How well is the project tracking to its dates? Color-coding works well for this. The color should be accompanied by both a reason and an action plan if it is not green:
  - ➢ Green - going fine
  - ➢ Yellow - okay, but worries present
  - ➢ Red - in trouble
  - ➢ It is fine to do gradients (yellow-green or yellow-red) to show trend
- You also want a list of any major changes in plan or overall risks that are affecting the project, together with mitigation strategies.
- Graphic progress reports by project can be helpful too

> ➤ Time-to-complete each project
> ➤ Velocity graphs (if doing Agile)
> ➤ Conventional percentage of complete tracking
> ➤ Confidence level in meeting dates per project (in percentage)

This kind of dashboard will help you understand— even for long lists of projects— what is going fine and what you should be worried about. The way teams fill these out and talk about them is often itself a clue regarding the team's health.

Projects for Clients

In companies where client work is done on a project basis, there is a need to track the status of this work— both for internal and external consumption. The external client view is similar to an executive summary. It is designed to abstract away the internal processes and at times, put a positive spin on situation:

- Project start date
- Stage 1 percent complete
- Stage 2 percent complete
- ...
- Estimated completion date

A similar but more detailed view can be available to an internal project team. However, a highly detailed view would be more appropriate for a project tracking system. This higher level view is meant to help other groups understand the general project status and load.

For the dashboard, we are also interested in the summary statistics:

- Total number of live projects
- Revenue involved with live projects
- Projects per client
- Projects in Stage 1
- Projects in Stage 2
- ...

Summary information is very valuable because project-oriented Business teams often focus so tightly on their own projects that they have no overall sense of how much work there is. Sometimes, the project work is not in Engineering but within an Operations group. But in those cases, the head of Engineering is generally responsible for the infrastructure and it is still valuable to see how heavily utilized the systems are from a business perspective.

Internal projects might be handled the same way, giving visibility to areas that are sometimes less noticed by executives. Having items like this available in the Engineering dashboard is an excellent way for executives who are more detached from operational work to understand what is happening "on the streets". It also helps to show how traditionally cost center groups, like operations, IT, or Engineering, impact revenue.

Process Monitoring

Whether the company's output is a service or a product, the work is implemented by a variety of processes, which might be implemented by Operations, IT, Engineering, or Business teams. These processes are a combination of infrastructure, tools, and human work and their efficiency and scalability drive the growth of the company. The human processes require some integration with a time-management system which tracks how long these processes are taking. This can be a sensitive area since people do not want to be driven like automatons. However, it is a good indication of how things are proceeding.

Story

It is worth noting that engineering project management tools and techniques work very well in other departments. Many departments have large projects with many components and tasks and lots of collaboration. At one company, IT adopted an Agile strategy leveraging daily scrum meetings. IT productivity shot through the roof and they were able to get their heads above water and start chipping away at the backlog of strategic projects.

Manufacturing Processes

The following are the metrics that help describe how well manufacturing produces products:

- Widgets per day, month, or year – broken down to different classifications (i.e. color and size)
- Quality control pass rate percentage
- Production line up time

Operational Processes

The following are the metrics for the operational aspects of a company:

- Customer service calls per day, month, or year
- Product return rate percentage, especially as a function of time since shipment
- Product installations per day, month, or year

Business Processes

The following are the key metrics for business processes:

- Projects analyzed per day, month, or year
- Average number of hours per standard project
- Average number of hours for special client requests

Metrics for a SaaS Business Model

With the new wave of in-demand SaaS (Software as a Service) applications, new metrics or dashboard charts are required to monitor the health and status of the application.

- Latency - time to ping key application URL from typical customer site
- Number of active users over time

- Number of peak concurrent users versus capacity
- Number of paying customers or users over time
- CPU utilization, memory usage, network I/O, and Disk I/O over time for each machine in the production environment
- Establishment of key thresholds to safely manage hardware expansion
- Total system uptime on a weekly and monthly basis compared to the customer service level agreements (SLA). Note that the system may still be considered available even though a component may have failed or failed-over.

Quality

These metrics will help you understand how much trouble customers have with the product and how responsive the organization is to pleas for help. It will also help you comprehend how productive your developers and your QA teams are. (We will discuss these more in the chapter on Quality Management.)

- Quality metrics as seen by the customers
  - Customer case trends (by severity and priority)
  - Percentage of cases escalated to Engineering
  - Average time to resolve customer cases at varying severity or priority levels
  - Reliability metrics
  - Percentage of cases resolved vs. cases delayed for a product fix

- Quality metrics as seen in Engineering
  - Defect open/fix/closed/deferred, cumulative, and trend by product
  - Defect backlogs
  - Regression rates (percentage of fixes causing regressions)
  - Code coverage statistics (test coverage)
  - Percentage of time spent on escalations and maintenance
  - Defect percentage by product area (cumulative and by release)

> ➢ Defect fix percentage cumulative by submitter and by product release

- Metrics on processes
  - ➢ Health of builds
  - ➢ Health of automated tests (percentage of test cases automated over time)
  - ➢ Code coverage of automated tests
  - ➢ Code quality metrics
  - ➢ Root-cause analysis (bugs caused by requirements error, design, or coding)

Product Adoption

The goal here is to capture the state of the installed customer base, by version and environment. The more details you can get on the environment of your customers and the trends of changes to that environment, the easier it will be to make platform testing and support tradeoffs. Create a chart for each product and for each active release (defined as still supported in field) of each product as follows:

- Number of active customers per month
- Number of customers by platform, database, or application server (helps to set priorities in QA testing for subsequent releases)
- Number of active installations by language (translation)
- Uptake rate of releases (graphed as the distribution of different releases as a function of time)

For realistic measurements of product usage and adoption, it is recommended that the product include a feature that calls home to the company. A key component of this feature is to offer something to the customer in exchange for their providing statistics. Some examples include:

- Check for updates, patches, and new versions
- Bug submission from within the product
- Product feature requests from within the product
- Accessing a customer support portal from within the product

- License validation, management, and extension from within the product

If statistics are being sent back to the company, it is important to allow the users to turn off anonymous statistics from their submissions. Even when they do this, you will still likely get enough data to determine usage patterns among your releases. Having an anonymous key that is generated during product installation is a good way to send completely anonymous data and still be able to uniquely identify a server. Some installations might also require the ability to perform the same activity where the server does not have direct Internet access. A common mechanism is to allow the product to create a payload that can be inspected by the administrator, to create a website for submitting the payload and getting a response back, and to make a page for decoding the response.

Customer Satisfaction

Customer satisfaction can be measured in several ways. Prognostics[1] make a solid business out of assisting companies in quantifying customer satisfaction. Their survey measures the satisfaction ratings and the importance of several company factors, including product innovation and health. Their advantage is that a company can compare its health against several other companies in the same industry. The service surveys a company's active users by asking them a set of basic satisfaction questions regarding support, product features, product quality, and loyalty taking two key measurements per topic:

1) How satisfied are you?
2) How important is this topic to you?

Large gaps between the results for the two questions are a reason for concern. The larger the gap, the higher is the degree of dissatisfaction. Many companies perform a Prognostics survey on a quarterly basis. With

---

[1] For more information on Prognostics, visit http://www.prognostics.com

the SaaS model where loyalty is measured by monthly renewal rates, one measure of satisfaction is the percentage renewals per month or year. A better measurement for evaluating SaaS products is to look at customer usage of the software over time to see if it is trending either up or down.

Innovation

- Patent filings (by country and including phase of submission). You should track the following:
    - ➢ Date of submission
    - ➢ Phase of the patent
    - ➢ Next milestone, deadline, or event (both the name and the date)
    - ➢ Brief summary of the patent and key claims
    - ➢ Primary inventor
    - ➢ Law firm or lawyer being worked with
    - ➢ Money spent to date

- New technology and processes assessment
    - ➢ The director or vice-president should always list disruptive technologies and/or techniques that can potentially improve the company's strategic position. The goal here is to monitor the advances and maturity of these technologies.
    - ➢ Time is one of the key factors of bringing the best value to the company during the adoption of a new technology. Adopting too early can add unplanned risks while adopting too late leads to a weaker competitive advantage. There is a balance to be reached in adopting any new technology and the leader should have a personal list of potential technology candidates. The same rationale can be applied to methodologies as well. The bottom line is that the leader has to recognize that the market is always changing and it needs to be monitored to detect new trends and forces.
    - ➢ Ideally, the leader should estimate from time to time both the value-added and the effort needed to make the move. Leveraging statistics from the installation base can help decide

when to adopt a newer version of a language or platform and drop support for an older release.

➢ List of potential risks related with Intellectual Property (IP) protection - Protecting companies' IP involves security processes and guidelines. The engineering leader should try to find ways to reduce the risk of leakage of critical information. Bear in mind that in a nimble technology company, protection is often a matter of combining forensic capability. Thus, you can identify the source of leaks with sufficient protection measures to make the leaks prosecutable because the Federal Bureau of Investigation will not help you if you have not taken sufficient measures.

Financial and Operational Metrics

In this section, we will look at some of the key ratios that describe both the economic health of the organization as well as the place of Engineering within the organization.

Revenue per Employee

Revenue per employee is considered a measure of maturity and success for a given company. Statistically, small companies average about $100,000 of annual revenue per employee up to $500,000 or more for large Fortune 100 class companies. For example, Microsoft often leads the software industry in revenue/employee with about $600,000 to $700,000 per employee. Another example is Google that is burning up the charts. According to Reuters, Google's revenue per employee is $1,166,644 as of August 2008.

Multiple of Sales (Valuation)

Company valuation is a factor of many statistics including:

- **Product sector**
  Hot sectors now include web community products (such as MySpace and Facebook), Open Source companies, and Service Ori-

ented Architecture (SOA) based companies. Companies in these sectors are given a premium valuation over those in weaker ones. It is common to find valuations of 10 times the prior years' revenue.

- **Growth rate**
  The higher the growth rate on an annual basis, typically, the higher the price to earnings (P/E) ratio and correspondingly, the valuation of the company. Google is a good example. During the fourth quarter of 2007, Google grew 51 percent (year over year). The company valuation (reflected by the P/E ratio of 33, as of March 2008) was $139 billion.

- **Perceived competitive advantages**
  Being in the right place at the right time with a unique product differentiator garners a premium valuation.

Multiple of Earnings (Valuation)

For a more product-oriented business, multiple of earnings is a common valuation method wherein Earnings Before Interest and Taxes (EBIT) are the standard earnings component to which multiples are applied in determining business sale prices. If EBIT shows no earnings, a multiple is sometimes applied to cash flow and even to gross margin.

Engineering Expense as a Percentage of Total Company Expenses (By stage of company)

As a company matures, the percentage of the research and development (R&D) expense decreases. Generally, an early stage startup spends 50 percent or more of its total operating expense in R&D, decreasing to low teens for a mature public hi-tech company. If the R&D expense is way out of line with these numbers, it may be a sign of trouble (i.e. not investing enough for the future or investing too much at the expense of short-term sales).

Product Management vs. Engineering Expense (For stage of company)

It is usual to have ratios of 10-1 or 20-1 for Product Management to Engineering, with the ratio typically increasing with the size of the company and the complexity of the products.

Developer to QA Ratios (By company type)

At one of our companies, we held to a strict ratio of 2.5 for Developers to QA. As a result, when the company grew, the QA team of 60 against 150 Engineers still met the 2.5 ratio. Some contend that there are higher economies of scale in QA testing and the ratio can be decreased as the company grows. It depends on the product, frequency of releases, ability to automate test cases, and other factors.

Developer to Documentation Resource Ratios

That same company also maintained a strict ratio of one technical writer for every four developers. Thus, as with QA, the Documentation team of about 35 against 150 Engineers still met the 4.0 ratio when the company grew.

Cost of Goods Sold (COGS)

This quantity is only relevant for hardware products. It reflects the total cost to manufacture one unit of a product. Since your business plan assumes a certain gross margin, your goal is to always keep COGS low enough to meet your gross margin targets. Companies often track this by making a graph showing projected COGS over the life a project to map out the impact of differing design changes on the final COGS. Note that it is possible to calculate something analogous for SaaS companies.

Service Margins

Generally, profit margins for products are higher than for service. If the product you are building requires too high levels of service, even if the resulting service business is quite profitable, you will still not meet your profit targets. Thus, a relevant consideration in designing products especially for the ones requiring customization or complex installation is to design enough serviceability into the product to keep your service margins as high as possible while still keeping the overall ratio of product to service margins sufficient to maintain your total gross margins.

Budget Reports

Budget reports show spending for labor, expense, or capital up to the current period, with projections of total spending as well as exit run-rate and comparisons with targets.

Culture

This will tell you your morale and ability to attract and retain key talent.

- Rating of company "fairness" on a scale between "meritocracy" on one extreme and "politically-driven" on the other
- Anonymous employee survey metrics such as employee satisfaction and employee rating of opportunity for advancement
- Turnover rates historically for each major job function and department
- Reports showing salary competitiveness (average salaries by grade versus industry averages)

Lessons Learned

Document adjustments made in the last few development cycles.

2. Product Definition

An engineering organization is only successful if it not only produces great technology, but if this technology also solves real customer problems and can be implemented and sold to those customers in a profitable way. The head of Engineering has a unique perspective of the costs and benefits of building different components and business feedback from Marketing and customers. The head of Engineering has a major role to play using this knowledge to work with other organizations in the company to ensure that their organization is building the best products that it can build with the resources it is spending.

In this section, we will look at all the challenges involved in identifying customers, understanding their needs, deploying appropriate development processes, and defining requirements for solutions to those needs, especially as it applies to the Engineering manager trying to form the connection between Development, Product Management, Marketing, and Sales teams.

2.1 Customer Understanding

Introduction

What role does understanding the customer and the market play in an engineering leader's job? Obviously, it is important for those in charge of technology to understand the people who purchase their products or services. What this means in practice is subject to debate. While even large corporations will say their companies are "customer-driven", not everyone agrees on who the customer is. At both large companies and startups, the authors have been in arguments about whether Engineering's customers are the people who purchase the products or services or if they are the internal business groups such as Product Management, Marketing, Sales, or Professional Services. This is a fundamental philosophical difference between a company, where all departments try to understand the end customers, versus a compartmentalized company, where each department focuses on their "internal customer" and only a few departments such as Marketing, Sales, and Customer Support focus on both the end customers and the market.

Practically, this philosophical difference is connected to how a company is organized and how decisions are made. An argument for having only the customer facing departments concerned with understanding the market and customers is that they have the most expertise. This view compartmentalizes departments into focusing on their areas of specialization, with their major concern of satisfying the internal groups they work with most immediately. This view seems to be present in larger companies where each department tends to protect their own turf. In those environments, the group that represents both the end customer and the market has a powerful leverage in decision-making. This can make them reluctant to share.

In this view, letting every department express their views on the market and end customers would be chaotic. While this kind of rigid separation of responsibilities can look efficient and well-organized, it fails to provide any checks and balances against internal departments that have biases. For example, if the Business groups are comfortable selling and supporting one type of product, they might be reluctant in transitioning to new products even if more neutral groups see this as necessary. In companies with a formalized Product Management function (typically under Marketing), it is common that the product manager will be responsible for colleting the inputs or feedbacks from all respective sources and consolidating that into a prioritized 1–N backlog list.

For Engineering managers, the definition of who their customers are mainly affects how much say they have in product strategies, product management, and requirements. If a company views that all employees should strive to understand both the customer and the market, then Engineering can bring these business points up in product discussions. While this can lead to more arguments, proponents of this view would say that this dynamic leads to better products and services. Certainly, it is more enjoyable, not only for the manager but also for Engineering as a whole. If Engineering is limited to how much it can discuss about the market or customers, it becomes more like a service group or a vendor. When that happens and Engineering is not a full a partner in product development, the best people will leave and the organization will start believing they can outsource all the technology.

The rest of this section will assume that it is important for the manager to understand both the market and the end customer. For those of you in a customer-driven organization that support this, learning how to see the business from more than just the technology perspective is important. On the other hand, for those who belong in a compartmentalized company, it is still critical for your personal development and career that you understand both the market and the end customers. While you might not get to express these views as often in decision-making, it is important you have your own opinions on whether your business groups are making the right decisions or not. Also, someday, you may work for a company that expects their head of Engineering to understand the market, so this is a good time to learn how.

The Customer Perspective

What is the goal of understanding a customer and why is this important? The fundamental issue is to understand a customer's perspective, business, and market. Companies are successful when their products and services address the needs of their customers. This is more complicated than it first appears.

But who really is the customer?

Anecdote

One of my first engineering jobs was with a medical equipment manufacturer, developing an X-ray image processing system specifically designed for cardiologists. It worked fine technically. It also did well in testing with cardiologists and was considered as a dedicated device for them. It was way cheaper than the general purpose X-ray systems. However, it was a complete flop on the market. Why? Because during that time period, the purchasing decisions for all X-ray equipment were made by radiologists. It was unclear to radiologists that a dedicated cardiology system made financial sense and the product approach emphasizes ease of use for cardiologists, rather than technical capabilities, which appeal to radiologists. The company thought they understood the customer by spending a lot of time with cardiologists but they did not understand the complexity of the market. The customer was the purchasing hospital and clinic, which had in it different stakeholders with independent perspectives.

To understand each stakeholder's perspective, one exercise is to consider it from their perspective. What does it take to get a stakeholder their next promotion? What is going to keep them from being fired? What is painful or difficult enough in their lives to spend money for to address the problem? How are the purchasing decisions made?

Customer Understanding is Key to the Entire Product Lifecycle

Customer adoption either makes or breaks a business. It is thus critical to understand the product requirements from the customer perspective. Recently, Mark Leslie, former CEO of Veritas, together with Charles Holloway, documented this viewpoint in their book *The Sales Learning Curve*. This is especially important for startups with limited cash or runway. They have limited time to find solutions that resonate with customers and solve a critical pain point. They need to hit their customer target audience without burning valuable cash as quickly as possible by planning on a few product iterations to test assumptions about customer needs and assist Sales in learning the product's "sweet spot". It's a waste of money to build a large Sales team before the product market validation is complete. There are similarities between this principle and the Agile model of merciless refactoring (i.e. learning from product prototyping early).

The process of a company engaging its customers tying to find the key pain points is hard to manage since there is a chance that the customers will focus on the short-term goals instead of the long-term ones. In order to allow the customers to share the product vision with you, the right context has to be set. There is a technique called "buy a feature" that can be used to engage in customer discussions where they will feel part of the decision-making process. This requires a number of customers' attendance in a meeting. At the beginning of the meeting, you will distribute a limited amount of fake money to each customer and present them with a list of all possible new features or improvements on your product or service. For each feature, there will be a price that corresponds to the cost of implementing it. There will be a facilitator for the discussion but it is important to let the customers lead the process. They can buy a feature as a group or individually. The ideal scenario is to spend the whole day in this process but there are cases where it is possible to implement this process at a conference with potential customers or even during user training depending of the type of product. Ideally, the attendees have a strong pulse on customer needs.

One common error in gathering a customer's feedback is to ask open-ended questions like, "Do you want free ice cream?" A more useful question would be, "Do you prefer ice cream or coffee after lunch?" The second question sets context and exposes a trade off.

The book *Innovation Games: Creating Breakthrough Products Through Collaborative Play* describes several techniques to help better evaluate the customers' needs for a particular product or service.

Product Requirements

Product Management plays the key role in gathering representative requirements use cases and stories. They have the primary responsibility of understanding the roles of the customers and audiences. Product requirements gathering or documentation means more than feature requirements. Information related to non-feature requirements or assumptions must also be captured such as:

- Quality expectations: What is an acceptable failure rate or "mean time to repair" and "mean time between failures"? What is acceptable when a component fails "customer data lost" or "customer needs to re-login but no data is lost" or "loosing data for a short period of time is okay"?
- Performance expectations: What is an acceptable latency for customer interaction? What is an acceptable "task"?
- Key requirements such as speed with which you can diagnose problems, maintainability, availability, scalability, traceability, and failover are often overlooked during an initial product definition cycle but are critical to success.
- Using the Agile model, the collection of simple customer stories or use cases is invaluable. However, they also have to be related to the concept of a user class or "role". Is this user an administrator, end-user, database administrator, or executive?

Of course, creating an accurate document of customer requirements or stories is worthless if there are process problems in the development cycle. The value of requirements traceability throughout the entire product lifecycle then becomes important. It is feasible to formally track each individual requirement through the development process (Definition, Design, Implementation, and Test) but it comes at a high price and few companies use a formalized requirements tracing process. At a minimum, most companies can perform some sort of simple root-cause analysis of all customer bugs and determine what percentage are related to requirements gaps versus design to coding bugs (a key measure of Product Management success). If the percentage of customer issues related to requirements gaps is high, then you have a problem either with the requirements gathering phase or the traceability process.

Gathering Customers' Feedback

Like the proverbial blind men and the elephant, customers' feedback gathered from different parts of a company is heavily influenced by both the perspective and the concerns of that group. This makes it especially valuable to gather feedback from a wide variety of sources so that the information can be weighed and evaluated to achieve a relatively unbiased understanding of the customer. For example, Sales might say the new features are too confusing, yet Marketing loves them and Customer Service does not find a high rate of complaints. This could be because the features make it harder to sell but are actually easy to use or it could be the early adopters are more sophisticated and the customer service issues will show up later. Marketing tends to always love new features and might feel it is just a matter of communication. Balancing these views and seeking other forms of information can help bring clarity to customer understanding.

Sales Feedback

Typically, sales feedback can come from a number of different channels that are normally managed by the Sales function. These include Technical Support, Professional Services, and Sales (Sales Engineering and Pre-sales). Each of these organizations has a different perspective or product interaction with the customer.

- **Support**

  Feedback from Technical Support is invaluable as it includes real world feedback from paying customers regarding both defects and areas of product enhancement. This information needs to be directed to the right organization, based on severity and prioritized effectively. This process is critical to company success and thus, it is highly recommended that you create a detailed flow or process chart for the steps throughout the entire process. It should document all the steps from customer case filing through Support, Engineering, and QA back to Support and back on to the customer. Responsibilities and response times should be clearly identified and set for each phase of the process in order to meet SLAs with the customer. Support is also frequently a source of pre-sales information. What kinds of questions does the prospect ask the Support team? What features are they using? What are the features that they do not understand or need help with? If the prospect is running into roadblocks or is confused, you know where work is needed.

If you're a VP of Engineering who also oversees the company's support function, you have a unique set of challenges. One of these is balancing the relative investment of new development against customer support oriented bug and feature development. There are several factors that help set this balance. These include company maturity (more mature companies with a large installed base must allocate a higher expense to support/maintenance), product industry, stage of company growth and business model (is it renewals based, etc.).

- **Professional Services:**
  The Professional Services team typically is involved with customizing the product above the APIs in order to enable customer success. As such, they collect their own feedback as well as their customers' on a regular basis regarding product extensibility, API documentation, API reliability, and ability to make upgrade safe customizations, among others. Like a support feedback, this feedback has to be documented and logged in a tracking system for future resolution. Professional Services is also a key in hearing about ways that customers would like to be able to integrate the product into their infrastructure but needs a more efficient API, a new API, or an extension to the current API.

- **Presales/Sales Engineering:**
  The pre-sales function, including Sales Engineering, typically deals with a wide variety of leads or sales prospects. Typically, some percentage of these prospects will buy the product. Statistics that document the

reasons why folks are buying (price, features, and performance, among others) should be kept. Likewise, a survey and a root-cause analysis that capture why folks are NOT buying your product should be done. If possible, it is best to track if they went to a competitor or not and what caused them to go to a competitor. This data should be fed directly through Product Management in order to prioritize and influence future roadmap discussions. When a prospect decides to purchase a competitor's product or service, try and track how long it is until they need to renew. Hopefully, your product will have adapted and you can take a shot at them the next time they go shopping.

Gathering Feedback as Part of the Product Lifecycle

Customer understanding is needed at nearly all phases of the product lifecycle, not just during requirements gathering. Once again, the advantage of the Agile model (release early and often) is that it allows you to quickly tune a product to customer needs, assuming the customer has the patience. Other tools and processes useful in gathering this feedback at various stages of product development include the following:

- Development of User Interface (UI) prototypes and surveys (important during design stage)
- A formalized beta phase is highly encouraged, assuming you can get a representative set of beta testers and with the various roles listed above
- Role of Human Factors and Usability Testing is critical in customer advocacy and formal Usability Lab testing with real customers. There is a fine art to professional usability testing. At RRRR Software, we were fortunate to have a dedicated team of Human Factors experts who videotaped the customers and prospects performing task-based product evaluations. These tapes were later analyzed in detail for UI efficiency, frustration factors, documentation, and online help effectiveness. Another great technique for getting early product feedback is the paper prototype. This is where you mock out your program on paper and have the customer interact with it.

One major advantage of having customer understanding permeate the product lifecycle is that there are explicit discussions and decisions on how a customer will react to the product. These models can then be tested against the customer's feedback after the product is released. This should help refine the customer's understanding and help point the way to future improvements. It is also a great way to find out related areas of a customer that your company might be able to help with.

Customer Forums

Another great mechanism for interacting with your customers and getting their input is the use of forum software for the web. Customers can log in, post comments, share feedback, ask for help, and provide help for others. Creating a rich ecosystem of customers is a great learning tool as well as a very valuable service for them. A rich ecosystem can also be valuable in the sales cycle. Many newer companies are using open development practices where their bug database and forums are freely available. This kind of transparency offers great visibility to the customers, lets them gauge the success of similar customers, learn more about the features, and get more comfortable with your solution. Another common trait of open development practices is a public demo server. Not all software is easily made into a public demo, but if it can be, customers can quickly experience for themselves what working with the software is like. This will actually help potential customers pre-qualify themselves before they start working with the sales organization. Customer forums are also a great place to solicit explicit feedback and reactions to new functionality, screenshots of new layouts, and product roadmaps. When asked and given a list of choices, many customers will speak up quite readily.

Customer Advisory Boards

Customer advisory boards can also play a key role in startups that do not have existing customers. The trick is to source and retain members that are representative of your target customer base. If you are a company targeting Fortune 500 companies as customers, it does not make sense to have an advisory board composed of small to medium business representatives.

Once product development is done and the product has been in a customer's hands for some months or years, another tool for getting the customer's feedback is the "Prognostics Surveys" which are popular in Silicon Valley. These surveys can be somewhat expensive but they can track a customer's feedback on issues like product fit to a customer's needs.

Processes and tools for customer feedback can be industry or product specific. As the head of Engineering, you and the other members of the executive staff should find creative ways to monitor the current and target customer base. Ask yourself these questions:

How else can we get Customer Feedback?

- How to capture this information
- How to share it with your team
- How to evaluate one individual versus others
- How to extrapolate from a single individual
- How to mine individuals for collateral input
    - Budget authority
    - Who else is a stakeholder?
    - Regulations or constraints
    - Sources of trust, reviews, and referrals
    - Ways to stay technically current
    - Peer groups— what do peers do

Next Steps

We can answer all these questions more deeply by taking a closer look at Requirements Management and specifically introducing the notion of the application scenario. This will give us a framework for formalizing not only of requirements but also of customer understanding itself.

2.2 Business Planning

Introduction

Why Business Planning?

Business planning addresses the fundamental question of how to allocate capital. Every company has goals of growing its revenues and earnings at a certain pace and has a certain amount of investment capital available to help achieve those goals. This capital can be invested in technology, new product launches, marketing, sales and channel, and partner development, as well as acquisition. Striking the balance between these is one of the ultimate responsibilities of the CEO of a company. Many engineering managers have little experience with or knowledge of how to make such decisions. This can be career limiting in a various ways. In any company, understanding the connection between technical decisions such as wanting to invest in a certain set of technologies and their impact on the company's broader financial strategy can allow Engineering management to interact with both the CEO and the Business team in a more productive way.

In a larger company separated into multiple divisions with a separate profit/loss responsibilities, a significant new career path opens up for a VPE— a promotion to be the general manager of a division, as opposed to just being the engineering leader. This is an excellent stepping stone for a VPE interested in becoming a CEO since this role has a CEO-like responsibility over business planning for the division. On the other hand, in a smaller company, particularly a startup in its formative stages, the VPE may be the founder or co-founder. The VPE may also need to play the CEO and/or Product Management roles as well as their normal engineering responsibilities. In this case, a clear understanding of the nature of sales, marketing, and infrastructure investments and how they need to be integrated with and traded off against technology investments becomes more crucial. Failure to have this understanding often results in the scenario where the manager says, "I know it in my gut." This mindset is the source of many "if you build it, they will come" failures.

What is a Business Plan?

The Wikipedia definition of "business plan" is: a formal statement of a set of business goals, the reasons why they are believed attainable, and the plan for reaching those goals. It may also contain background information about the organization or team attempting to reach those goals.

As such, the process of business planning from an engineering perspective involves:

- At the macro level, a business plan allocates a percentage of expenditure by department, largely based on the stage of company maturity and industry. For example, early stage startups do not need a sales function and as such, the percent of expense by Engineering may be as high as 50 percent of the total expense.
- Defining product scope at a high level as well as the time frames for product staging or evolution. This usually takes the form of a high level product roadmap or timeline with coarse grain dates and high-level features
- Providing personnel and capital requirements (timing/cost details) to meet the product scope above (ideally down to a monthly level). This includes monthly staffing curves for full-time and contract positions as well as capital equipment purchases (hardware and software) and other expected expenses such as travel and entertainment, incentives, and overheads
- Engineering also provides a key role in competitive analysis during the business planning cycle (i.e. defining the value proposition). How are we going to position ourselves feature-wise and technically against competitors A, B, and C?
- Ensuring that any assumptions or dependencies are noted and monitored over time

Most importantly, the business plan has to be perceived and treated as a living document and maintained as assumptions inherent to the plan are either validated or negated over time. This is where most companies fail. Competition changes while technology trends come and go and sales channels may be harder to establish than expected. When planning for competition, Guy Kawasaki recommends, "It's a race, and we're going to work like hell to reach escape velocity. That's the bottom line." A good company has frequent product strategy meetings to fine tune the business plan or if necessary, throw it out and start over. One of the authors, for example, has bi-weekly high-level strategy meetings in his company. Guy Kawasaki, in his book "Reality Check", recommends that one person creates the business plan and does so over a maximum of two weeks. This helps insure that the company is willing to adapt the business plant to reality instead of sticking to a document that may no longer make sense.

Engineering Role in Business Planning

The engineering leader is the "voice of sanity" or "voice of reason" when companies are looking to achieve specific objectives. The engineering leader should evaluate every projected target and product for feasibility and risk. In this way, not only does the engineering leader need to support the objective, but they also need to be confident that the product development organization is capable of meeting those objectives.

Aside from maintaining alignment with the business, the leader also needs to support the business's overall goals. They must be accountable in delivering the results that are demanded of the product organization. This requires a careful assessment of both sides. A manager who is strictly careful, cautious, and risk-avoiding only-willing-to-provide-high-confidence-projection does not serve the business if that costs the business its agility. However, a manager that signs up for every objective with a "can do" attitude risks loss of credibility and respect of both superiors and subordinates if the organization is not able to meet those commitments.

Both the head of Engineering and the VP of Product Management need to be extremely aligned and able to work very well together. This relationship between Product Management and Engineering can make or break an organization. If both trust each other's ability to perform their function and deliver, then the organization has a solid and functioning core. If lack of trust or respect exists on either side of this relationship, the company will be consumed with internal politics and will be unable to look externally, where the attention must be focused.

As Dwight D. Eisenhower said, "Plans are nothing; planning is everything." An engineering manager should remember this especially in performing estimation. It is critical that plans be constantly updated to reflect updates about the business climate, whether they are about technology trends, emergence of common or best practices, competitive situation, or specific customer direction. Any source can affect the business's plans. A company that is not agile is— almost by definition— less likely to be successful than a company that is organized to be one. The engineering leader's role is to constantly assess feasibility, risk, and potential solutions and to increase the communication channels with every other department of the organization.

As mentioned earlier in Chapter 2, some of the organizations that have the best market and customer understanding are:

- Customer Support
- Professional Services (for the companies that have this function)
- Competitive Marketing
- Sales engineers
- Product Management

Channels with each of the above can provide valuable sources of information regarding specific deployment guidelines and constraints, specific product likes and dislikes, usability feedback, performance suitability, and other information that usually are not directly gathered by engineering organizations.

The Planning Process

The Business Plan from the Engineering Standpoint

From the Engineering standpoint, the business plan is straightforward. Over some planning period, it will articulate a set of engineering deliverables based on some timeline at some assumed resourcing level with some set of personnel skills and risks. It will also assert that timely delivery of those items, together with actions taken in the rest of the organization, will meet the revenue targets indicated in the business plan. At the end of the day, as the head of Engineering, you have to convince yourself that the plan is doable and that if done, both the customers and the company will be satisfied with the results. To achieve it, you have to work through the market opportunities, the technical challenges involved in meeting those opportunities, and the resource situation available.

Figuring the Value Proposition

Identifying and reviewing the definitions of each type of customer is a critical business planning effort. As the company learns more about the critical features needed to serve each customer, the product should change in a direction that maximizes the overall financial return. The assessment of financial return is not a trivial task but it needs to be understood as much as possible. The better quality you get from this assessment, the more likely the company is to succeed.

Furthermore, it is important to note that the infrastructure needed to execute the plan can change substantially, depending both on the type of customers you are going after and on the pricing point of the company offerings. An organization that sells a $100,000 solution is different from one that sells a solution using the software as a service model and charges $500 a month for it.

The engineering manager has to work with Product Management and group features in "minimum marketable feature sets". This process allows a better analysis of financial return.

A typical situation is the assessment of a project that needs to have features A, B, and C to position well at one market segment. During the initial phases of development, the company evaluates this area as a key segment and these features are high priority. These features are dependent of each other.

At one point in time, it is clear that there are other market segments that seem to be more profitable than the original one. If both features A and B are done and feature C is incomplete, what is the best course of action? It should be the one that brings a better financial return within an acceptable time horizon, for example, within a year. In making this decision, it would be nice to have a dollar amount in each feature. Reviewing the resource allocation in order to maximize the financial projected cash flows is also important.

The book *Software by Numbers* by Denne and Celand-Huang describes a technique to schedule work using a model based on the time-to-market, the effort to build, and the projected cash flows for each feature.

Planning and Estimation

One of the challenges in doing business planning is to estimate effectively how much effort is required for different kinds of projects. There are three ways on how to do this effectively:

- Have a good understanding of the organization's productivity
- Understand the capacity of the organization
- Have a decent approach in estimating complexity of projects

Beyond mere gut feel, productivity is easily measured if you are doing iterative development and if you can track both the accuracy of the developers' estimates for their pieces and the actual rate at which features get done in each sprint or iteration. This is one of the real benefits of iterative development— one gets a very solid sense of how much can be done in one unit of development time. The capacity of the organization is related to the number of your developers who are already working on committed projects and at what pace they will roll off those projects as they complete. A simple spreadsheet is often a good way of tracking this as it draws up "swim lanes" for different skill sets, showing how people are loaded and how they become unloaded.

Once you understand how many available people you have and how much work they can get done, you then need to estimate how hard each piece will be, assuming you have the right skills match. A good technique is to have a couple of people form an estimate and simply average them. If people have been doing iterative development for a while, they will usually have developed a relatively good sense of how much can be done in one sprint. The key challenge is to decompose large systems and estimate them even prior to understanding the resolution to often difficult technical problems posed by those systems. This can get tricky but this is where experience and judgment come in. You have to make a guess because the business plan depends on it.

Identifying the risks is also an important part of business planning. If there is an unexpected event that delays the product release by a quarter, what is the fallback plan for the Sales force? As a manager, you should think about questions like this. If you can anticipate the effects of your group's actions on the business or sales side of the organization, your challenges and concerns will be received with a more open mind than if you simply create obstacles for the Sales team. When you are done, you should have a set of estimates of effort, schedule, and risk for the set of business alternatives being discussed.

The Rhythm of Planning

Companies usually organize themselves around a fiscal year. During this year, there will be an operating plan comprising a revenue plan designed to generate a certain amount of growth as well as a spending plan designed to produce that amount of growth. The business plan then will define the product development activities undertaken in that year that support the spending and revenue plans. A good way of looking at this is to differentiate between long-term investments that have a horizon beyond the current year and tactical investments with an immediate payoff. Therefore, having three rounds of discussion over the course of a year is a good way of structuring the business planning discussions.

The first discussion, which is held two-thirds of the way throughout a year, focuses on long range "big bet" investments. This set of discussions forces alignment on long-term sales and technology strategy. Held right at the end of a year, the second discussion aims to produce a complete plan for the upcoming year. An agreement on what will happen in the next 12 months should be settled here. Lastly, the third discussion taken one-third of the way into the next year is focused on tactical adjustments to the operating plan based on knowledge from the organization that tries to execute the plan to date. This cycle allows a balance of long-term and short-term thinking and keeps everyone focused on building realistic plans. It encourages converging on and maintaining an executable plan.

In a startup, this cycle may appear a bit different because planning is more dominated by the need to get to particular milestones such as profitability or the next round of funding, rather than to deal with roughly similar annual planning periods. Nonetheless, those milestones will appear either as short-term or longer-term goals as well as an organized set of meetings that cycle between long range planning, detailed execution planning, and tactical refinement.

Moreover, such meetings work better with adequate preparation. It is very important to circulate the main ideas before the meetings so that everyone can prepare properly. When the actual planning discussions take place, there should be relatively few surprises and everyone should arrive well prepared to present their views and have informed discussion.

Reality Check

Product Management will be pressed during the planning process to identify target market opportunities as well as suggested programs for going after those opportunities. The Engineering head will be responsible, in turn, for determining the relative costs of going after those opportunities. The perpetual challenge here is to balance the aggressiveness needed to be financially successful with the realism to produce an achievable execution plan. There is a natural tendency for Product Management to over commit and the engineering leader to under commit. Neither extreme is desirable. There is very little substitute for the development manager taking the time to thoroughly understand the market dynamics involved and to form their own judgment about this tradeoff. In most cases, the product managers will never be technical enough to properly assess the technical risk. On the other hand, engineering managers are fully capable of learning the business aspect. By understanding the business dynamics, the technical manager is in a position to give a more informed judgment as to which courses of action are both desirable and feasible. By building this understanding and delivering results based on it, the engineering manager also opens new career paths for themselves in terms of moving more towards the business side.

Another important point for the engineering leader is the fact that the engineering organization needs detailed and realistic plans more than the product managers do. There is a natural temptation for Marketing to content itself with rather hypothetical and-then-a-miracle-happens plans. In many cases, it is the head of engineering that not only needs to drive to create good execution plans, but also has to make sure that there is an effective planning process that converges on effective and executable plans. This means reaching agreement on plans that have enough detail about market goals and which affordable and doable technical plans can enable the achievement of those goals. If the engineering leader has an understanding of and sympathy for the business perspective of the Sales and Marketing folks, they will find it easier to make themselves heard while trying to get the right conversations going. The key thing to avoid is not to be the techie who "just says no". One needs to be able to say "yes" to the right things and speak intelligently to the business viability as well as the technical viability of one's proposals. Again, the engineering manager is not just responding to particular questions; they should also be helping frame the entire planning process to make sure it produces a good result. You should help design a good planning process so you can help design a good plan.

2.3 Requirements Management

Problem Statement

Requirements pose a special issue for Engineering Management because it is where their relationship with the Marketing/Business teams gets tested. The problem domain determines the nature and stability of the requirements, which in turn influences the relationship and the processes used by both the Business and the Technical groups. In heavily constrained problem domains such as highway construction, requirements are extremely detailed and stable. This led to the evolution of the traditional development processes. Software is often on the opposite extreme, with requirements that are comparatively vague and fluid. This has motivated the development practices toward Agile processes, which attempt to change the ways that Business and Engineering teams work to accommodate this uncertainty.

We will go over some typical management problems that occur with respect to requirements definition. We will then look at an ideal model for generating requirements and on how to apply that in different settings.

Case Study

When I worked at Acme Corp. in the Systems division, we were constantly instructed to support new operating systems, drivers, databases, and applications on the range of Acme Corp. hardware, ranging from laptops to eight processor machines. As a result, we supported approximately eight different operating systems on six to seven different hardware platforms with the entire device driver and database development and testing that goes along with each new operating system. The combination of supported platforms was enormous. On the other hand, there was no one in Marketing or Sales for that matter who was accountable for the return of investment on a per-platform basis. No one's job was on the line if a particular platform failed to become profitable. As a result,

Product Marketing wish lists strained Engineering resources with requirements from poorly managed product configurations, thus, de-focusing Engineering from more profitable product combinations.

Requirements Management Approaches/Challenges

Requirements are sometimes described as a contract between the Business and the Technical teams. However, requirements documents are seldom written as a detailed legal document. They also do not always require review or signatures to make them active unless you are dealing in a government context or have adopted strict software engineering methodologies like Capability Maturity Model (CMM) levels 3–5, which we will discuss more in a later section. Viewed in this context, a lot of the misunderstandings and problems with requirements come from the fact that they attempt to instantiate the agreement between groups without the detail and formality of a legal document.

With the relationship between groups not strictly dictated by binding agreements, reaching an understanding between the groups on the nature and scope of the requirements is critical. Without ground rules in this area, either team is free to criticize the other team for not doing their part. Product development will then proceed badly. It is equally important that Product Management, typically the creator of the Marketing Requirements Documents (MRDs) and use cases, consider the requirements from all possible sources including existing customers, prospects, engineering (technologies/re-factoring), and Sales Engineering. In addition, there must be an open forum for the relative prioritization of these collective requirements that balances short-term sales needs with long-term strategic goals.

Large Companies

Large corporations can suffer from the requirements becoming too much like legal documents. In an attempt to legislate away any misunderstandings or disagreements, the requirements documents become nearly as formal as contracts, with extremely detailed sections and sign off at every stage. When the problem is well-defined, highly constrained, or when many vendors and sub-contractors are involved, these detailed requirements documents can make sense. Some industries such as biomedical devices, pharmaceutical products, or civil engineering can require both detailed requirements and design documentation. However, for industries and problem domains that are not heavily regulated and have short product lifetimes, this kind of requirements can kill innovation. These larger companies are less likely to adopt Agile practices such as a "living backlog list" or 1-N prioritized feature list. Also, you should be aware of the squeaky wheel symptom. This is normally exhibited by a more vocal and passionate advocate for a given product feature that disproportionately influences the priority of a given feature over more worthy ones.

Anecdote

> At a large multinational computer manufacturer, the requirements for all products were long and detailed. When they started to purchase Original Equipment Manufacturer (OEM) products for resale, they did not adjust their requirements. The requirements made it so difficult to approve the product that it could not be released until past the normal end-of-life for a PC product. This meant the company was reselling the older generation of product, losing out to their own supplier who could provide the current generation to the market. The requirements process was so broken that it even broke products that they did not develop at all.

Startup Problems

Another classic problem is when the Business teams have no experience with requirements, which is common at startups. In those cases, they view requirements as marching orders that Business teams give Technical teams, rather than as a joint effort to find the best tradeoff between business and technical issues. This problem is especially bad in the software industry because the work appears to be so easy to define. With hardware, manufacturing, or regulated industries such as biomedical devices, there are enough constraints in the problem domain to convince most business people that requirements require a shared effort. In the software industry, however, it can appear that the software directly implements the business vision. This can then lead to Business teams mistaking the graphic user interface (GUI) for the product so that the requirements documents become an attempt at a UI design, from people without any training in the area.

Every startup also has the problem of changing requirements. It is typical that during a four to six month development effort, new requirements come in from sales prospects or the existing customer base that are important for revenue. At ACME Corp. where one of us worked in the late '90s, a high priority feature added by the CTO late in the development cycle of more than 300 person staff year release had delayed the overall release by several weeks at the cost of investor confidence. In the past, these new requirements were simply added to the head of the list without any evaluation of the opportunity cost or return of investment (ROI) of other affected features.

The "backlog list" concept promoted in Scrum and Agile practices addresses many of these issues. The list is a living document that maintains a 1-N prioritized list of all candidate features, typically driven by Marketing but with input from Sales and Engineering. A new requirement "candidate" is inserted at the proper "priority level", based on ROI, effort, and timing. The next release is easily defined as the top "X" items on the backlog list. This provides instant visibility to the E-Staff of the tradeoff decisions regarding "creeping elegance". Assuming that each requirement line item has an associated high-level estimate of effort, the rough timing of the release can be easily calculated. At the same time, it is important to document within the 1-N list what we call "horizontal goals" and not just features. These include quality targets, time-to-market, interactivity, scalability, platform support, human factors, third-party application, and tool dependencies. Many software releases have missed customer expectations by not looking at release or product requirements from all relevant perspectives.

It is also important to weed out of the MRD the "how" statements and leave only the "what" statements. Too often, a somewhat tech savvy marketing manager will try and assert design level information in the MRD, when this is best left to the expert/s— the engineers in this case. In the end, alternative implementations that are potentially creative may not get considered.

The best requirements come from a partnership between the Business and the Engineering teams. This should produce a document that allows latitude for creativity and innovation that leads to the mutually agreed upon goals for both sides. The Business teams need to do their part in understanding the industry, market, and customers' wants while the Engineering teams have to focus on the architecture/technology challenges and production issues. Each side should be free to learn more about other areas. Both sides also need to engage in an open and honest discussion. Executives need to do their part in ensuring that requirements process is done effectively with the right spirit of cooperation since problems in this area can cause not only a product but also an entire company to fail.

A challenge common to startups is where the requirements of a single big customer will command all the Engineering resources in a release to the exclusion of all other requirements. To avoid this, the common practice is to identify the source of a requirement— for example, client X or prospect Y or CEO/CTO. A release goal can then be set as for instance: 60 percent existing customers, 20 percent new customers, and 20 percent product vision. When the release goal is specified in this manner, it adds transparency to the effects of scope creep. It also makes clear as to where customer-facing parts of the company may need to engage in tactical customer management to support strategic goals for the business.

Startup Anecdote: Confusing defining requirements with designing the GUI

Inexperienced business people often mistake defining requirements with designing the software, especially the GUI design. I was the VPE at a startup that designed a simple new feature for a desktop application. This feature intended to display a name list, which could be clicked for a detail view of each name. Engineering wanted requirements that would define what data was needed, which data would appear in each screen, and explain how to deal with missing data. However, Business felt they should design the two screens.

Engineering would build prototypes, which were reviewed by different subsets of the business managers who would often disagree and reverse the decision of whoever was not present. While business managers enjoyed their feeling of control, the Engineering team felt frustrated and demeaned. Worse, the GUI discussion was so distracting that none of the more subtle issues such as data quality problems were ever addressed. The proposed GUI ideas were technically impossible and precious time was spent proving this to the business managers. In the end, it took nearly two months and over 25 person-hours of meetings before the Business team felt they had given their "requirements", and Engineering decided the business rules on its own.

Requirements Management Infrastructure

A good requirements management process must have proper support infrastructure. We have never seen a good requirements management process based on just Microsoft Word, Excel, or even a Wiki. It must support the ability to slice and dice the requirements repository by priority, customer, product area, degree of difficulty or level of effort estimate, and time frame desired. Wiki does not do this. Neither can Word. Excel is not centrally sharable or guaranteed current. Your best bet is to go with a specialized commercial requirements tracking system, which are available from many vendors.

A good Requirements Management System (RMS) must:

- Be centrally sharable
- Allow slice and dice
- Always be current and authoritative
- Support what-if scenarios for release planning
- Be able to carry associations between:
    - ➤ Customers and application scenarios
    - ➤ Application scenarios and use cases
    - ➤ Use cases and user stories
    - ➤ User stories and implementation tasks
    - ➤ User stories and acceptance criteria
    - ➤ User stories and acceptance tests

Requirements Management for Visibility and Traceability

Overview

Motivation: In this section, we will look at how to construct usable requirements. Whether you use a specific formalized requirements management system or just Excel, most organizations publish their requirements using Marketing Requirements Documents (MRDs) and Product Requirement Documents (PRDs), which describe the market opportunity and the proposed product meeting that market opportunity, respectively. In many cases, these organizations simply expect engineers to respond directly to these documents or spreadsheet forms. These organizations and processes implicitly assume that engineers do not require detailed problem understanding. In practice, this leads to engineering tradeoffs that are frequently non-optimal, as PRDs and product managers cannot anticipate every possible issue an engineer may encounter.

Problem: The Engineering Development team formulates the best possible guesses when issues and tradeoffs are encountered. These guesses are not based in customer problem context because such context often does not exist. In this section, we will introduce a lightweight process that allows an organization, including its Product Management staff, to capture customer problem context as well as to use this context in forming the basis of product decision-making from high-level strategic direction to detailed feature specifications.

Approach: We use the application scenario artifact, which is a simple way to capture the job function or responsibility area of a customer stakeholder. Using a corpus of many such application scenarios allows a product planning or management team to readily identify the specific target user or market that a product is intended to serve. Even more, it is readily apparent which markets and users are NOT the intended customers for a given product. Each application scenario motivates a set of use cases. Each use case motivates both functional and non-functional requirements. These artifacts are an epistemological foundation for designs, test plans, user documentation, and other product artifacts.

Results: Projects that adopt such user-modeling artifacts use this understanding to systematically capture customer understanding and to provide plan and status visibility and traceability throughout product development. Moreover, capturing this information allows product road-map benefit analysis with respect to specific customers or markets, since each engineering task is traceable to a specific customer need.

Conclusion: If an organization feels their Product Development team lacks sufficient end-user-context and/or user-problem understanding or if customers indicate that specific product releases barely meet their needs, the organization may want to consider adopting processes based on explicitly modeling customer problems and needs. Such situations are more commonly found in product version 1.0 (i.e. new products). Application scenarios are very useful artifacts to capture such context.

Basic Concepts

Application scenarios:

- Address a problem space
- Motivate multiple use cases that together resolve the problem of the main stakeholder
- Are derived from real people with real problems and issues in real organizations with real budgets and with real decision authority
- Are a good way to collect information on every stakeholder a company representative comes in contact with
- Can be used by both Sales and Support to characterize their contacts or users
- Drive use cases

Each can review each other's representations of application scenario and fill in missing understanding. Core use cases are the basic necessary use cases in order to viably resolve the problem. Use cases worthy of having are those that address the second order issues.

The following is a requirements object model for information flow:

- Customer => Application Scenario
- Application Scenario => Use Case/s
- Use Cases => Functional Requirements
- Use Cases => Non-Functional Requirements (and informed by Customer and Application Scenarios)
- Requirements => Design (and informed by Application Scenarios and Use Cases)
- Use Cases => Acceptance Tests
- Requirements => Unit Tests

Application Scenarios

Application scenarios are described in Geoffrey Moore's seminal book *Crossing the Chasm*. They are simply these five questions:

- Who is the primary stakeholder?
- What is the problem?
- How does this person address the problem without us? What is the typical day in the life of this person?
- How does this person address and resolve the problem using our product/s? What is the new day in the life of this person?
- What are the differences?

Discussion: When talking about the primary stakeholder, this must be a real person. Do not make up this individual. There are plenty of times when we can use our imagination but this is not one of them. Understanding real customers means you have to find one or more of them (prospects will do). This is the most important part of the application scenario so it will ideally take three or more passes through it before you feel you have properly characterized the person/s:

- Skill set
- Education
- Likes and dislikes
- Responsibilities
- Collaborators
- Respected inner circle
- Budget

- Decision-making style

The second most important part of the application scenario is the problem. If solving the problem is not going to make the customer's job significantly easier, get the individual a nice promotion or raise, or if failure to solve the problem does not risk the person's job, the problem arguably is not important enough to motivate the individual to find a solution (the one you are selling). The problem is more than a single task. The distinctive problem is the achievement of some goal or maintaining some metric. The problem must clearly be important to both the individual AND the organization that employs them. There must be substantial pain to the individual and the organization that your product will eliminate.

Thirdly, what are the methods currently employed to either address or partially address the problem? Why are the methods deficient? What resources are required to utilize the current methods? On what metrics are these methods falling short? You should characterize all dimensions. Look at the following:

- Skills required
- Staff
- Time
- Budget
- Space
- Communications
- Approvals
- Additional supporting infrastructure
- Things being done
- Things not being done

Afterwards, you should imagine the individual's life and environment once your product has successfully addressed the problem. Note the same dimensions as described above. You have to describe the new situation. What should be immediately apparent are the differences between the previous two points. Your product may have some disadvantages like short-term costs but it should have an overwhelmingly large set of compelling advantages over the current situation. Your product could be eliminating staff, saving cost over the long run, saving time, and reducing required skill levels, among others. These are the important advantages that will eventually work their way into your product positioning and messaging once your product is ready for prime time.

When writing application scenarios, reflecting on the other stakeholders that interact with the scenario's central figure is a good way to generate other application scenarios. Clearly, every individual could be the subject of at least one application scenario since an individual typically targeted by a hi-tech product usually holds more than one area of responsibility. Thus, not only can one document multiple scenarios per individual. Also, it is sometimes surprising how different scenario authors will have different interpretations of an individual's responsibilities, hence, the need to document the scenario author as part of the scenario production. By examining a scenario's subject as well as understanding the collaborators like direct reports, boss, peers, and interdepartmental collaborators, the set of application scenarios can also grow nicely. It is important to realize that a purchaser of a system has very different product evaluation criteria than the user, the user's boss, and the CEO. These stakeholder concerns are very important to capture, as what may be a compelling product for one may raise new problems for another.

Application scenarios are just a fancy way to describe how each individual in an organization could think about the customers and prospects they come in contact with every day. Asking these questions (in your own mind at least, if not in actual direct interaction) puts one in a conscious mental framework of learning about the business and the business's impacts on its customers. Asking these questions needs to be a way of doing business for every employee of a company. Wanting to know this kind of information about customers should be a burning desire for every employee of an organization. What is the potential impact if everyone in an organization had this level of understanding about the company's customers? Now, what do you do with application scenarios?

Another interesting aspect of application scenarios is: according to whom? You need to make sure that the source of the application scenario and its story is well tracked. Also note how well the scenario writer knows the central subject of the scenario.

Use Cases and Application Scenarios

Application scenarios describe an entire responsibility or problem area that must be managed well by a stakeholder. For example, a Chief Information Officer (CIO) has a responsibility to provide 24/7 operations for all of an enterprise's business-critical applications. These are many use cases, not just a single use case. Clearly, they must:

- Interact with other stakeholders
- Recruit administrators
- Acquire equipment
- License software
- Assign work

Application scenarios organize conceptual structures or containers for use cases. They relate use cases so that together they form a product that delivers value to a specific application scenario.

A company accustomed to thinking in terms of application scenarios to understand its customers, prospects, partners, users, and all with whom it comes in contact with ends up with a rich knowledge base of many application scenarios. This enables many data-driven (evidence-driven, if you are into Harvard-speak) decisions so you can:

- Easily sort out which application scenarios are in the "sweet spot" of your intended or delivered application or upgrade
- Identify key and compelling value propositions that will communicate your product's advantages against your competition
- Determine which media outlets you will use to advertise to reach these stakeholders (potential customers) based on understanding the aspects of the individuals described in the application scenarios
- Determine many operational and environmental guidelines, compatibility, and interoperability requirements
- Find out what application scenarios are to be set aside for the next version or minor release
- Make proper tradeoffs in the course of product development because your engineers have a good understanding of the key stakeholder concerns and needs, as encoded in these application scenarios

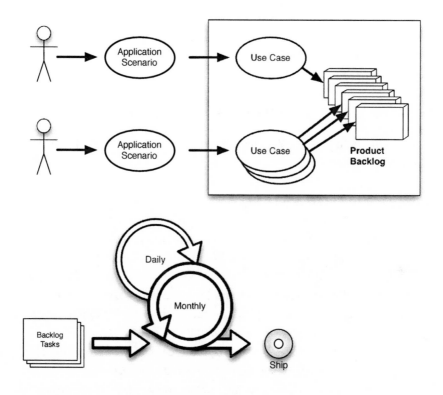

Prioritization by Use Case

Use cases are an important artifact introduced by Ivar Jacobson to organize and motivate requirements. In many organizations, independent requirements would be prioritized independently based on the degree of difficulty, availability of skill set for development, and clarity of specifications, and other criteria. However, the realization that many requirements are interdependent got lost in this practice. For example, in order to perform a function (use case), it may be necessary for all 14 requirements to be implemented. If two out of the 14 critical requirements are omitted, the use case would not be functional and the product may as well not have the other 12. If the critical two are left out, the time spent developing the remaining 12 would be wasted. Without explicitly encoding these relationships among these requirements, the team loses such understanding of these prioritization tradeoffs and then delivers a non-optimal product since the effort spent on those 12 requirements could have been spent implementing the complete form of another smaller use case.

So, the summary recommendation is that one should prioritize by use case and not by requirement. It is easier, faster, and more effective. It also results in better product.

Working with Application Scenarios

Once you have the application scenarios defined, a clear algorithm emerges for decision making.

- For every stakeholder you come across, seek to understand their problem to be solved, their upside and downside for solving or not solving the problem, and their particular constraints
- Create application scenarios that simply and effectively capture a key stakeholder's interest
- Use application scenarios to understand your serviceable market
  - ➢ Weed out those specific application scenarios that do not represent the "sweet spot" of your product offering
    - ▪ Examine these for possible follow-up on product offerings, if the immediate product succeeds
  - ➢ Focus on those specific application scenarios that are smack in the center of your product "sweet spot"
    - ▪ Examine these for characteristics of stakeholders that assist in determination of your market
    - ▪ How many such stakeholders are there?
    - ▪ How much do they wield in terms of budget authority, decision making authority, staff influence, and executive influence? What must they avoid at all cost?
    - ▪ How is your solution going to get them their next raise or promotion? If this is not the case, it is likely too weak to be actionable.
- Use the surviving application scenarios to derive a set of use cases that together address the application scenarios they are motivated from
- Use the use cases to drive a set of user stories if you are doing Agile
- Use the user stories to drive sprints and iterations
- Use the application scenario to drive a set a non-functional requirements

- Use the application scenarios to refine your understanding of each stakeholder at each contact point
  - ➢ Every individual in the company who encounters a stakeholder— be it a customer, prospect, ex-customer, or lost prospect— should author an application scenario.
  - ➢ The production of application scenarios should become part of the way a company does business— it is just the way you think about the market you serve.
  - ➢ Examine each application scenario to learn about the stakeholder's:
    - Budget
    - Decision authority
    - Manager's concerns/key decision criteria
    - Upside for success
    - Downside for failure
    - Ability to create options
  - ➢ Other side-effects that come out of these application scenarios are:
    - What materials, newsletters, magazines, periodicals, or reviews does this stakeholder read, hold, credible, disbelieve, or scoff at?
    - What education level has this stakeholder achieved?
    - What are the deployment constraints imposed on a potential solution in this stakeholder's environment?
    - What other systems and actors must the solution interact with?
    - What are the stated success factors?
    - What are the implicit or hidden success factors?
- Use the use cases and application scenarios to drive user documentation
- Use the use cases and user stories to drive test planning

Customer Understanding and Application Scenarios

We can now return to the question of customer understanding and recast it in terms of application scenarios.

In the best of all possible worlds, you have a customer-partner-program (CPP). This is different from a Customer Advisory Board (CAB), which meets infrequently. A CPP meets at least once a month in a group setting for two hours. In this way, CPP members can share among themselves their application scenarios, specific stakeholder needs, most important features, and usage concerns. This is a fertile ground for capturing application scenarios and their derivatives.

Second choice: If one cannot create and maintain a CPP, you should have all of your customer touch points like Sales, Support, and Marketing capture their specific customer interactions in application scenarios. They should get used to thinking of these five questions for every new individual they meet.

Third choice: If one cannot get your Sales and Support people to create these application scenarios, regularly debrief them at least once a week. To fulfill your role in Engineering or Product Management, you have to ask the basic questions that define application scenarios and try to document them as a way to assist the field in retaining this kind of customer understanding.

Fourth choice: If you do not have the option to do any of the suggestions above, you have to realize that you are going to make many tradeoffs in the wrong direction. You should be comfortable with this reality. Do not expect to make good decisions in the absence of good customer understanding and then be surprised when your products miss the mark(et).

2.4 Product Vision and Project Vision

Product Vision

Sometimes, we hear CEOs refer to "vision" as this ethereal fluffy nice-to-have. However, that is an uneducated view of what a product vision is. One of the best treatments of product vision is probably available in the Rational Unified Process (RUP) inception materials. It includes:

- Succinct problem statement
- Target market
- Key value proposition
- Key product features (so it is clear we are solving the problem)

Additionally, the product vision should describe the timeframe involved to set the context and to better define the opportunity.

How Product Vision is Developed and Who is Involved

The product vision is a Product Management function. However, while Product Management is a part of Engineering in some organizations, it is distinct in others. If there is a CTO, then product vision is almost certainly their responsibility. In smaller and less structured organizations, the VPE often owns the product vision and less commonly so in larger organizations. In some larger companies, the Product Managers will report to the VP of Product Marketing. The Engineering management role, with respect to product vision, will therefore vary both with the size and the stage of the company.

Role of Engineering Leadership

The role of the head of Engineering in some ways is to negotiate with the CTO or product manager at the high level regarding the feature set and scope that will get the company to deliver marketable features as soon as possible. In that sense, the product manager focuses on the "direction" while the engineering leader focuses on the "path". If these perspectives are combined, this will lead to a natural negotiation between the VPE and product manager in order to refine the vision. The final goal of this interaction should be to define approximately the sequence of efforts that will produce the greatest value in a specified time. The value, in most cases, translates into revenues or into moving the company into a strategic position that could lead to a competitive advantage.

One sure thing is that the engineering leader best distinguishes between the product vision and its physical realization (i.e. implementation). While the product vision is being defined, the engineering leader cannot be "drinking the Kool-Aid". The head of Engineering is responsible for the realization of the product vision and thus, they play an advisory role in its definition.

Whoever owns and drives the product vision must count on Engineering to deliver it. The technical leader must give realistic assessments about their team's ability to deliver the product in the agreed and expected time span. The technical leader has to predict and communicate resourcing requirements to deliver the product (e.g. hire new staff skilled in necessary technologies; acquire any needed software tools or components through purchase or build, and other possible resourcing changes).

Time scales vary in size of company and industry. Generally, in larger companies, the product vision goes out for longer periods like three to five years than in a smaller company wherein it usually takes 12 to 18 months. Highly competitive and fast changing marketplace results in shorter time scales (i.e. Internet). Industries with long product delivery cycles (i.e. hardware systems and semiconductors) have longer period in their product vision. Longer time scales are inherently riskier since there is more possibility for change.

Communicating the Product Vision

The engineering leader must intimately understand the product vision and be able to articulate it to the rest of Engineering to create a shared understanding for everyone in the department. Getting the support and commitment of the entre engineering organization to the product vision is critical to successfully delivering the product roadmap. The engineering team must feel that milestones and deliverables are credible and achievable; otherwise dissention will arise.

2.5 Feature Set vs. Time-to-Market

Introduction

"Features, schedule, quality— pick any two" so goes a popular saying among many engineers. In many ways, it indeed reflects the tradeoffs that often get made. The lesser time available to do a task, the more triage needs to be done as to the amount of functionality delivered and, in extreme cases, the quality of the system. During the dotcom boom, many companies focused entirely on features and schedule at the expense of quality. One of our companies' CEO liked to rail against the 'Tyranny of the Or'. What he means by that is that he does not want to choose between features and quality, he wants both! Is he being unreasonable about this? Hardly.

One of the key roles of an engineering leader is to act as a bridge between Engineering and Business. Any investment in technology of the company aims to produce a certain return in a certain span of time. The challenge many organizations face is that the people who understand the business value and opportunity of a technical investment do not actually grasp the issues and risks involved in implementing it and those who understand the technology have a vague understanding on what the business goal is. This mismatch is a real problem. It tends to result in complex designs that fit poorly within the given time and budget parameters. The ongoing challenge for Senior Technical Management is to make sure that the Requirements Management process produces a realistic and sufficiently nuanced account of what is required to succeed. They should also check if appropriate development methodologies are applied. The goal here is to understand the business requirements well enough to create a minimal technical design that meets the business goal and then have a development process flexible enough to implement this design while dealing with whatever surprises come along the way. Generally, this implies helping the requirement gatherers fine tune their requirements to reduce them to the minimum required and then carefully matching the technical solution. Maintaining this fine balance is the key in making products that work well for the users in an acceptable time frame. At the same time, it is important to monitor the technical risks in a plan and make sure those risks are properly communicated.

In addition to the process issues, success in this arena obviously comes from building a successful relationship and communication channels with all the involved parties. It also requires great sensitivity to both the business needs and the limitations and challenges of the technical approach. In larger organizations, this becomes challenging because it is harder for the higher-level managers to know all the details involved. Thus, it is very important to listen closely to and recognize what the people from both Business and Engineering are saying. Being able to grasp and communicate both technical limits and customer requirements, even when obliquely stated by a person from the lower ranks, is a key talent for a manager.

There are a couple of good approaches in optimizing both feature set and time-to-market simultaneously, which can be applied either singly or together.

Requirements and Solutions

Having a proper solution focus is one of the most basic answers to the puzzle. Most customers do not buy a product because they want the product. Rather, they buy it because it serves as a solution to some of their problems. Oftentimes, technology companies tend to get so focused on how nifty their products are that they lose focus on the problems being solved. As a result, when customers talk to a Sales team, they will often find themselves wanting to stop the Sales people from talking about all the cool features and instead get them to focus on the customers' own issues. The consequence is that in many organizations, devising a solution for a customer is an improvisation done by the field force post-sale. But this setup is intrinsically inefficient. The usual underlying product is fairly complex and in many cases, only a part of its functionality will be required to solve a given problem. If one can clearly understand the problems and create a product to exactly solve them, one can often build a simpler product than if one tries to solve general problems. By simplifying, one can exactly meet the market need while still being fairly quick about it. The key challenge is that both Product Management and Engineering should have an accurate enough customer understanding to correctly define salable solutions.

In this case, the head of Engineering needs to help push the organization to clearly understand the solution space. Aside from not stymieing future development through an overly narrow implementation, the leader also needs to make architectural tradeoffs to keep the schedule in. This can be hard particularly for startups whose main asset is having some major new core technology. But in those cases, it is important to get hold of some practical solutions that will drive sales growth beyond the core of early adopters.

Incremental Requirements Refinement

If the organization is doing incremental development, it is possible to use incremental requirements refinement to optimize features against schedule. The trick here is that almost any high level requirement can be divided into a set of parts, which vary in importance and difficulty, even if the total requirement itself is very significant. With this, if you implement only the important parts of the key requirements, you can often meet many functional requirements with a fairly modest schedule. Doing this requires a deep grasp of customers' needs, a disciplined approach to incremental development, and a willingness to reprioritize on a regular basis. Success here depends on the company's ability to prioritize needs. This will not work if all requirements are regarded equally high in importance. When that happens, it is mostly a sign that only a few requirements are well-understood. The sign of a correct set of requirements is in fact a detailed notion of what is important and what is not.

These two techniques can be combined. For example, if a company wants to enter a new market, it can subdivide the space into different solutions and prioritize those by implementing first the most important ones. Within each solution, use cases are prioritized. This also applies to those within the individual little features. Doing this carefully yields an entire roadmap for how an entire feature set is incrementally delivered, producing value at every point on the way.

When releasing a new product becomes inexpensive, development schedules can be adjusted for frequent small releases. This is typical in Internet and software businesses that are hosted rather than deployed at a customer site. In both those cases, there is relatively little cost to a release since the environment is controlled. Any upgrade is managed internally and thus, there is no cost in supporting the old release. The upgrade is an easy "push", requiring no consent from customers. The ability to do frequent small releases greatly benefits a business since it lets you get features to market as soon as they are ready. However, you get into a cycle of just incremental changes and you never get to undertake large changes, such as architecture or schema that do not fit into your regular cycle.

In practice, there is a common rhythm to the product releases even without doing pure incremental development. It is typified by an evolution like this:

- 1.0: Ship it
- 2.0: Make it work
- 3.0: Make it work right
- 4.0: Make it work fast
- 5.0: Make it work small
- 6.0: Make it work better than the competition

This is an obvious simplification but many products follow this pattern quite successfully. Basically, you need to decide which mixture of feature, innovation, and quality are required for the target customer mix at every stage of a product's maturity curve. Early adopters are more enamored with the concept and can stand some rougher edges. As a company moves up the adoption curve to more conservative and demanding customers, higher degrees of refinement in both quality and features are required to remain competitive. The main risk is excessive compromise early on. If you misjudge the feature set, you will either get a toy product or miss the market window. Also, if you misjudge the quality, you will get a reputation for flaky 1.0 products. This brings us to the topic of risk management.

Risk Management

Risk management changes greatly with the size and stage of the company. Having little or no money in the bank, startups can afford to take enormous risks since they have so little to lose. As a company gains success, balancing its risk and reward becomes harder. The company must come to a consensus on a corporate strategy for this. It can be difficult to explain to a Business team that if they press extremely aggressive requirements and schedules, they bear joint responsibility with the Technical team if the schedules slip or if the quality is bad.

However, the opposite scenario is also dangerous. Large multi-nationals are sometimes so risk adverse that they barely get anything done. For them, the opportunity cost is harder to measure than the cost of making a mistake. This can mean that your career progresses more by getting less done, so long as you never make a major mistake. It is important for engineering leaders to clarify and test the corporate consensus regarding risk tolerance, especially since the Chief Financial Officer (CFO) and the VP of Sales may not share the same opinion. Ideally, the CEO will broadly and overtly express a position to the entire company regarding feature, timing, and quality imperatives. As the company evolves, assessing the corporate risk tolerance on a regular basis— more specifically, quarterly— is also important.

There are some general guidelines subject to specific product or market exceptions that are typical of early stage companies.

- At early stage companies, time-to-market is critical as cash flow is limited. Thus, it is important to constrain the initial requirements to fundamental features only and validate them with the prospective user base, as soon as possible. At a prior company one of us had joined as a Director of Engineering, the VPE explained that "the quality of a product that does not ship is zero". That was his way of saying that he— and presumably the rest of the executives— felt that time-to-market was the most critical for that stage of the company "life-cycle".

- As the customer base begins to grow, the company must begin to address any outstanding quality issues. Otherwise, its ability to gain reference accounts and quotes is affected and the cost of maintenance begins to eat into product development funding. Also, the best way to kill a young startup is to gain a word-of-mouth reputation for poor quality products.

- Once the basic features and quality are relatively "under control", the focus usually turns to adding new platforms and reducing footprint, performance, scalability (depending on product), usability, and human factors.

Mismanagement

The techniques described here work well with reasonable people. Unfortunately, many people who are promoted to higher managers do not know these. The issues around features versus time-to-market are a real litmus test for the wisdom of one's superiors. If you find yourself in a situation like this with your immediate boss (i.e. the CEO), then it is best to quickly get the support of your peers— especially the VP of Sales— on your side and have them become advocates on your behalf. We have personally found that the CEO values the input from the VP of Sales more highly than other executives since they have a direct and quantifiable impact on the CEO's success. We would also contend that a CEO who wants all three— features, quality, and time-to-market— might not be in touch with the customers' needs and priorities. If neither the CEO nor the VP of Marketing can support you in making these tradeoff decisions, it would REALLY be a bad sign that the company may not truly understand their prospect or potential customer base.

2.6 Encouraging Innovation vs. Tactical Objectives

Introduction

Managing the tradeoff between encouraging innovation and meeting tactical objectives is a continual struggle for every engineering organization. Caution will dictate avoiding innovation and taking the tried and tested path. A high achieving development organization, however, will always try to innovate and implement new and cutting edge techniques.

In this chapter, we will look at ways of institutionalizing innovation in your organization. We will discuss these two main areas: how innovation factor into the day-to-day operation of the organization, especially for smaller organizations, and how certain kinds of innovation via dedicated research labs can be institutionalized.

Innovation and Your Team

When should you encourage innovation and when should you be cautious? Reining in your Development team can be demotivating but it may be the right choice. On the other hand, there are times when innovation can produce breakout results and set you up to meet long-term strategic goals. The answer depends on a number of factors including:

- How much slack do you have in the schedule?
- Can you schedule the time for innovation?
- Do you trust the developer/s to meet the schedule?
- Can you mitigate the risk around the deliverable?
- Are the costs fully understood and can the company afford it?
- Are other executive stakeholders bought in?
- What is the medium/long-term risk of not delivering this "innovative" feature?

- With innovation usually coming at the price of product quality, can you afford the risks?
- Some companies are driven by true research and development effort where innovation must be factored into nearly every new product line to survive. Chip foundries and disk drive makers come to mind here. What kind of company do you work for?

Promoting Innovation

Lab or No Lab

Committing to solve problems that you do not understand on a product roadmap is a behavior that introduces and increases risk. We prefer to identify problems that have no known solution and invest in discovering answers through an explicit activity track we refer to as research. When done in iterative development, there are frequent timely occasions— at iteration boundaries— to review research results and decide whether to put those results on the product roadmap or not.

There are a variety of ways in managing research. In larger organizations, you can create a dedicated research lab, which we will discuss more below.

Fellows programs and senior contributors, whose judgment and alignment with company objectives have been proven and are unquestioned, can be excellent ways to encourage relevant research. However, this is typically impossible in smaller organizations.

Some accommodation to individual research directions should be allowed in reasonably sized organizations, although this must be reviewed and authorized with an eye towards relevance to the business.

Engaging the Engineers

In smaller organizations where creating a "lab organization" would be impossible, the VPE should encourage the discovery of possible innovations during the spare time as long as there is no compromise on the milestones. There should be a clear distinction between committed work and innovation efforts.

Typically, the CTO at a given company has the responsibility to drive these efforts, with visibility and oversight from the VPE. They have the responsibility to look out several years across the technology horizon and look at trends in technologies, tools, and competition in order to provide direction to the research and development staff.

If each engineer spends some time thinking ways of improving the product, some new approaches to improve or solve problems will arise. These ideas should be documented in an informal way and shared with the team. These documents will form a "pool of ideas" that could be reviewed in meetings with the product manager. This process gives Engineering the chance to explore ideas without adding risk to releases. In any case, it is important to separate efforts related to possible innovations from those required to fulfill milestones. The interaction between people focusing on addressing business needs with people capable to innovate creates a powerful cycle. This allows Engineering to participate and the product managers to validate new ideas with customers. In some cases, these innovations may have no direct customer benefit but they may enable the product architecture to scale a few more years. Nevertheless, the engineering leader must be a key advocate for these changes with the rest of the Business team so as not to "dead-end" the product-line.

Engaging your engineers also means tasking them— through weekly 1:1 meetings, personnel reviews, and other interactions— with staying on top of the latest technologies that affect the company. This takes time and money. You should encourage your team to attend relevant conferences and to allocate some part of their time to research and not just to implementation. You have to build this time into your staffing schedules.

Also, you should have a reward system in place for innovation, whether it is a bonus for patents or spot bonuses for great ideas.

The Lead Horse

One technique that we have successfully used in the past is having a "lead horse" function. Assume a group of seven developers working on a product. The product is released approximately every six months. The lead horse starts the next cycle (project) two months prior to the shipment of the current project. The lead horse can be a single person or a team of two. They are in charge with staying within the product vision but not held tightly to a priority list of features. They can innovate and prototype during this time. It is expected that by the time the remainder of the team come off of the last project, the lead horse team will have figured out new material and will have reduced the risk of implementing this new material through prototypes. These new items can be offered up to the Product Management for consideration in addition to the top down requirements. The lead horse role is a plum role and can be used to reward particularly great contributors on the previous project. This technique requires that you have:

- Enough excess capacity (10 percent or more)
- A large enough team (does not work well with a Product team of three people)
- Long enough development cycles to accomplish an interesting task

The benefits of this include:

- "Researchers" are still working on and are responsible for tactical delivery of some items so they stay close to the mainline— no ivory tower syndrome
- Ability to "hide" innovation costs in the product development budget
- Ability for anyone who makes a big enough impact to do cool stuff and to try out ideas

Innovation Pipeline

There is a similar technique that we have used to allow the refinement of product features in a way that resembles a pipeline where in the first stage, both the product manager and engineering head, with the help of prototyping developers, create and recreate simulations of what the implementation should look like. The team repeats this process until everybody is happy with the idea and the simulation of how it is going to work. The engineers would work as consultants, helping to identify risk factors and engineering challenges. They also can be source of ideas to be explored and validated with the management.

The work done during the first stage serves as an input for the traditional development stage where real applications are built. The main advantage of this approach is that the requirements get validated by the management and refined by several prototyping iterations. This approach also helps Business select the ideas with more possibility of returning real value for customers instead of just "gold plating" the product with nice features but no strong value behind them.

It is important that the engineers understand that the goal at the first phase is prototyping and not architecture planning. This helps the engineers embrace several changes requests and feature refinement efforts. As efforts to design any type of infrastructure increase, there will be a natural resistance of throwing out the old designs and starting with a new approach.

Risks

The major risk in encouraging innovation is to spend effort on activities that do not contribute to the bottom line. The main issue is that almost all innovation exists on a somewhat longer time horizon, increasing the possibility that the end point will no longer be aligned with the company's needs by the time it appears.

Anecdote

I was managing the Development team of an enterprise software company when I was asked to take up a small research team to work with the CTO to prototype a next generation predictive analytics engine to replace the existing one. One of the challenges faced by the company was addressing the customers' needs in new verticals with the existing engine. A new vertical generally required one major and one minor release for general acceptance—

a huge development cost. There was also a big professional services cost to customers from configuring the current engine, which was brittle to noisy data and was poorly generalized outside the original industry vertical. This new engine promised to vastly simplify the configuration and to be stronger to data quality issues. It was believed that the business was about to take off and that the current system would quickly become inadequate as we grew the customer base and the number of industry verticals we served.

We set an aggressive six-month schedule and devoted two star developers for the project. However, concurrent to this effort, the company tried to deliver a major release to a key customer. The release fell behind schedule so after three months, we had to stop the project to help with the release. After the release was done, we finished the prototype of the new engine and presented it to the company. Although the results were every bit as good as promised, the new engine was never productized and the effort was essentially wasted. What went wrong?

The company was not in a position to invest the necessary resources to re-architect the software. The company was losing money and having trouble acquiring new customers in a stagnant economy. The new engine was not a drop-in replacement for the old engine and coming on the heels of a difficult and poorly planned major release, there was no appetite for another big release without any new features for users. Setting up a research team to develop next generation infrastructure can be successful only if the business itself is sufficiently strong to afford it. Otherwise, innovation can only be factored in from within the common engineering schedule. Generally, caution should rule in a negative business environment.

There was no necessary stakeholder buy in at the end of the project. Professional Services felt like it had its hands full with the current system and all its warts. Also, it was not ready to think about retraining to a new system. Sales understood the need to bring the services cost down but their greatest difficulty was just closing deals on feature or functions. Thus, a big effort for feature or function parity was not very compelling. Product Management was struggling with usability issues and was also focused primarily on the UI. They already had a big laundry list of features for the next release, so they also were not bought in. Engineering understood pretty clearly what the cost to productize would be. This should have been communicated with the other parts of the organization earlier so the decision not to invest could have been made before wasting six months of effort. Keeping the other executive stakeholders informed and bought in should happen continuously throughout the project. If the business climate deteriorates, you will very likely lose that buy in and should consider cutting the project. Completing a successful prototype does not mean the project was successful. Cutting your losses early can be a better outcome than completing the prototype and not productizing it.

The decision to invest in the effort was made based on optimistic predictions on the business. The underlying assumption was that the business was about to turn the corner. Even if we were "early" with the prototype, productizing it could be delayed until the business picked up and greater resources were available. Unfortunately, neither did this glowing business scenario materialize nor did delaying the productization of the prototype become a useful mitigation. The main code line was a moving target; hence, the value of the prototype depreciated with every product release as it further diverged from the target it aimed to replace. Mothballing a prototype is a feasible risk mitigation only if the requirements are static— a somewhat rare occurrence. If you cannot afford to productize the prototype, then you should seriously question why you are building it.

Not all innovation efforts have as much cost or risk associated with them like the example above. However, in all cases, a very disciplined decision making process should be applied to ensure winning outcomes. This chapter will help formulate the framework in which those kinds of decisions can best be made.

Research: Finding Solutions to Hard Problems

For purposes of this discussion, we define "Research" as a technical work that goes beyond the normal scope of development, requires some novelty or greater depth in its solution, and is part of Product Development. From a management perspective, it is a technical challenge, whose solution involves either major risk or substantial rewards, or both. Research is a greater unknown than the normal product development— the timelines are more non-linear and unpredictable because it is difficult to recognize when insight will lead to solutions.

Clearly, it is very risky to depend on the uncertain timing of Research for product schedules. However, there are cases where this is unavoidable. Research can give a company a big competitive advantage by providing IP, patents, and trade secrets. Startups often make Research the crown jewel that justifies their entire existence. Sometimes, an entire path of development hinges on a novel solution in a very specific area. For many reasons, Research may be required.

The easiest way to manage Research in a Product Development environment is to make it independent of the product timelines. This requires a product roadmap which can proceed without Research, but that is improved or accelerated if the Research works out.

It is important that the team doing Research stays engaged with the Development team. When the Research is not explicitly part of the product roadmap, there is a tendency for the Research to lose touch with the product needs. Research itself can then become the "product", but it is a product without customers.

The best way to structure the relationship between Research and Engineering is through the regular roadmap process. Generally, the roadmap will describe both long-term and short-term objectives. Within this context, Research will identify long-term but not short-term objectives. The long-term objectives are specific areas of focus in the research, leaving the group some latitude to decide on specifically what projects to undertake at any particular time. The aim of each group in Research is to produce some deliverable, whether it is a paper or a prototype. Once a project gets to the point of producing a prototype, the Research group needs to transition the project to the regular Development groups where at that point, its further development can be managed via the normal roadmap process within development. The key metric to watch out for is that a useful number of projects from Research are actually making this transition. The subtlety here is that with radical research, many dead ends need to be considered before success is achieved, thus, making it hard to quantify what an "acceptable" success rate is. A good way of mitigating this risk is to partner with a university to lower the exposure to potentially huge numbers of unproductive efforts, while not closing the door to the successes when they do happen.

Notice that this model hopes for but does not guarantee that a particular piece of research makes it into the development roadmap at any given time. Making regular development cycles dependent on particular pieces of research is extraordinarily risky. This should only be undertaken if there is no alternative and/or one has some *a priori* reason for believing the effort would be successful. Business needs to adjust both their expectations and timelines to reflect the risk Research introduces. Both Marketing and Sales need to recognize the risk of heavily promoting features that are at risk. Production, Customer Service, and QA teams need to understand where the additional risk is and how they can help deal with it. If it is so important and budget permitting, it may also be useful to run multiple efforts in parallel, in the hopes that one succeeds. While this obviously takes more staff, it reduces the risk by not forcing a premature choice between likely possibilities. This is common in the defense industry with two or more companies delivering product prototypes to a "bake-off" stage at which point, the customer "grades" a winner and awards production dollars. Managing competing teams requires everyone to focus on the larger goal of advancing the product roadmap. Teams working on the Research path, which is not used, need to know if their contribution was important and valued.

Research labs can be extremely valuable by providing an opportunity to invest in long-term projects that will become crucial in the future. However, these are not enough since they would never survive any tactically based short-term investment plan. Research labs can also establish partnerships with universities that can bring more innovation to the organization as well as make recruiting easier by raising the profile of the organization with new graduates. This is particularly valuable when a company establishes new sites in other countries. Also, a research partnership with a local university can greatly improve the applicant flow. Be sure to clarify any IP ownership/copyright issues with the university in advance.

Finally, to make sure the lab gets adequately funded, you should determine what percentage of your budget you want to spend on the lab as part of your business planning. You also have to make sure that tactical considerations do not cannibalize the funding. The big factors you want to look at as a manager in starting a lab are the following:

- Do you need long-term innovation?
- Are academic contacts valuable to you?
- Do you already have researchers who can benefit from working in a lab environment while making a responsible use of it?
- Do you have adequate ability to manage this?

Success metrics include: number of journal articles published, patents filed, number of academic partnerships, and after a while, number of innovations fed back into product development.

2.7 Licensing for Royalties

Introduction

While there are many ways to distribute and sell a product, deals that involve licensing technology to someone— as an OEM or through related means— constitute a special class of concern for the engineering leader who may be called upon to help negotiate such agreements. In this chapter, we will look at some of the issues involved in negotiating such license for royalty agreements.

Business Considerations

OEM deals are an excellent way of expanding your business. You can get an annuity business with great revenue for a relatively small expenditure. You effectively leverage your customers' sales and marketing force if you do the deal correctly. For example, one large company generates six percent of its revenues from a deal of this kind using two full-time employees. Once established, it is hard to be replaced in most cases. Support is simplified because you are dealing with engineers and not end-users. The following are the circumstances you should watch out for:

- If your customer is a small company, get a large pre-pay. They may not be there in a year or two.
- Make sure there is a term limit. Be careful of perpetual licenses.
- Be careful of the assignment clause. For example, you sell a license for your cool widget to Joe's Garage Software who will then use it for all of their products. Six months later, Microsoft bought Joe's. Can Microsoft use your item for all of its products?
- Figure out how you are going to count usage. It is fine not to count if license files and keys are going to make it harder for the customer. Just make sure that you are dealing with reputable people. Licensing is a volume game in most cases and missing a few end-customers out of millions will not matter.

- If your OEM is much bigger than you are, be careful about expensive requirements such as an accessible documentation or Radio Frequency Identification (RFID) tags that you had not counted on!

Contractual Language

There are several considerations when dealing with licensing issues. These issues are often as important to the licensee and the licensor. These considerations include:

- **Rights to sub-license product to partners or distributors**
  As a licensor, you usually do not permit the licensee to sub-license the product, except under rare circumstances.

- **Access to source code**
  Unless you are an open source company, this is not typically granted.

- **Distribution and management of license keys (if applicable)**
  If you are the licensor, you need to make sure that you adequately control and protect the product distribution via a capable licensing tool, if necessary.

- **Audit process**
  Most licensing contracts require the ability to audit the licensee and verify the number of distributions for accounting purposes.

- **Branding and trademarks**
  Ideally, you have to ensure that your brand, trademark, and copyright assignments are required to be evident in a customer's product.

- **IP rights**
  These are usually non-negotiable and must be excluded. Exceptions include open source companies.

- **Warranty limitations**

  Most licensing agreements delineate time-based warranties with specific timeframes— for example, 30 to 60 days from date of delivery to licensee— for notification of critical issues to the licensor. Once the notification is made, there are contractual timeframes to respond to the issues with an adequate response before the licensor can be considered in breach of contract.

- **Liability limits**

  Limit the financial liability to a specific amount. In some cases, this equates to the licensee fees. In addition, most agreements prevent money damages that result from the use of or the inability to use the product.

- **Assignment**

  As the licensor, you usually want to require the licensee to request prior written approval before assigning the product to other entities. Assignment makes the auditing process more difficult.

- **Usage models**

  Define the usage models. Is the licensee able to use the product in a hosted model (i.e. an Application Service Provider (ASP) or is it only an individual product license?

- **Rights to future enhancements and releases**

  Make sure these are mentioned in contract. In many cases, a new major product release may warrant a renegotiation of the royalties.

3. Product Engineering

The title "Vice President of Engineering" by its very name implies leadership of purely engineering concerns. In this section, we will discuss all the engineering implications of building, deploying, and maintaining products. We will look at the roles of people on the team, the methodologies we use, and the different disciplines that can contribute— from software and hardware engineering to project management, testing, and documentation.

3.1 Software Engineering

What is Software Engineering?

The IEEE defines Software Engineering as "the application of a systematic, disciplined, quantifiable approach to the development, operation, and maintenance of software."[2] These three areas encompass a broad span of processes and methodologies. Software development processes includes the following elements:

- **Activities and steps**
    - Requirements
    - Architecture
    - Design
    - Implementation
    - Testing
    - Deployment
    - Support
    - Maintenance

- **Development models**
    - Agile
    - Clean room
    - Iterative
    - Rapid Application Development (RAD)
    - Rational Unified Process (RUP)
    - Spiral
    - Waterfall

---

[2] IEEE Engineering Management Society, "EMS Mission," IEEE, http://www.ewh.ieee.org/soc/ems/?menu=1&page=3

  - ➢ Extreme Programming (XP)
  - ➢ Scrum

- **Supporting disciplines**
  - ➢ Configuration management
  - ➢ Documentation
  - ➢ Software quality assurance (SQA)
  - ➢ Project management
  - ➢ User experience design

This is a huge range of topics which are often hotly debated and about which much has been written. In this and in the following chapter, we will discuss these from the standpoint of the practical needs of senior engineering leaders in different kinds of organizations who try to optimize the performance of their teams.

Activities Within Software Engineering

Requirements

One thing most of us have learned about requirements as they affect software development is that ***requirements change***. No business can afford to invest the financial resources, staffing, time, and opportunity cost to exactly specify— with 100 percent accuracy and confidence— what the product need of the company will be in the delivery timeframe of the contemplated product. Doing so would require a specification team to be not only inhumanly detailed, organized, thorough, disciplined, cross-functional, and competent, but also prescient. A company that expects that it will not learn anything while executing a project is sadly lacking trust in the ability of its Development and Operations teams to improve upon the initial requirements and plan. The head of Engineering, together with their colleagues and subordinates, must create an environment in which sets of processes or practices are ***expected to be learned*** from the execution of product development plans. These new insights and knowledge need to have a way of making the plan and its product better.

Architecture

The architecture must *be as simple as possible, but not too simple*. Architecture is critically dependent on both the culture and the other non-technical aspects of the organization. In an environment that specifies 100 percent of requirements *a priori*, it is sometimes believed that architecture can be tailored to that specification. The defensive posture of Development upon completion is, "we built what you asked", although in fact, what got built was what was asked at the start of the project and not necessarily what was required for business success.

In environments that expect that the business context— and therefore, product requirements— to evolve or change, Development expect that the underlying architecture must occasionally change. This change must be driven by the first-class objects and concepts that need to be supported by the product. Resisting architectural change and "hacking" these objects and concepts into a schema or design that was not originally conceived to embody them is ill-advised. It introduces excess complexity and leads away from simplicity, maintainability, implementation-hiding, and other good development principles. It is also a mistake to complicate the architecture from the start in order to accommodate unknown future development. Too often, those unknown future requirements do not materialize as expected and the development effort spent to accommodate them is uneconomical and inefficient.

The important thing to understand is that architecture is always going to be made up of a series of compromises and the engineering leader's role is to either make the compromise decisions or properly inform them.

Design

There are two ideas here: functional design and technical design. Functional design covers the user-facing experience, encompassing UI, aspects of information modeling, and user modeling. Functional design is driven by Product Management and may include stakeholders in Sales and Professional Services. Technical design, on the other hand, describes the architecture and functional components that will deliver the specified functionality. Technical design is driven by Engineering and may include stakeholders in QA and Product Management.

Implementation

Implementation is the software's initial coding. This phase usually reveals gaps in the requirements and surface issues in the design. The role of the engineering manager here is to make decisions on how these are addressed, considering the ultimate effect to the project schedule and deliverables.

Testing

The engineering leader's interests and concerns with respect to testing are to come up with a product that meets the objectives of the company and its customers. From the company's standpoint, the product must achieve the goals originally set out in the product vision— revenue, competitive positioning, and functionality. On the other hand, from the customers' perspective, the product must represent sufficient benefits wherein the customer's ROI expectations are achieved. The aspects of the product that erode these goals are those areas which do not meet functionality and quality needs.

Therefore, an engineering leader must ensure that functionality and quality objectives are clearly understood, defined, and met. These are typically the objectives of the testing process. A solid test plan considers many factors besides basic feature testing. A great test plan includes validation of scalability, stress, boundary conditions, usability, platform, 3rd party interfaces, API, and negative (error injection) testing to name a few. The template for a test plan should include these topics.

Deployment

Deployment embodies those aspects of the product, or other services and products, which assist the customer in realizing the product's expected benefits.

Support

Once the product is deployed and is used by customers, issues will arise. These are support issues raised by customers. The challenge for Engineering is to allocate sufficient bandwidth to address customer issues, which are usually of high priority and often require immediate attention. The difficulty is compounded by the fact that they arise at very unpredictable times. Large organizations will have a group in Engineering dedicated to support. In small organizations, however, the frequency of support issues usually does not warrant a dedicated full-time equivalent (FTE), so the bandwidth will come from the development group and will impact development schedules.

Maintenance

Usually, a major product release is followed by one or more maintenance releases that provide fixes to bugs that were either left unfixed in the major release or discovered after the release. Small feature requests are also usual fodder for maintenance releases.

Development Processes

The flow from idea to shipped and supported product depends on the context, development process, or software lifecycle. This lifecycle varies greatly with the company's size, maturity, and target markets.

We can dissect this lifecycle into a sequence of processes: the development methodology, which governs the technical construction of the product; the release management process that governs how the technical work is delivered to the field; and project management process, which provides the communication and coordination glue that pulls it all together. (In fact, the fourth process is the technical architecture itself, but since this is a book about Management and not Engineering, we will not belabor that here, except in so far as it is directly influenced by the development methodology.)

Having a reasonable choice of methodology in each of these areas and appropriately skilled teams executing on each of them is at the heart of effective engineering management. In succeeding chapters, we will drill down into these areas in great detail. But all these approaches are answers of some kind and before we go there, we need to be clear on the question they are trying to answer.

Organizations fundamentally choose their processes based on two criteria: scale and risk profile. Generally, a very small organization where all the people are highly skilled and located together in the same room can be highly productive in a completely informal manner with almost no process involved. But in modern commercial contexts, almost all interesting projects involve teams of some reasonable size that are often geographically distributed. It is well-known that communication overhead between people increases together with the number of people and with the square of the distance between them. The more communication is required, the more effort has to go in coordinating people and keeping everyone on the same page. This forces greater formalism in processes. Likewise, the lower the appetite for risk, the greater the need for the project to be absolutely and predictably successful, and the more structure is required in the processes of coordinating the project. Once this greater degree of structure is added, productivity is inherently reduced. The struggle to maintain productivity as process and communication overhead goes up is at the heart of all arguments about methodology.

Difference between Software and Hardware Engineering

Engineers who are mostly involved in hardware and systems development might wonder why there are so many discussions in the industry about software development methodologies when there is so little argument over hardware development methodologies. In fact, if one does an Internet search for those terms, the results will be almost all about how the software development methodology affects the hardware development. Understanding this can give some perspective on the overall issue of Product Engineering.

Hardware and systems development tends to involve integration of components with very strictly defined interfaces or conforming to strictly defined standards— most of which are not under Engineering's control. If you are developing an integrated circuit, you are constrained to using components that are defined by the materials and the fabrication process. Also, your own interface must be very well defined ahead of time so that customers and partners can design in your product. If you are developing board or box level systems, then most of the hardware components, whether they are chips, hard disks, interface cards, or power supplies, match to a myriad of industry standards. Hardware and systems design is an integration effort in combining components— which are complex subsystems— and meeting or helping to shape industry standards.

Another characteristic of hardware and systems development is the high cost of producing prototypes. Test wafers and prototype circuit boards are expensive to produce and do not often exactly represent the final manufactured product. Prototype systems frequently do not have the exact chassis designs, thus, cooling and grounding are only approximate. Many phases of this work are done in simulation. However, this can also be an expensive process, especially if the system design changes drastically over the course of development or if the system is dependent on a new component that has not been fully characterized.

Finally, hardware and systems development almost always has a strong dependence on vendors and manufacturers. A design can easily be superior in performance but impractical if the manufacturers cannot maintain the tolerance needed in a cost-effective way. A cutting edge system product can often depend on a vendor of a cutting edge component, which makes the product dependent on both the development and the manufacturing of that component.

Consequently, development processes for hardware and systems design have fewer degrees of freedom than their software counterparts. Many of the product requirements need to be well-defined ahead of time because of the need to conform to standards— both standards for components you use and the standards your customers expect from the product. Even a dominant hardware company like Intel cannot arbitrarily change industry standards such as power supply voltages or interface standards like Peripheral Component Interconnnect (PCI) without working closely with many other vendors. The cost of iteration or prototyping designs is fairly high both in money and time. This implies that design decisions can be difficult to change or refactor, since these changes will affect other parts of the system.

Similar constraints apply to the development of products in a regulated industry such as military or medical products. The need to meet milestones and produce documentation to conform to regulations restricts the flexibility of development processes. Similarly, the high cost of rendering physical prototypes, which are essentially free in the software world, severely constrains the number of iterations between product definition and product release. In these constrained worlds, the development process is what the software industry would consider the "old fashioned" Waterfall approach. While these development processes look tedious compared to software development processes, they are the reflection of a different development environment. Even the most extreme software development zealot does not believe that a very large system such as an aircraft carrier can be built using software development processes.

Software development is less constrained, even for the software that goes into system level products. Taking advantages of these degrees of freedom can lead to higher efficiency and better quality. For example, in the punched card programming days, the cost of an iteration or run of a program was fairly high. In a school environment, one would submit their deck and it might be an hour before it could be run. Often, it would take hours before one could get their printed output. That environment was more like a hardware development and one would spend more time planning each of the iterations because each step required much effort.

Today, even fairly large programs can be run quickly on hardware dedicated to each developer. It becomes more efficient to do more iterations because they are faster and cheaper, provided you put enough thought into each iteration so you are not just flailing away. The software methodologies described in this section show different ways to use the greater degree of freedom in software development to improve the process.

However, as software development processes differ from hardware development processes, there is a possibility for friction to form within the organization. This explains why it is important for an engineering manager to understand the different development methodologies, no matter what type of product they manage because both software and hardware development elements impact all companies. Most hardware companies have some software that goes along with it such as utilities, design aids, simulation models, firmware, or device drivers. Understanding how software development may be improved can help make the hardware more competitive. Software companies need hardware to run and many of the elements of hardware development are reflected in the way IT or network operations runs the infrastructure. IT works in the same kind of constraint-driven world as hardware development, which produces a more risk adverse approach. An engineering leader should understand how different departments approach work differently. This can be a strength if a company can use the best process for each type of work and combine them smoothly.

Risk Tolerance and Development Process

Risk is a measure of the uncertainty around a variable. In software engineering, there are internal and external risks. Typically, an engineering leader needs to manage three interlocking internal risks: schedule, quality, and functionality. On the other hand, there are also external risks including people, company objectives, and market conditions. These are the factors that have little to do directly with the managed risks but are absolutely critical to keep an eye on.

Risk in a product release refers to the uncertainty around meeting commitments on any or all of those variables. Uncertainty in one variable can usually be traded off with another one. A common example is dropping features in order to meet a schedule commitment. Alternatively, a schedule may be allowed to slip in order for all the required functionality to be completed. Another unfortunate common alternative is sacrificing quality in order to ship all the features— some broken— "on time".

Different projects and industries have varying risk tolerance. In video game development, for example, there is almost zero tolerance for schedule risk. Typically, a game has to hit the market in time for Christmas and the console makers have very strict deadlines for accepting games for certification before the holiday season. Another example for this is in the aerospace industry where there may be zero tolerance for quality risk when human safety depends on software. The risk tolerance in a particular business or for a specific project is a key factor in determining the most suitable development model to apply.

Story #1

My first job out of college was working for SSS designing databases for flight simulators. These included the visual 3D model of the earth and celestial features to train the space shuttle astronauts. The National Aeronautics and Space Administration required SSS to comply with a rigorous set of development methodologies including complete requirements traceability in the entire development process from testing to deployment. Considering that pilots are now able to completely certify and achieve their license solely by flying the simulator, a more rigorous software development process is warranted as lives are at stake. Likewise, in healthcare, life support, mission critical systems, and hardware oriented design, vendors are more likely to use CMM Level 4 or 5 practices or a traditional waterfall model and likely not Agile practices. In systems like this, the product simply cannot be designed in an iterative fashion as with Scrum or Agile models.

Story #2

My first job out of college was working for RRR on their installer. Installers on shrink-wrapped software are interesting creatures. They are the first-hand experience of the user and need to work on every system without modification. Most software systems these days have some capability to update themselves in the field. This usually requires that the installation process be completed successfully. When you are working on an installation package, you need to be very careful that the system can complete reliably. When you are working on an installation package that is designed to run on a potentially virus infected system and/or makes modifications to the kernel on the system where it is being installed, you need to be even more careful. Based on the technological sophistication and risk profile of the user of the product feature, the product risk profile can be changed. For some cases such as the installer for a retail anti-virus package mentioned above, if there is an error on the screen at any point, there may be no second chance.

Some of the top risks are based on the targeted environment for the software. If you are targeting professional organizations with regimented IT policies, then you have a very different set of risks when compared to mass-market shrink-wrapped software. Another key risk area is the volume. Enterprise software that has a low number of customers will not incur the same number of customer support issues as a product that is installed in hundreds of thousands of locations around the world. To put a more definitive point on it, try comparing the customer backlash that you would expect with a bug in the administrative console for an enterprise email solution with a similar bug in a popular desktop application. In one case, many workarounds will be found and discussed by the community. In the latter case, a huge number of support tickets—automated or otherwise— will be generated.

Anecdote

While working at TTT, I had a customer support case handed to me by a VP. It took me a while to figure out what was going on. The installation package had failed for reasons that were far beyond what I had expected to happen. After a while, I determined that the end user had downloaded and installed five competing anti-virus packages on their system and a few utility product suites. All of these packages modify the kernel and, generally, should not be installed on the same system. In addition, between the downloads, installations, and updates, the user had run out of space on their primary disk drive making Windows unstable. This is the kind of issue that you need to consider and plan for in a mass-market product that will rarely, if ever, come up in an enterprise product.

<u>Next Steps</u>

From here, we will probe into the problems of choosing a development methodology, how we manage the software lifecycle, and how we maintain finished products.

3.2 Roles and Responsibilities

Building a hi-tech product requires many different people with different skill sets to collaborate. In this chapter, we will look at the various roles one might find in a development organization. Naturally, how these roles are instantiated will vary with the scale of the organization. In a startup, a single person might occupy many of them while in a large organization; there may be whole teams in a given role.

Management	
People Management	Concerned with hiring, training, and growing the team's performance
Product Management	Defines requirements for a product and acts as an interface to customers and field folks distilling and prioritizing needs
Product Marketing	Publicizes the product and generates leads
Release Management	Manages lifecycle of product releases and the integration of individual projects into that product. Works closely with the Program Manager and the Product Manager to coordinate release scheduling, tasks and interdependencies. Ensures all release level specific process documentation (MRDs, PRDs, Use Cases, Test Plans are done and approved as needed.
Program Management	Drives progress, resolves problems, and coordinates schedules, tracks progress, documents, meetings, and communications for an entire product
Project Management	Similar to program management but focused more on a particular team or subsystem
Software Development	
Software Architect	Very senior developer who does large scale system designs
Software Technical Lead	More senior developer who mentors junior developers and coordinates technical work for a group
Scalability Lead	Centralized or distributed role— ensures that architecture can meet demands of large customers

Security Architect	Drives security architecture and security audits for organization
Software Developer	General worker bee engineer
Database Engineer	Specializes in information design such as data modeling and tuning of Structured Query Language (SQL) databases.
Performance Engineer	Focuses on design, execution, and triage of performance and scalability tests
Tools Developer	Focuses on design and operational aspects of tools to support the rest of organization
UI Designer	Specializes in human factors design and testing
Hardware Development	
Hardware Architect	Very senior developer who does large scale system designs
Hardware Technical Lead	More senior developer who mentors junior developers and coordinates technical work for a group
Packaging Lead	Leads packaging design including mechanical, usability, cooling, power or electromagnetic interference (EMI) requirements, safety, and certification
Security Architect	Drives security architecture and security audits for organization
Hardware Developer	Designs, integrates, and lays out the hardware for the product
Engineering QA	
QA Engineer	General engineer with QA background who creates test plans, develops test cases, works with developers on new features, runs tests, and helps with escalations
Automation Developer	General software developer focused purely on automation development
Test Execution Technician	Hardware savvy person who sets up test rigs and monitors running automation
Manual Tester	Semi-skilled test engineer who executes manual test cases
Technical Publications	
Editor	Senior writer who does information design, and style guides, and the like
Writer	Someone who interviews a developer, reads design documents, and somehow creates usable documentation from it

Publication Production Specialist	Technician who monitors assembly and publication of documents
Artist	Graphic artist who works on pictures, icons, and layouts
Manufacturing / Production	
Manufacturing Lead Engineer	Plans, directs, and coordinates manufacturing processes
Manufacturing Engineer	Develops manufacturing processes and equipment and coordinates suppliers
Production Workers/ Technicians	Executes the manufacturing, packaging, and shipment of product
Purchasing Agents	Coordinates activities involved with procuring goods and services such as raw materials, equipment, tools, parts, and supplies
Production QA/QC	Coordinates testing and inspection of products and incoming components
Customer Service Representatives	Confers with customers to provide information, take orders, cancel accounts, and manage complaints

3.3 Development Methodologies

Process, Methodology, and Growth

When a company is formed, the founders are usually experienced technologists who simply know how to build stuff that works. Life is simple! As the organization and the product grow, things become more complex. More communication is required among people. Interfaces between different areas of the product need to be more clearly specified— both technically and organizationally. As a result of these needs, we create processes that govern the interactions between people and systems. These processes unquestionably help us to be more productive in larger settings. However, they also take away freedom and flexibility that existed when the company was smaller. By creating more rules, we give up flexibility for efficiency.

To understand this, let us go back to the first modern large corporations, which were the railroads of the 19th century. They needed to assure safe operations despite the long single tracked routes, no good telecommunications, and a largely uneducated workforce. They accomplished this by creating detailed processes to be followed on pain of termination. The result was the prototype of today's large organizations— very efficient but stiff and hard to change. The large hi-tech organizations of the '50s, '60s, and '70s are also seen as having developed from this same heritage, creating workflows and habits that made the organizations productive but unable to adapt quickly when business conditions changed.

This creates today's dilemma of how to create a scalable organization that retains the flexibility of a small business. The concept of "agility" refers to how we attempt to solve these problems. As an organization grows, it will apply more formal approaches to process models in its other departments. While many activities in a company can be described using process models, the fundamental process in most engineering organizations is the development methodology and it is here where the agility battles are fought first.

In this chapter, we will generally look at agility, development methodologies, and process models.

Development Methodology

Why the Selection of a Development Methodology is Important

The development methodology is the single most important factor that shapes an engineering organization. Depending on what development methodology you choose, it will attract different types of engineers. It will also help define the way the organization engages itself with the rest of the company.

The development methodology is in some ways connected with the kind of product and industry in which it will be applied. Choosing the right model depends on a number of factors including:

- Product industry
- Product class
- Release cycle duration
- Customer quality expectations
- Phase of company funding
- Team skills and training
- Company culture

Software Development Phases

All software development moves through essentially five phases:

1) Requirements
2) Design
3) Implementation
4) Testing
5) Release

The requirements phase is about defining what the software should accomplish when it is completed. The design phase describes how the software will be built. Implementation is the actual building of the software. Testing is done to verify if the software behaves correctly. Finally, the release phase determines if the software is ready for general use.

The different software development methodologies describe different ways of moving through these phases, with varying amounts of feedback between the phases and iterations before reaching a final release.

Waterfall Development Methodology

The Waterfall development model represents one end of the spectrum of development methodologies. This model is entirely sequential. The development project does not move to the next development phase until the current phase is entirely completed. For example, there is no design work until requirements are fully completed and "signed off". Once the design is started, requirements cannot be revisited. The design is given to programmers for implementation only after the design is completed. In the later stages of the implementation phase, the works of different programming teams are integrated. Once the work is all integrated, the software is tested and debugged and finally released.

The main argument in favor of the Waterfall model is that fixing a defect earlier in the development cycle is more efficient than working on it later. In other words, it is easier to fix a paragraph in a requirements specification than to rebuild a component derived from a flawed requirement. For this reason, the Waterfall model emphasizes getting the requirements and design correct before starting implementation.

Another argument supporting the Waterfall model is its emphasis on documentation. If engineers leave, then new engineers can quickly pick up the knowledge they need from the requirements and design documents.

However, the main drawback of this model is that requirements usually change either because market conditions change or because later phases of the development cycle reveal new or changed requirements.

Because of this, organizations that use the Waterfall model almost invariably do so in a modified form.

General Process Models

In larger organizations, it can make sense to formalize processes beyond just the pure development process. There are a couple of approaches to this. Let us define process here simply as a description of how people interact to solve a certain problem. We will describe a couple of these and show they complement but do not replace specific development methodologies.

ISO 9001

The ISO standard is a simple framework for verifying process compliance. Its value is very straightforward— a company will be compliant with ISO 9001 if, and only if, it does what it says and says what it does. This implies that all major activities follow a process. However, this is not prescriptive. The process can be vacuous, counterproductive, or downright evil. None of those matters to ISO. All that counts is that the existing process is followed. The major reason for adopting ISO is simply for business reasons: notably, to claim ISO compliance in markets where that matters. It also easily works with any development methodology because it only asserts that you follow whatever process you adopt. In that sense, it encourages you to steer away from New Year's resolutions about the things you wish you did but did not really adhere to in favor of only adopting practices you can actually stick to.

CMMI

The CMMI is a rich process framework developed by the Department of Defense, in conjunction with the Software Engineering Institute at Carnegie Mellon University. It provides a way of categorizing all different kinds of processes and assessing the sophistication with which an organization approaches those processes. Like ISO, CMMI by itself does not tell you how to do your development since it just assesses how sophisticated your organization is. CMMI is a requirement in certain industries, especially in the defense sector. It is most useful outside of those areas if you have a large and diverse organization and if there is a need to bring greater consistency to the organization. In this case, doing the assessment is very helpful for understanding both your strong and weak areas. It is a great tool in driving process improvement efforts. Where it falls down is that the official certifications are notoriously easy to game and the fact that someone is Level 5 certified means very, very little about their real state.

There are three important and helpful ideas in CMMI. First, CMMI supplies a way of classifying the sophistication of an organization at attacking any given activity:

- Level 1: Initial – People do their tasks without any particular plan
- Level 2: Managed – Basic project management techniques applied and see repeatable results
- Level 3: Defined – Organization has defined processes for this activity and follows them
- Level 4: Measured – Organization measures these processes
- Level 5: Optimized – Organization learns from these measurements

Secondly, CMMI provides a classification of all of Software Engineering into 22 process areas and hints as how these levels apply to each. What is good about this is that you get a nice framework for studying your organization and seeing what areas your organization is better at than others. To do this, begin by checking how in each area the organization asks the question, "How do we want to do this?" Having asked that, you should see if the resulting answer is followed. If yes, check if it is measured. And if it is, you should find out if the organization has the courage to listen to the measurements.

CMMI recognizes that in a larger organization, different groups may need to answer some of these questions differently. It therefore allows the organization to define a base process that serves as a minimal *lingua franca* across the organization and then permits specific processes tailored from that base process for different teams.

All in all, this gives an excellent way of organizing your process improvement activities, provided you do not get too hung up on paperwork. In cases where CMMI is required, the official CMMI requirements for mountains of documentation on the processes can be problematic. In practice, what matters is the basic sequence of: identifying what we want, doing what we want, measuring it, and lastly, learning from the measurements. This is the important spirit of CMMI and it will benefit almost any development methodology.

Thus, CMMI is still not a substitute for any of the specific development methodology issues raised in this chapter, just because it can work with almost any of them. (Well, maybe not pure XP, but that should be obvious!)

Agility

Most specific modern development methodologies that propose alternatives to the classic Waterfall model fall under the Agile umbrella. Agile methodology evolved as people noticed how highly effective the best small teams of good developers are and how exponentially worse most large programming teams are. Noticing what was different between effective and non-effective teams, a set of best practices has been codified as the Agile Manifesto[3]:

We are uncovering better ways of developing software by doing it and helping others do it.

- Through this work, we have come to value:
  - ➢ **Individuals and interactions** over processes and tools
  - ➢ **Working software** over comprehensive documentation
  - ➢ **Customer collaboration** over contract negotiation responding to change over following a plan
  - ➢ **Responding to change** over following a plan

- That is, while there is value in the items on the right, we value the items on the left more.

---

[3] See http://agilemanifesto.org/ for more information.

This manifesto leads to a set of 12 Agile principles[4]:

- Our highest priority is to satisfy the customer through early and continuous delivery of valuable software.
- Welcome changing requirements, even late in development. Agile processes harness change for the customer's competitive advantage
- Deliver working software frequently, from a couple of weeks to a couple of months, with a preference to the shorter timescale.
- Business people and developers must work together daily throughout the project.
- Build projects around motivated individuals.

Give them the environment and support they need and trusting them to get the job done.
- The most efficient and effective method of conveying information to and within a development team is face-to-face conversation.
- Working software is the primary measure of progress.
- Agile processes promote sustainable development. The sponsors, developers, and users should be able to maintain a constant pace indefinitely.
- Continuous attention to technical excellence and good design enhances agility.
- Simplicity— the art of maximizing the amount of work not done— is essential.
- The best architectures, requirements, and designs emerge from self-organizing teams.
- At regular intervals, the team reflects on how to become more effective, then tunes and adjusts its behavior accordingly.

From this basic understanding, a variety of practical methodologies have evolved. Both the promise and the problem with Agile is its hostility to traditional bureaucracy. This feeling is easily perverted into the belief that "anything goes" and that random and willful behavior constitutes Agile. This

---

[4] See http://agilemanifesto.org/principles.html

is a **giant** misunderstanding. **Agile methodology implies a great deal of discipline.** If you see a chaotic team, they are chaotic, not agile. Another set of confusion comes from the great variety of these methodologies, the weird jargon they have spawned, and the religious debates between their adherents. None of these are useful to the engineering leader.

What is useful— and thus, important— are the basic core of beliefs and a very workable set of practices that all modern software organizations should have. If done well, it creates better quality products, faster, more predictably, and with a happier team. While this may seem a strong statement, bear in mind that Agile is not in detail terribly new; it is mostly an accumulation of best practices. Adopting even significant parts of these can yield great benefits.

The following are some of the core Agile practices that are typically constant across all flavors, albeit sometimes obscured by strange terminology:

- Trust and collaboration between product managers, users, and developers
- Highly flexible and non-confrontational planning practices
- Development scheduled in short iterations of identical length
- Flexible and negotiated implementation targets per iteration
- Continuous prioritization and risk assessment
- Early and continuous software delivery
- Focus on keeping daily builds good
- Focus on comprehensive automated tests, kept green at all times
- Just enough documentation
- Just in-time documentation
- A well-managed backlog
- Clear acceptance criteria
- A clear rhythm of iterations spanning years

We will explain the useful parts of Agile (Scrum, Spiral) as well as its less useful parts (XP, RUP).

Core Agile Model

All Agile methodologies have two things in common. First and foremost, developers and users are empowered to collaborate closely and build plans that work for them, rather than having plans imposed top-down. To realize this, the development schedule is characteristically sliced into a series of iterations of constant length, from one week to one month in length, depending on the scale of the project. All schedules are based on fitting tasks into the iteration. The team maintains a backlog of things to do and some notion of which iteration they go into. At the beginning of each iteration, the team decides which tasks to do based on a careful reprioritization and risk assessment. In particular, riskier pieces are prioritized over the lesser ones. Then during the iteration, the team strives to keep a working daily build. For all new features, automated tests are built. As much as possible, these automated tests are run against the daily build and the attempt is made to keep them running. QA works side by side with the developers in helping with the system level testing. The developers, for their part, are responsible for writing all their own unit tests. At the end of the iteration, every team member needs to have a well-defined deliverable to show off. Then, the cycle repeats.

This model requires Product Management to be intimately involved and be willing and able to help in the regular reprioritization process to make sure the team is building the right stuff.

Generally, only enough documentation is built to satisfy the needs of the external constituents. For the team's use in the current iteration, it should be no more than that. Schedules, as much as possible, are done collaboratively with the developers, asking each developer how much they can do in the next iteration. At the end of each iteration, everyone receives feedback as to how over or under ambitious their plan was, allowing people to tune their estimation skills. It is important to make the iterations run no longer than a month because, otherwise, the developers cease being able to make accurate estimates.

The advantage of the iterations is that it greatly reduces risk for large projects. Keeping things working all the time diffuses the problem of the awful integration phases that many large traditional projects kill their schedules after the putative "code complete" date. Keeping the programmers involved makes for honest schedules that can be kept. Keeping the product managers involved all the time prevents bad surprises and at the same time, allows for adjustments due to changing business and technical issues.

So far, so good. But how do we apply it in practice? We will give brief overviews of the methodologies. If you want to try one of them, it is important to read up on them in detail, talk to people who have done it, and be thorough! In spite of the apparent informality of these approaches, they need to be followed rigorously to work. If done in an inconsistent way, nonsense will happen!

Extreme Programming (XP)

XP was the original Agile methodology. It includes all of the above plus a couple of extra twists:

- **No Designs**
  XP believes there should be no designs of any kind. The customer should always be with the team physically. XP firmly believes that everyone should be collocated. Plans should be drawn on a white board. Engineers should code new features and show them to the customer immediately. If changes are needed, the code gets refactored. The design should always be simple and understandable to the team.

- **Planning game**
  In place of standard designs and requirements, XP has a very different approach. The planning phase includes the exploration, commitment, and iteration phases typical of more classic methodologies. One main difference is that unlike the typical MRD, XP requirements are based on user stories. These stories are usually task-based and have the benefit of forcing the development team to think like a customer. The typical MRD— while it is commonly feature-based and not task-based— does have the benefit of documenting orthogonal requirements including performance goals and platform requirements that cannot be captured in a two sentence "story".

- **Sustainable pace**

   XP permits no overtime. It feels programmers do their best work with enough sleep and that risk management and reprioritization are the keys to managing the schedule, not cramming in slipshod work at the end.

- **Pair programming**

   XP believes that programmers should do all work in pairs. Design, coding, and testing should always be done together. This is based on the observation that if two good engineers who get along well collaborate, they can often do great things.

Advantages of XP Practices

   For conventional business applications where the technology is simple, there is an abundance of small features to implement that depend highly on understanding a customer's detailed requirements. XP is a completely functional model.

Disadvantages of XP

   The biggest problem with XP is that its adherents are so dogmatic that they fail to see where the model breaks down. This dogmatism can totally interfere with a rational discussion of the limitations of the model. These limitations are:

- With its opposition to design and formal documentation, it has no real answer both for large projects that require multi-site coordination and for the complex issues that require numerous analyses before one can meaningfully code anything. On the other hand, if one is adding simple UI features to a business application, then the XP processes can work fairly well for keeping users and engineers aligned.

- Pair programming is an acquired taste. It sometimes makes perfect sense when: one does very high risk changes; one wants to work with a trusted partner on some technical brainstorming; and when one tutors a junior employee. The downside— especially when it is required— is that the two engineers need to be socially compatible and smell about the same and the work needs to be complex enough to keep both of them engaged. If there is no good chemistry between the engineers, pair programming can be a painful experience.

- If you suffer from indecisive product managers who flip-flop a lot, premature implemented work can result in a great deal of rework. Again, the more complex the user requirements become, the more legitimate reasons there are for changes to the user design. Having the engineers program this in parallel before these have gelled adequately can lower productivity.

- While rational schedules are certainly a good thing, overtime is still a periodic necessity. Time is money! When it is crunch time, people need to have the proper level of urgency. At the same time, it is certainly correct that too much rush-rush is responsible for many quality escapes.

Thus, despite the XP being a lovely idea, it becomes hard to implement in many environments when it insists on some overly simplistic approaches,

Test Driven Development Methodology

Test Driven Programming is an outgrowth from XP methodology but is not logically connected to it. The idea is fairly straightforward. First, we believe we should always have a working system. Second, we believe that every part of a program should be subject to an automated test. It can then follow that every action on the part of the engineer should be immediately subject to an automated test. The logical conclusion of this line of reasoning is that prior to making any code change, the engineer should first design an automated test case for it. This test case will fail as expected because the code to support does not exist yet. When the code is then finished, the test will pass.

This approach has some benefits. It forces engineers to decide up front how to tell if they are done or not. It guarantees that micro-feature-by-micro-feature everything works exactly as it has to. It has been shown experimentally that for very junior and less experienced engineers, this approach causes them to produce higher quality code than they would otherwise.

The approach clearly falls down though in many areas. It only works for fairly stand-alone bits of functionality. Any time the functionality of a system is dependent on the interconnections between numerous pieces of code and on some fairly complex architecture, it would be impossible to create a realistic test case up front. Real time systems with parallel processing and interrupts, or hardware interfaces are typical examples where this does not work at all. In real life, this is a powerful tool. It should be used as part of a sensible unit test strategy especially in those places where it makes sense. And no more than that.

Scrum

Scrum is the most practical and scalable form of Agile. It is generally a kinder and gentler form of XP, allowing— but not requiring— some of its more "extreme" aspects like pair programming.

Distinctive for Scrum is its reliance on a short daily meeting (the Scrum) where everyone understands the day's priorities and resolves blocking issues. Scrum can work with big teams by allowing each team's daily meeting to send a representative to a Scrum-of-Scrum meeting wherein problems across teams are resolved. The daily meeting idea is often hard to accept for teams trying it for the first time but it is very empowering. By swiftly answering questions and removing roadblocks (i.e. assigning engineers to fix automation failures), it maximizes the team's productivity. The meeting is coordinated by the Scrum master who can be elected by the team or simply be a program or project manager. While collocation is good, it is not strictly required.

Scrum has a reasonable answer for how to accommodate complex designs within Agile methodologies. Agile always wants work to be timeboxed and for there to be a deliverable at the end of the iteration. For design problems, the deliverable can simply be a specification, even an incomplete one that has been published and reviewed with someone, either peers or a manager. The key thing is that the engineer has signed up to do some part of the design work and that there is a check if the work is indeed completed. By simply requiring all work, no matter what type it is, to produce some deliverable to show that the work was done and done well, even large scale design tasks— and, in fact, many non pure-development tasks— will easily fit into an iteration model.

Spiral Methodology

Spiral methodology is a compromise between iterative development and Waterfall methodology. It also structures development into a series of iterations yet allows for a full design-implement-test cycle inside of the iterations. This is in fact the most realistic way of introducing iterative development into very large and complex systems. Pure Agile, especially XP, is almost always only applicable to fairly small and algorithmically simplistic environments. In any kinds of large system, there are major requirements for design work to coordinate tasks between modules and teams as well as the need to do complex integration testing. In this context, the Spiral model allows breaking down a very long development cycle into a series of mini-Waterfalls. This provides many benefits of iterative methodology in terms of reducing risk, allowing lessons to be learned and, at the same time, providing more flexibility. It also gives a context for further experiments with methodology because individual teams within an iteration can adopt different approaches— for example, one team might do full Agile. However, all will still work as long as it fits into the overall iteration scheme.

By allowing a smooth interchange between traditional Waterfalls and modern Agile approaches and by providing a good way to break down big projects, Spiral methodology is the most commonly implemented form of Agile development in large commercial systems.

Rational Unified Process (RUP)

The RUP is a relatively complex methodology promulgated by the nice people at Rational Software. It is an eclectic mixture of all of the above, wrapped up in rather intricate verbiage. If you have a large organization, which is easily mesmerized by consultants and if you think that COBOL is unfairly maligned, then spend money to have Rational teach you how to do this. Otherwise, do not do this.

Evaluating Methodologies

To Agile or Not to Agile

Generally, if your requirements are very stable and are entirely known up front, a Spiral approach works the best. Basically, it is just Waterfall with enough intermediate milestones to avoid integration hell. On the other hand, if there many technical risks and/or poorly understood customer requirements, the full Agile approach is indicated.

When Creating a Hybrid Model Makes Sense

The most important thing to remember about Agile is that it is a collection of best practices. These best practices can often be used independently of one another. Notice also that most of the arguments against any of the pure methodologies are almost always in fact fully justified. In practice, any real organization needs to customize a methodology suited to its technologies and culture, picking and choosing from the best of the different methods.

Generally, one of the most straightforward approaches to this problem is by starting with a Spiral methodology and within the iterations implement Scrum as the organization is interested in it. If you then apply the general Agile methods of continuous build, test, integration, prioritization, and risk assessment with daily meetings, you wind up with a good mixture of the best practices of all the different methodologies. You can then also allow different teams to go further into Agile as they desire— this is itself an Agile approach!

However, whatever approach you take, you should still define your organization's process and follow it rigorously. The discipline of doing this well is what makes it work. Conversely, it is very hard to make a case to do any of the above approaches purely and in isolation from the rest. The real world does not match the theoretical confines of the methodology zealots. It is important to note that the original XP project was cancelled before it was completed!

Adopting Agile

Adopting agile well is not as easy as it looks. First, you should do your homework, understand well the proposed methodology, and determine if it will fit your organization. Second, you have to sell it to the organization. Developers will think it is a management trick at first but once they see you allow them to drive the process, they will come on board quite enthusiastically. Product Management is an easy sell since Agile gives them more opportunities to change their mind— for better or for worse. The hardest sell is Engineering Management due to its apparent loss of control. For one thing, developers determine schedules, not pointy-haired bosses. A traditional project also has huge specifications and vast-detailed schedules. Unfortunately, they are always out-of-date and at best, comforting lies. Thus, you need to retrain management to appreciate the accuracy and currency of the high level schedules one gets in a well-run Agile project. They may be shorter but they are better since they bring precision and accuracy in line. The same applies with the documentation. One needs to show the Management team how they retain control via the regular risk assessment and prioritization processes. One also needs to teach Management how to lead without micromanaging, which is goodness in and of itself. Once you have got people sold, people have to be trained. If you are switching big bang, you will need formal training sessions and you have to spend a lot of time getting people to do the process correctly. You need to watch out for typical beginners' mistakes such as:

- Vague and unverifiable stories in the iteration wherein you cannot tell afterwards if they have been done or not
- Hopelessly optimistic schedules for the iteration
- Failure to pounce on the problems in the daily meetings

An alternative to the big bang approach is to sneak it in piecemeal by first doing Spiral and then bring in the Scrum elements one by one.

Other Factors

Beyond your basic framework, additional decisions will be market-enforced. Therefore, if you are a military contractor, you may have to implement CMMI. You may also have to do ISO for marketing reasons. Your engineers may want to do something like XP or Test Driven methodology locally. If you use the flexible approach advocated here, you should be able to accommodate any of these without too much trouble.

Some Metrics

- Engineering productivity (ULOC /mo) (= uncommented lines of code per month)
- Schedule adherence (Actual versus planned)
- Quantitative survey of product features and functionality versus customer needs

Anecdotes

Happy Example - J2EE application

The target application was a highly customizable J2EE/Ajax Call Center application with 70 people working on it. It had a vast array of features and its releases took far too long with painful integration phases, protracted QA phases, major quality problems, burnt out teams, and very unpredictable schedules. The test phases completely dominated the schedules where in the Waterfall model, only six weeks were given for Development versus four months for QA.

To tame this, we adopted Scrum. We automated most of QA. We ran daily builds and made sure the automation passed. We set up a daily meeting to monitor the tests and to review any decisions that needed to be made, questions to be answered, and problems to be solved. We divided the work into one-month iterations and built our master schedule around fitting tasks into months, not assigning times to tasks. The developers were asked to flesh out in detail what went into each of the iteration. Product Management got to help do the prioritization each month and agree or disagree on what was in or out. QA worked side by side with the developers on test plans and new tests for features completed in the iteration. For the next major release, we needed one month of QA instead of four. It shipped on time and it worked. Product Management was delighted because we dropped no features at the last minute and, in fact, added quite a few things late in the game. We were all amazed it worked!

Automated Build/Test Environment

The application in this case is the entire development environment for a very large embedded operating system. There are around 80 people involved in five different locations, representing five different organizations. Again, Scrum is used. We do monthly iterations, daily meetings, builds, and test stuff. We engage heavily with customer representatives on a weekly basis and let the developers drive schedules. We work crazy overtime when it is needed and give comp time to make up for it. The approach has greatly increased productivity, morale, and customer satisfaction. Interestingly, we have not told anyone we are doing Scrum. Most of the people involved are still unaware of this.

What Not To Do

Selecting a development methodology depends heavily both on your team and your company. There are times when this might be out of your control. In very small or very early stage startups, you might find yourself initially struggling to establish the basic best practices. I headed up Engineering for an early stage startup during the dotcom era. I had development staff in China, Hong Kong, and the US. Three out of four of the US team left just before I started— the first in a series of unpleasant surprises. I found that there was no source code control system. There were also no QA and staging servers, with developers directly editing with notepad on production systems. The code was different on each country's servers— even before localization— with different features and options. I spent most of my time working to instill the basics of development— some kind of documentation of what features are suppose to be, basic source code control, and the startling idea of testing new code on something other than production. Some developers rebelled and went to the CEO, claiming that all this "bureaucracy" was slowing down development. I left this position because the CEO supported their existing "semi-random scramble" development methodology since it had seemed to be more energetic and "dotcom", back when that was a positive description. It is a bad sign when the head of Engineering is unable to control their development process. A business environment that does not trust the VPE to be fully in charge of this is ultimately a bad situation.

3.4 Project Management

Introduction

What we mean by project management is the organized communication required to coordinate the activities of multiple people and teams working together on some common objective.

Project management is a core management discipline required to successfully build most non-trivial systems. While there are many books on this topic, we will discuss in this chapter some of the key project management skills every engineering manager needs as well as how project management as a discipline fits into the development organization.

Basic Skills Needed in Project Management

There is a minimal set of project management skills every successful manager needs to master. This includes effective meeting management, planning, and tracking.

Meeting Management

Surprisingly, many managers are not good at running meetings, which is a key skill for keeping an organization productive. If you poll developers in many companies, a common complaint is that too much time is wasted in pointless meetings.

You need to conduct meetings to keep people in sync but they can easily multiply and become a substitute for work. A real trap for a senior manager is that as an executive much of the day is spent in meetings. This can lull one into a sense that this is all there is to do in the day when in fact, a senior manager wants engineers doing development and not just giving status updates!

The first thing to consider about meetings is how to avoid having more meetings than necessary. Thus, before you call a new meeting, you should ask yourself, "Is this meeting really needed? Can it be combined with any existing meetings?" Often, a few longer and larger meetings can replace a number of smaller meetings, especially if the goal is just to keep some senior leader such as you properly informed. Another trick is to use Wikis and blogs to publish status information. This can often reduce the need for a whole class of purely status related meetings. It is a good practice to regularly review the set of meetings being held in your organization and look for opportunities to rationalize and streamline them. (We will discuss in the Communications chapter the best practices for when you do want to have frequent meetings.)

Planning and Tracking

No matter what the kind of project you are working on, making the group define up front the success criteria as well as the next steps is a good practice. This would turn the simplest projects into a basic set of milestones you can track. You can then monitor these milestones for both progress and problems at regular intervals, which can happen via meetings or offline. The key thing is that the involved group working on an organized activity should have an agreed upon statement regarding what will happen next and when will it happen. The basic principle is: "Say what you will do, do what you said you would". When people get stuck, their situation and— at the same time— the mitigation plans need to be identified quickly. While this sounds simple, the basic discipline of rigorously sticking to these principles is what allows groups to get the task done in a transparent and reasonably predictable way.

You need to communicate the plan once you have it. This involves telling what the purpose of the project is, who is doing it, what the deliverable is, when the deliverable is coming, what dependencies the project has on other projects, what problems might be stalling the project, and what risks the project entails to itself or to the organization. Wiki pages and PowerPoint presentations are common tools for doing this. A good discipline is to always keep an up-to-date status page or presentation and keep that updated on a continuous basis, in which case, one always has something to point interested parties at.

Project Management in the Organization

For projects of any interesting size, it becomes useful to start having dedicated project managers. There are many ways of doing this and the individuals involved often have different titles. In many organizations, both the first and the second level managers spend much of their time doing project management. As complexity increases, there can also be full-time project managers who do not have any people management responsibilities. These can be devoted to particular projects or parts of products or to working on entire products or releases of products. The names for these positions can be confusing. Some companies call those working on the entire product as "release managers" while others as "program managers". On the other hand, those working on the small pieces are variously called "project managers" or "program managers".

Typically, a dedicated project manager does all the basic project management actions described above but on a much larger scale.

A key function of a project manager is to accumulate all relevant overview and status information about the project and be able to communicate status on the project to all interested parties, whether this involves publishing to a web site or making presentations at meetings.

A second function is to actively work cross-group dependencies and issues and identify what meetings are needed to be held or to require the people invited to existing meetings to resolve those issues.

The most interesting activity a project manager needs to do on larger meetings is to formally create and track the schedule of the project. There are a variety of ways of doing this. On large systems, Microsoft Project is the most common tool. This is useful if you have to track the actions of particular individuals and groups in very great detail. However, it is very time-consuming and should only be undertaken if you have enough project management time available to absorb the administrative overhead involved. Notice that Project itself does not scale very well and it usually needs to be mated to some backend— minimally, Microsoft Project Server— to allow for effective simultaneous use by multiple teams. Notice that on extremely large industrial projects like entire airport terminals, there are even more powerful tools such as Primavera that are useful. But only go there if you have thousands of people working on a task.

Many projects, in fact, can be tracked well using Microsoft Excel. Generally, there are real advantages in using the most lightweight possible process. This is especially true if you are doing Agile development where detailed plans are only worked out a short distance in advance. Radical XP teams indeed try to just rely on with what they can write on a white board; those of us who live in geographically distributed worlds have a hard time reading whiteboards on the other side of the world!

For people doing larger Agile systems, there are a variety of nicely specialized project management tools. But even then, you should think about keeping it simple! It is better to have a simple schedule, which is up-to-date, readable, and believable both to the team and the management, rather than having a big and impressive Project schedule that is generally disconnected from reality. A good technique is to create a spreadsheet with tabs by project and for each project, create a list of tasks describing the name, description, dates, status, risks, priority, difficulty, and impact of each one. Such spreadsheet can be used both for planning as well as for status tracking. A single spreadsheet of this kind can easily manage even the work of teams comprised of 50 members without too much trouble.

An interesting management question is: "How many project managers do I need?" This is a function of the scalability and bandwidth of your management team. As your organization grows, you need to regularly review with your team how they are doing with their time-management. If you see your staff having a hard time staying focused on strategic objectives because of too much communication struggles on tactical projects, it is probably time to add more Project Management staff.

Project Leadership

Driving Projects Forward

Being the head of Engineering, you act both as a leader and a manager. You are supposed to lead and not just watch your projects! Without strong leadership, a project often stalls under the weight of bureaucracy and other roadblocks or just simple inertia of an organization. Therefore, one of the most important roles of a leader is to move projects forward.

First, let us be clear that this is more about organized leadership— that is, leading your organization and your company in a structured way such that they achieve results. Hence, this definition is in a broader and higher level and the activities include pushing actions forward, gaining consensus, driving to decisions, getting buy-in from other departments, and getting leaders amongst your reports to drive projects forward successfully.

Gaining Consensus

Before a project can move forward, a leader must first gain consensus from all stakeholders that the project is worth doing. This often entails many different skills and probably is the most difficult task for a technical leader. The skills involved here include:

- Ability to communicate clearly
- Ability to sell an idea (or a dream, if the idea is hard to quantify)
- Ability to analyze its benefits
- Ability to navigate the political landscape
- Many other soft and hard skills, depending on the organizations, size, and players

To the novice leader, it might seem that consensus is optional. Sometimes, a person new in a management role may feel that it is a sign of weakness to seek consensus and that a strong leader drives forward regardless of what others think. This is, however, a grave mistake. A truly confident leader is always willing to listen to what their staff says. Consensus leads to better teamwork and more productivity since people will actively use their creativity and talents to promote a mutually agreed upon goal. The alternative can lead to what is sometimes called a "death march", where people work on a project because they are told to but they do not believe in the project's purpose or approach. When there is poor transparency in the organization, there are times when the entire project team openly talks about the futility or meaningless nature of the project, with only the upper management unaware of these views. Building consensus builds morale and teamwork and it is the only way to inspire talented professionals to put their hearts into their work.

A prerequisite for gaining consensus is to be clear on the benefits of the proposed project. Before pushing a project forward, a leader must be completely convinced of the benefits. Otherwise, it will be very hard to convince others. Sometimes, it is not that easy to quantify benefits, especially for relatively subtle changes like better user interfaces. In those cases, an important skill to learn is to assess the benefits in terms of identifying a particular user and activity that will be noticeably improved by the proposed action. If you can articulate those user level benefits, consensus will be easier to achieve.

Driving Decisions

Project teams will frequently stall when they reach some difficult decision point, particularly when that decision requires actions from other organizations or senior management. At times, a team will not even be fully aware that it is being slowed down for simple lack of perspective into the larger organization. Part of your role as a leader is to monitor the projects in your organization and recognize this kind of situation. It is your job to help drive these problems down by helping the team get in touch with the right people and by clearing organizational obstacles. That includes working with other people from Senior Management to insure alignment on goals as well as protecting your team from political vicissitudes. Again, this requires discipline on your part to monitor project progress, recognize these issues, and then have the personal courage to attack them promptly.

Organizing Teams

A clear management responsibility is making sure you have the right teams working on your projects. This means you have to ensure you

are providing adequate resources to make the team succeed at their assigned goals. It also entails providing enough management bandwidth to
handle these projects. If the project has a cross-functional aspect, you need
to guarantee that other teams are signed up to provide the right time and
attention. You have to maintain perpetual vigilance to make sure that the
organization remains healthy, especially in fast growing organizations. If a
team doubles in six months, it would be very easy for people to get overloaded. This can quickly impact the team's productivity. Keeping your
management structure scalable and with adequate bandwidth is critical to
keeping your projects on track.

Transparency

You have to remain vigilant if the teams are accurately reporting
status. This means being honest about problems and clear about goals. If
you see signs that people are hiding problems from you, you have to jump
on it! Even worse is a mediocre project leadership where there are muddled
goals and vague statements of progress. You have to firmly insist on public
review of specifications and to be clear on verifiable deliverables at milestone boundaries. At the same time, you also need people to feel safe about
reporting bad news. You should praise those who deliver these.

One of the key challenges for the engineering leader at all times is
determining when to delegate and when to dive in. The quality of both the
project reporting and the work being reported are the things you have to
stay on top of. When you see projects getting off-track, you need to jump in
and figure out why the team is having a hard time with their project management. Is it due to the lack of resources? Is it political problems or poor
management? If you have a good discipline on clear project status reporting,
you should be able to generally decide which things you can leave to your
staff and where you have to go into fire-fighting mode.

Assessing Progress

One of the main purposes of most project tracking and scheduling
mechanisms is to document how well a team is tracking to its stated
schedule. Since wanting to report good news is a human nature, this leads to
a fascinating problem which is a standing joke in software development—

almost all software projects quickly become 90 percent complete, completely on schedule, and then get stuck there. The last 10 percent of the work always takes the other 90 percent of the time. Since as the head of Engineering you need to assess progress, make decisions about where to put more resources, change schedules, and change features, it is then critical to accurately know the state of a project. The 90 percent of the problem entirely gets in the way of this. What should you do about it? There are a couple of techniques:

- First, measure progress not against how much work has been done, but about how much is left. So if a schedule calls for 10 weeks and you are eight weeks into it, ask the engineers how much time they need to finish it. If the answer is five weeks, then you are 66 percent done and not 80 percent.

- Second, try to avoid building overly long unverified schedules. This is the downfall of the Waterfall approach because it tends to lead to very long blocks of work with little insight into what is going on inside of them. The iterative model separating things into fairly short chunks with verification of the results makes schedules more accurate because at each iteration boundary, you can tell exactly where you are and you can make many little adjustments instead of a big one at the end. Also, most people are better at estimating the next two weeks than the next six months, so the iterative model encourages more accurate scheduling.

Another good attribute of iterative development is that you can collect metrics on how many of the scheduled pieces a team can do in an iteration as well as how long they take in the end. When fed back to the team, the resulting metrics will help them make more realistic schedules. It can also produce a nice velocity metric that predicts how soon the total project will be done.

A third drastic approach applied on large projects is Earned Value Management. Being labor intensive, this approach should not be used without adequate support. This follows up on the first idea above about always thinking on how much work is left to do. Basically, you assign a financial value to the complete system and to all work as it is being done.

You know how much work has been completed and how long it has taken you to do. You also know the revised estimates of how long the rest will take. This will tell you how much value you have produced, how quickly you are producing value, and how much value you still need to produce. You can then calculate velocities of how many dollars per month value are produced and how many still need to be produced in order to meet the deadline. Remembering that the labor of all engineers costs more when your product is late accurately tells you your productivity as well as its financial implications. Assuming your program managers can calculate all these numbers, it provides an excellent and accurate model of your progress in terms of when you will finish and how much it will cost. This approach is mandated on many Department of Defense projects and should be seriously considered if you have the financial sophistication on your staff to handle the model. However, it is probably NOT a good idea for most startups.

Conclusion

Despite the fact that there are dozens of tools and methodologies to help measure project progress, none of these will be successful if you have not achieved consensus and transparency. If people do not believe in a project, they will give the status reports necessary to protect their career. All project management tools depend on the following principles we have described: driving projects forward, building consensus, driving decisions, organizing teams, and having transparency.

3.5 Release Management

Introduction

Generally, most software and hardware products are built from some code base multiple snapshots of which are releases to the public. Therefore, our basic unit of currency in Engineering is normally a product release. You can have many products and many releases of each product, sometimes all at the same time.

Release Management is one of the most challenging aspects of Engineering Management because it is the discipline that causes these releases to get delivered to the customer! It combines a couple of different functions such as:

- **Planning** - What releases to make and when
- **Team Building** - Assembling the groups to work on a release of a product
- **Program Management** - Coordinating and monitoring the master schedule for the release
- **Coordination** - Managing dependencies between teams
- **Organizing Launch** - Making sure that Engineering coordinates with other business functions on the launch of the release
- **End Game** - Leading the difficult final phases of a release to ensure it actually releases
- **Maintenance** - Organizing maintenance activities on releases
- **Obsolescence** - Managing end-of-life on products

This is a rather broad charter! It requires a complex set of both technical and political skills, great determination and communication skills, and above all, a good sense of humor. Particularly in larger organizations, assignments can make or break careers.

Product Lifecycle

The release manager is essentially the program manager of the product lifecycle. The product lifecycle is a generalization of the engineering development process, broadened to include the full scope of business activities involved in creating products. Generally, any product has to move through the following phases:

- General roadmap or business plan
- Specific product concept
- Detailed requirements
- Detailed design and schedule
- Implementation
- Launch preparation
- Early shipment
- Maintenance
- End-of-life

While all these steps occur in some form for just about any product, their exact nature depends massively on both the kind and the scale of product and the nature of the engineering methodology chosen. Also, a small company will have easier time than a big one. We can look at some typical cases:

Large Operating System or Enterprise Software Releases

In this case, all of these phases exist as well-defined separate entities. Typically, products are supported long after their release so it is necessary to maintain multiple branches of them in parallel since different customers will be on different releases. In this scenario, managing the maintenance burden and timely end-of-life planning are critical. Releases are usually large, complicated, and fairly well spread out.

Hosted Web-based Software

In contrast, many hosted applications are built in very short releases from a single code line. Both maintenance and end-of-life are irrelevant because the previous release is always entirely replaced by the new one. On the other hand, the short time between releases can become a challenge here, especially with respect to more radical changes.

Shrink-wrapped Applications and Devices

Since many purely shrink-wrapped systems cannot be updated in the field, there is no maintenance per se but huge pressure to get everything perfect the first time. Additionally, there can be huge schedule pressure if it is a consumer product where releasing in time for key seasonal dates (e.g. holidays or tax time) is crucial to the success of the product.

Multimedia Projects

Some web sites are more graphic-oriented projects than true technology projects. In this scenario, large quantities of the work may be done by contractors, in which case Release Management becomes very involved in the actual assembly and maintenance of the team. A release manager may become more of a producer than just a program manager.

Obviously, this little survey shows that there are many variations here around a couple of questions:

- One team, many teams?
- One company, many companies?
- Few big releases, many little releases?
- Many branches at once, just one branch?
- Does it have to be perfect the first time?
- Will it stick around for a long time?

Naturally, the bigger and more complex the project is, the more hair-raising it all gets. Program managing giant projects on the order of Microsoft Vista represent some of the most extreme management challenges anyone may ever be exposed to.

We will next look at the different aspects of a release manager's life. Note that while presented in a somewhat Waterfall-like fashion, in real life a release manager is semi-randomly buffeted between all these tasks in an endless kaleidoscope of fun.

A Note on Process

Release management in a larger organization is generally simplified by publishing a standard product lifecycle with defined checkpoints and a regular set of criteria for moving from one point to the next. But remember that the purpose of this exercise is to remove needless conversations from the system to not create more paperwork! A good lifecycle is easily understood, flexible, and easy to follow with as little overhead as the organization can bear. Never collect signoffs for the sake of collecting them! Do not do this:

Anecdote

At one company, the IT director felt it was his moral imperative to block releases that deviated in any way from the process. He would walk around the company carrying a baseball bat and the release documentation. On one occasion, he triumphantly interrupted my meeting with the CTO to declare a release rejected and then tore the documentation and throw it at our feet. It did not matter to him that the error was a simple date typographical error and it was someone else's release. The point is that often, IT feels it is their duty to resist releases to "protect the company" and that both Engineering and IT must find a way to balance this with the need to make progress.

Release Planning

The first order of business for the release manager is to convert a general roadmap or business plan into a viable release schedule. This is a simple diagram showing a timeline of different releases for different products. It is so simple yet so hard to make! Based on understanding the company's business needs, technical capabilities, and levels of support, one has to divide the work to be done into reasonable releases which have dates acceptable from a Sales and Support standpoint. This planning has to consider multiple needs. Development has a fixed capacity and one cannot schedule more projects through a certain phase than there is staff for. Product launches have to be coordinated with Marketing and Sales activities such as getting in the channel for Christmas in a consumer product. Releases aimed at existing customers also have to honor commitments made by Support to customers. One also needs to consider when customers are interested and willing to take on new releases. At the same time, schedules have to respond to what Engineering can deliver. In environments where multiple releases are supported at once, the support burden posed by the existing releases can become quite onerous. This requires working with Support to set up strict end-of-life policies and retire support on older product, which in turn requires that there are clean upgrade paths for important customers.

Settling these schedules often requires tremendous effort for an engineering leader, particularly as there will often be huge pressure to over commit. A real advantage of Agile processes is that by allowing for flexible reductions in content, they can make it safer to commit to aggressive schedules. Also, having short release cycles where that is practical removes a lot of pain from these discussions.

Release Drivers

As part of this process, one needs to understand the following dynamics that govern both the generation and destruction of releases:

- New features require new releases.
- Vehicles are needed for bug fixes.
- New releases introduce new bugs so customers often want bugs fixed in patches to old versions.
- The bigger the customer, the slower they are to upgrade. Consumers may want to upgrade all the time— enterprise customers may want to upgrade every few years.
- If too many old versions are maintained in parallel, maintenance releases will cause bottlenecks in sustaining Engineering and QA.
- Large customers will demand custom fixes just for them.
- You may have a matrix of platforms (i.e. underlying software like database, application server, browser as well as underlying hardware

configurations) on which you must assure the product operates correctly.

There are various approaches to this problem:

- Create staged releases:
    - ➤ Beta/first release— aggressive customers, only the development platform is supported
    - ➤ Second release— more conservative customers, certify other platforms
    - ➤ Maintenance phase— only a lessening number of bug fixes
    - ➤ End-of-life

- With hosted software, you can avoid many of these issues but instead face the challenge of finding enough time to test non-trivial changes in the face of the short release cycles. However, this is usually a simpler challenge and the software industry as a whole is moving increasingly toward hosted solutions.

Parallel Releases

One of the harder tasks for the head of Engineering working with Release Engineering is working on more than one release simultaneously. Most organizations can focus on only one thing at a time. Most will find it difficult to make progress on a longer-term objective while being focused on a shorter-term goal. If the organization wants to do very large scale long-term changes in a system in parallel with shorter term releases, the engineering leader has to work hard to create isolated resources to work on the longer term project that will not get cannibalized by the shorter-term ones.

Patch Strategy

Properly fitting maintenance into product development is crucial. Full releases are fairly heavy in weight and having a lightweight approach to manage quick fixes can help unburden resources for more major development. A basic component of this is having an effective patch strategy for getting point fixes to customer without requiring full-scale releases. To wit, there should be a clear delineation between what can be shipped in a patch release, what requires a point release, and what requires a major release. Customers need to know what to expect in different releases and what planning is needed to apply patches and upgrades.

Patch releases are the quickest to turn around, thus, they are generally used to get important bug fixes or even feature requests (e.g. as part of acceptance for a major new customer) into customers' hands. Since you tend to have many patch releases, one of your worries is the future upgrade cost. Therefore, the code released through patches should not require special upgrade effort. Ideally, only logic changes will get released through a patch. Schema changes or changes in a public API, among others, should not be part of a patch release because of their heavier upgrade (and testing) costs. Upgrade cost is of course less of a concern with hosted software.

In comparison, point releases and major releases each require more time and effort. Point releases are commonly rollups of patch releases along with some minor features and low severity bug fixes. They may also include certification across other software/hardware platforms or other languages. Major releases, on the other hand, are the vehicles for significant new development and they provide the greatest release management challenge.

Regular Patch Release Schedule

It is important for customers to determine when they can expect fixes to be able to plan for timely upgrades. When a customer is on an actively maintained product line, there will be frequent small and large fixes that customers need. Having regularly scheduled maintenance releases helps set customer expectation about timeliness, priority, and reasonable fix rates. If there are regularly scheduled maintenance releases and you tell the customer that the fix is in the next maintenance release, most complaints about priority will be defused. Getting a fix during the official release before the next official release is difficult to push for. Naturally, if it is reasonable to provide a patch release to get immediate relief to the customer, then that should be done.

Regularly scheduled maintenance releases offer several key benefits. They provide predictable timeframes for releases, thus allowing the customers to plan for upgrades and updates. Knowing when the releases are coming and what the rough amount of effort is required to upgrade to a new release allows them to plan the efforts involved on their side and set expectations with the users. Regular maintenance releases also help Engineering and QA planning. They know what to expect and are encouraged to provide plenty of fixes in each patch. They also make the workload predictable and reduce risk around the release by limiting the scope of new features to be delivered in any one release.

Why Release Planning is So Painful

In reality, release planning is often a painful process. The trouble is that almost all organizations have a bigger appetite for product than what an engineering organization can ever deliver. Ultimately, the biggest fights any engineering manager faces are against efforts to over commit the release plans. These battles are usually abetted by too much optimism from the engineers. The result is invariably projects that slip their schedules as reality catches up with them. A usual sign of overcommitted projects is that they get past their earlier milestones with various things unfinished. The product turns out to have many gaps when it enters QA. As developers finish development at last, QA needs to redo testing and— low and behold— the test phase extends. It is easy to mistakenly identify this situation for a QA, quality, or productivity problem. In the first place, it is a release planning problem for having made a bad schedule. The reality though is that these bad schedules are often driven top down by Senior Management and are hard to avoid.

The best medicine known against this phenomenon is the Agile approach of building content incrementally because in this scenario— through the process of continuous prioritization— there is always a working product with the most important features. This strategy works as long as there are smaller slices of content that can be discarded at milestone boundaries to meet the schedule. If this approach is workable, it can allow very predictable product releases, without requiring particular acts of rationality on the part of one's fellow C-level staff. If this approach is not feasible, part of an engineering leader's mission is to work tirelessly to improve the organization's process maturity. This is a codeword for making the organization more honest and realistic about constructing release plans.

Conceiving the Product

Team Building

This step occurs mostly in very complex multi-organization or largely outsourced projects. Basically, Release Management needs to ensure that all the required players are assembled. This can range from outright hiring contractors to simply working with other teams— either in one's own company or at partners— to make sure that appropriate resources and contacts are available. Later in this book, we will discuss working with partners as a special case of this. From a budgetary standpoint, this can also include feeding information from the release schedule back into company-wide financial planning to properly allocate headcount.

Program Management

Release Management owns all status and communication for the release. This starts with the master schedule for an entire release. This involves working with all the involved teams to get their schedules created and integrating their updates into the master schedule. Furthermore, all issues need to be tracked and followed up on. After design documents are generated, they need to be collected, reviewed, and published. The release manager ideally needs to publish the schedule, current status, risks, and issues to all comers along the way. On large projects, there are infinite questions and demands for status. Having Release Management centralize this reduces a lot of communication overhead.

Product Concept

For new product introductions, it is important to have a well-defined concept for the kind of that product as well as the people who will work on it. This is all about identifying the teams that have a stake in the product and making sure they are collaborating on requirements. You cannot have viable requirements documents if some stakeholders are unaware that they are supposed to be generating requirements! The key thing for Release Management at this point is to make sure that all relevant parties are aware of the project, there are planned resources for it, and that they are able to proceed with requirements generation.

Requirements Generation

Having the organization agree on the requirements for a product is very important. In the Agile world where iterations are quick and customers work closely with developers, this is easier. However, for any system that has large iteration costs such as hardware, it is imperative to create a reasonably good set of requirements up front. While this is mostly a Product Management function, Release Management needs to make sure that appropriate progress is being made. As Engineering responds to the requirements with an implementation plan, there should be coordination back to Business that the proposed plan meets both business and financial needs.

Dependency Management

On large systems, different teams will depend on one another. One instance is when these dependencies are surprises. When one team needs another team to do something substantial that was not budgeted for, it can cause major management headaches. Tracking and resolving dependencies is a major release management task. In fact, simple spreadsheets work quite well for these tasks. The difficult parts are finding all the dependencies and making sure that groups address each other's dependencies, rather than ignoring them. This is particularly the case with cross-organizational dependencies.

Launch Preparation

Launch preparation revolves around all the activities needed in launching a product. This means looking at what all organizations outside of Development have to do and coordinating their schedules. Marketing will schedule advertising and publicity. Once television coverage is bought, you cannot easily change the ship date! Both Sales and Support teams need to be trained. For hardware products, there is a more complex process of verifying readiness for transition to manufacturing, manufacturing pilot processes, and the like.

Sales

The Sales team needs to be trained. This is two-fold: the Sales force needs to understand whom to sell and how to sell the product. Sales engineers have to understand how the product fits into solutions and how it needs to be configured.

Marketing

Marketing collateral needs to be prepared. This often requires collaboration with Development to ensure that schedules match exactly.

Professional Services

Professional services needs to be brought up to speed up both installation and configuration processes. Development needs to make sure that the training materials exist and that the installation actually works.

Support

Development usually needs to make sure Support is trained on answering questions and that escalation paths are set. Many customer support contracts require an escrow agreement wherein the product source code is store at an off-site 3rd repository (Iron Mountain as an example). In the event of a company default, the customer acquires access and rights to the source code.

Manufacturing

Anything that goes into a box— be it hardware or shrink-wrapped software— has extra steps around the creation of a bill of materials, integration, and testing of the manufacturing process, and hand-off to manufacturing. Since many of these functions are usually outsourced, this requires an extra level of coordination.

Finance

Appropriate SKUs need to be created and have pricing lists entered in the finance systems so that orders can be booked.

Technical Publications

Any manuals, user guides, or other technical publications that need to be released together with the product have to be ready at launch time.

End Game

The end game is the high-stress period when the project needs to converge and ship. This phase is all about watching defect find and fix rates, identifying and managing ship-stopper bugs, and the like. Typically, the lack of convergence between find and fix rate is in conflict with the published schedule, causing the release manager many headaches!

There are the critical checklist items that should be done or considered before declaring victory:

- Virus scan of all product deliverables
- The product test results meet minimal levels of acceptance (Zero P1 bugs and X P2 bugs, for example). X depends on the company and product class.
- TOI or Transfer of Information detailing release deliverables and support implications complete and delivered to all related organizations (SE, Support, Sales, etc.)
- Escrow media delivered to off-site repository.
- Final review of process documentation, looking for last minute product gaps (MRD vs. PRD), although it should have been done earlier.
- Marketing has updated product collateral and price list.
- For SaaS products, the implications of launch have been factored into infrastructure scalability requirements and sufficient capacity is availability for projected growth.
- An independent security or VTA (Vulnerability and Threat Analysis) has been done for the product (especially if SaaS).

End-Of-Life

The last thing Release Management does with a release is to work with Support and Sales on end-of-life milestones. Usually, there are three such milestones:

- When the product is no longer sold
- When no more maintenance releases are produced
- When all support ends

The goal of these milestones is to control the quantity of releases being actively supported while smoothly moving customers onto newer releases where they will presumably have a better experience.

3.6 Maintenance and Operation

Introduction

In this chapter, we will look at the development activities that follow the shipment of a product. The characteristics of this work depend fundamentally on the kind of product. If a product is shipped to a customer and updates are later also shipped to the customer as follow-on, then we call the development work behind those updates maintenance. If, on the other hand, the product is delivered entirely over the web, then the organization has to assume responsibility for operating the product as well as delivering updates via the web. So in addition to maintenance, the organization has an operations burden.

Maintenance for Traditional Products

As head of Engineering, you will be asked most of the time to focus your teams on creating new features for new products. But, invariably, you will have to set aside a certain amount of time to work on fixing bugs reported by customers or to make enhancements to existing products because of hardware changes and the like. This work can easily become a huge internal drag on the organization because it eats up a large chunk of its resources. Since you are rewarded to build new features, the net result is a huge apparent drop in the productivity of the organization. Generally, developers do not enjoy doing maintenance and if they spend too much time working on it, they can become very unhappy. In particular, very senior developers are often asked to help solve difficult problems and can easily get bored or burnt out from doing too much of the task. At the same time, customer satisfaction is dependent on producing high quality products and on meeting customer expectations. Thus, it is critical for an engineering leader to always be very aware of the actual percentage of effort going to maintenance and how to balance that against new feature developments.

Demands for Maintenance

Typically, there are a couple of drivers for maintenance work. First there is the need to fix bugs, especially customer generated ones. Part of the release planning process is to carefully decide how and when to fix these. Notice that not all customers and not all their issues are equally important. It is important to work closely with both the Support and Product Management teams to understand the following:

• Where they have already made commitments to customers
• Where they explicitly are not making a commitment
• Where the matter is still open

Be careful on what you commit yourself to and then, deliver precisely!

A second source comes from a platform support matrix. If your product works against a broad array of third party hardware and software components— particularly, if there are multiple combinations of these— you need to define a platform support matrix as part of your requirements planning process. Since other vendors will be continuously updating their products, you will need to update this matrix too and then update your product to match. Again, it is critical to work closely with Product Management and Support to understand field needs regarding this. A good way to clarify this problem is to think in terms of solutions. A solution is a particular customer problem that is addressed by using your product together with others in some interesting configuration. Understanding what solutions are sold and applied in the field helps you scope down the number of combinations you need to support.

A third source of maintenance comes from the need to back port changes. Typically, if a product is shipped to customers (as opposed to a web-based product), especially enterprise customers, you will find serious clients who are slow to upgrade to a new release. To accommodate them, you may need to back port key features to older code lines. This is very expensive and should be minimized at all costs. This will require you to work with Product Management to understand the business case for doing this.

Finally, a significant maintenance burden is working support on customer escalations. Usually, when a customer encounters a problem that Support cannot handle, it will get escalated to Engineering. Resolving these issues, even if they result in no bug or feature reports, can be very time-consuming.

The net result of all this is a large set of demands to do work other than new feature development. Once you have done the due diligence to understand exactly what your maintenance needs are, the next step is to plan how to execute the maintenance.

Controlling Maintenance Costs

Many organizations struggle with how to handle maintenance work. There are a couple of models. One model is to just treat it as a tax on the team. With this, a schedule simply assumes that staff is available only 65 percent for new features, 10 percent for vacation and sick, and the rest for maintenance. Another approach is to create a whole separate maintenance team, often in a lower-cost labor market. This approach is tempting on the surface but has two snags to it. First, it only works if your older products are well-documented. Otherwise, your maintenance team will do a poor job in problem-solving. Second, they will notice after a while that you are giving them the nasty work and you will be blessed with high turnover. Either way, your productivity is likely to be a good bit lower than you would like. In general, doing offshore work just for the sake of doing maintenance cheaply is not a good idea.

A better alternative is to give maintenance work to new teams or staff as a training exercise and then move them to new feature development. This will give them more motivation and it actually scales better. This method works in any geography and using more junior staff, in fact, controls your costs. If you want to do less maintenance work, it is up to you as the engineering leader to work with your fellow executive staff to do a better job of release planning in lowering the amount of maintenance work you have to do. In reality, the best thing you can do here is to make sure your teams produce high quality work that requires less maintenance!

Platform Support Matrix

A related problem is controlling the size of the platform support matrix. The major factor here is the sheer cost of testing huge ranges of configurations. The drivers at this point are both the amount of hardware and the labor required. You can control this in a number of ways. First, many hardware vendors provide labs you can visit to do testing. Utilizing these facilities can obviate the need to buy a lot of obscure hardware you only need for isolated tests. The labor costs are harder to manage. Obviously, if you automate these tests once a configuration is available, the tests can be easier to execute. The deeper trick is to form partnerships with your key vendors and get them to do more of the testing for you. This is harder to do if you are in a startup but as you become more established, your vendors may be quite interested in expanding their market by interoperating with your product. They may also be willing to help you with this testing. This is a fine thing to investigate with your Product Management staff.

A more challenging aspect of platforms support is official vendor certification. This is mostly important with certain large vendors such as Microsoft. Typically, Product Management will determine if having such a certification is essential to the ability to sell the product. You need to carefully examine the requirements for certification. Depending on your product, they can either be easy to meet or very costly. Look before you leap!

Controlling Support Costs

Customer escalations are a tricky thing in an engineering organization. They are usually emergencies and since everyone wants to make it right for the customer, all the stops are unexpectedly pulled out and the best programmers are asked to help. While the customers are made happy, it is easy for escalations to become a huge distraction for an organization.

There are a couple of things the head of Engineering can do to help in this situation. First, make sure that Support is involved in the development of new products from the beginning. It is important that designs are verified to make sure that the product will be easy to support (e.g. if it has good logging). Second, Support needs to be trained in each new product and be provided with troubleshooting guides. Support should be encouraged to develop Level 3 staff that can manage more complex escalations. Support also needs to create a knowledge base of all resolutions so that existing resolutions can be reapplied to recurring calls on the same problem. Doing all these things will greatly lessen the flow of issues into Engineering. Notice that many of these are not pure Engineering activities but require an engineering leader to actively collaborate with Support management.

Within Engineering, you should ensure there is an orderly workflow for handling customer escalations. There should be a defined escalation path from Support to Engineering. It should be clear which individuals are contacted when. While any engineer should be willing to help with important issues, you have to make sure you are fair in distributing the workload. You also need to resist the temptation to overuse your most experienced engineers. This latter point is important. More experienced folks can solve problems quickly; however, they tend to be burned out if called on to do it too often. It is also not scalable. Having more junior people involved— perhaps with coaching from the more senior ones— is an excellent way to improve the skill level of the younger staff while keeping your more senior staff available for more innovative work.

A good approach for distributing your Support workload and maintaining your development schedule is to create a rotation from your engineers to act as Support leads. You can have an engineer assume the Support lead role for a month with the rotation known several months in advance. Pick the rotation so that the Support lead is not on the critical path of any deliverable and adjust their development schedule to allow for the time they will spend on Support. You may still have to draw on other staff for customer escalations requiring development but the lead role is distributed and you can plan more effectively.

Root-Cause Analysis

A deeper approach to the support problem is to study the pattern of customer escalations and to look for weaknesses in the product. Trying to prevent customer escalations by eliminating their root causes is one of the best ways of reducing this cost. A good approach here is to have engineers do a root-cause analysis for all customers' bugs and escalations, through which one can identify the cause of the issue and what might have been done to prevent it. If in each release of a product you knock off the top five causes of customer escalations, the number of both bugs and escalations will be reduced.

Custom Requests

A related challenge is how to handle custom requests from large customers. In most large companies, this is handled through the professional service engagements. In small businesses, this may come straight back to Engineering. You need to treat it as a Professional Service engagement even to the extent this comes back to Engineering. There is a subtle customer management issue going on here. If a customer's request is a general one that will affect everyone, then— by all means— treat it as a bug or feature request and just do it. But if this is a one-off for this customer— no matter how important they are— it is also a distraction and you are better off charging for a professional service engagement.

The big challenge with existing products is balancing sustaining work against new development.

Operation

When you provide a product directly over the web, you are responsible for operating the web site and delivering the updates. Over the last few years, the growth of SaaS-based applications has been significant. Companies like Salesforce.com, NetSuite, and others have seen significant growth and much of it were at the expense of their traditional license or subscription competitors. This development in the market has required a different view of traditional software maintenance activities. In particular, we need to look separately at the problems of running the web site and those of updating it. We will discuss web site operations in a later chapter.

From the standpoint of software development, there are many advantages and some challenges to the SaaS model over the license distribution model, from the perspective of both the vendor and the customer. These include:

Advantages

- Simultaneous deployment of changes and modifications to all users with no need to ship patches to customers individually and only one "version" to support.
- Since the vendor hosts it, the customer does not have to deal with the entire infrastructure-related issues (hardware, operating system, application server, database, maintenance, and upgrades) with a traditional on-premise implementation.
- Economies of scale can be applied to the hardware infrastructure and thus, effectively lowering the cost on a per-user basis.
- A customer's proof of concept stage is often simplified, since they do not need to deploy or configure bulky software components.
- Using a SaaS-70 compliant vendor to host your in-demand application also has its own pros and cons. For a small company, it may save the cost of IT database and server administration experts but at the expense of increased monthly operating costs.

Disadvantages

- A SaaS site is a common target for hackers and phishers who may maliciously attack your site. It is a good practice to perform regular independent security audits of both the platform infrastructure as well as the application. These tests determine if a hacker can obtain inappropriate access to other user's data and/or subscriber information, make unauthorized changes, bypass business logic, hijack user accounts or escalate privileges to site admin from normal user, and many others.
- All or nothing availability. This makes schema changes and major patch updates more "mission-critical". Many companies maintain a "staging" area just for this reason. The "staging area" is a separate production-like hardware environment— typically a scaled down version of the production environment— where software modifications can be exposed to targeted beta users without adversely risking the production environment.
- There are unique design implications when considering a SaaS product usually not required of a licensed product, in particular the need for multi-tenancy in architecture design or the appropriate

"firewalling" of one user data, as well as the need for improved audit logs on a per user/customer basis.

- Visibility of "downtime". When a major SaaS vendor goes down, it is highly visible and often reported in the newspapers at the expense of the vendors reputation and credibility

- Scaling hardware can be a challenge as thorough knowledge of the inherent bottlenecks and thresholds of the application architecture must be gathered. For example, at what level of "user load" does the application server physical memory need to be increased? How many database machines are required to meet minimal latency requirements and how can they be brought online seamlessly without affecting active users? There are literally dozens of infrastructure, tuning, and configuration parameters that must be "balanced" to maintain an efficient product environment that optimizes the cost/user. Typically, the vendor needs to maintain an average of 40 percent overhead in infrastructure to cope with peak usage demands.

- The end-user has less access to their own data in a hosted model than on-premise. Customers may require you to provide them raw data to load in their own on-site data warehouse in order to meet their reporting needs.

3.7 Builds & Tools

Scale, Complexity, and Productivity

As a manager, a major concern is how to keep your engineers productive. In this chapter, we will look at some of the major processes that keep development efforts productive as well as the infrastructure required to implement those processes. We grouped these efforts together because from a management standpoint, they often fit well together organizationally. These issues all become steadily more crucial with both the growing complexity in the product and the increasing number of developers working on it.

As more people work on a system, the tasks have to be divided among multiple individuals, whose work needs to be integrated. As the number of people goes up, the effort required to do this integration increases combinatorially. In many traditional software projects, the integration phases take more time than the actual component development work. The most efficient way to build any kind of non-trivial system is to practice continuous integration and to construct an entirely working system daily. Then, that system needs to be tested as completely as possible and all major issues should be resolved immediately. The idea is that on any given day, one has an at least potentially shippable product. The key advantages of doing this is that: blocking problems that stop developers from working are addressed immediately; management always knows what is and is not going well; and integration issues are resolved as they appear rather than later in the process when many things are already cast in concrete. Implementing such a scheme requires three things:

- A daily build that assembles all the pieces into a complete product
- An automated test suite that can test the build
- A management process to monitor and act on the results

At the same time, one needs to understand how the daily build or test process interacts with the individual developer's personal development process. If the personal development process is ineffective, it is hard to make the global process effective.

A key responsibility of the head of Engineering is to make sure these processes are effective! If you allow backsliding on these matters, your organization will pay in a big way through reduced developer productivity.

Personal Development Process

The lowest level in the development environment is the personal development process. The first thing a new hire encounters is the piece most often neglected— the documentation on how to do development. Having updated tutorials and references on how to work in the environment is the key to making new hires productive and to helping existing employees during technology transitions. A good way of keeping this documentation updated is via a specially designated section of a Wiki with a frequently reinforced focus in the organization on the importance of keeping this current. And what do we put into this reference? The personal development process has to cover the following seven main areas:

- How to create a new workspace
- How to compile the system
- How to configure the deployment environment
- How to test the code
- How to debug
- How to submit changes to source control
- How to work with the defect tracking system

This process depends on a set of key tools: the compilers, debuggers, source control system, and the defect tracking system. While different organizations will make different choices about these tools for a wide range of factors, there are a couple of constants.

Source Control

Generally, source control systems cause many controversies. The developers will usually despise them and always pine for a different one. Note that all these systems are annoying and the switching cost is very high. You should ideally just say "no" to such requests. You need to keep a couple of things in mind. First, large distributed organizations will need to use heavyweight tools like ClearCase or Perforce simply because of the scale of their branching needs combined with the need to manage bandwidth on international Wide Area Network (WAN) links. This does not apply to smaller organizations because there are many modern tools like Subversion that easily handle their needs with less moaning from the developers.

A second consideration is security. Once your organization gets large enough IP protection, it will become a major issue for your lawyers, as do activities like ISO 27001 compliance. In this case, you will need to make sure you have adequate logging, security, and partitioning. Again, with source control, you have to think about the tradeoff between developer convenience and your need for advanced branching, security, and WAN management considerations before moving to one of the "big" systems like ClearCase.

Build System

Your engineers should decide on a standard way of building each module from its parts, both in terms of the technology used (i.e. Ant, make) as well as the standards for creating the scripts. This is important not only from an ease of maintenance and training aspect, but also from the standpoint of later integrating these scripts into a nightly build.

Defect Tracking Workflows

Defect Tracking

A defect tracking system is simply a database of records about problems in the product. Engineers often think of it as being just a database. This is a misnomer though. Defect tracking systems are the basic workflow systems in an engineering organization. Ideally, the defect tracking system should exactly mirror the workflow of the organization in terms of how requests, bugs, and incidents are brought in, evaluated, assigned, addressed, verified, closed, and rejected. Engineers will oftentimes complain about the defect tracking system and will want a different one. In most cases, these complaints pertain to the application not matching the workflow. The fix is to make the workflow match. Changing to a different database is rarely the answer because the workflow is always heavily customized, even if the application itself is off the shelf. In choosing a tool— and there are many out there— the first consideration is your ability to tune the product to how you do business.

The Bug Lifecycle

Even the smallest organization should formalize what is the nature and life of a defect. Getting this right is at the heart of a repeatable development process. While every organization will embellish these records, here is a common core of fields describing a defect:

- **Identification and description**
  - ➢ Number
  - ➢ Short description
  - ➢ Detailed description
  - ➢ What module it is in

- **Workflow**
  - ➢ State: new, open, fixed, closed-fixed, closed-duplicate, closed-no-fix, or closed-not-a-bug
  - ➢ Priority: 1 - emergency, drop everything, 2 - ship stopper, 3 - fix in release, 4 - fix eventually
  - ➢ Severity: 1- customer down, 2 - impacts developers, 3 - feature broken, 4 - nit, 5 - enhancement request
  - ➢ Owner
  - ➢ Release to fix in (could be multiple)

- **Activity record**
  - ➢ History of all actions performed on this defect

Notice that there is business logic here. There has to be an owner but this could change as module and state change. One state may only lead to specific other states. This logic is often both complex and contentious. In reality, most defect systems eventually become more workflow systems rather than databases. The need to model this workflow means that there is a high barrier to changing the system once you have selected it. This explains why one needs to design this process well and make good choices about the tools.

The Daily Build Process

Build System

You will need a master build script that can assemble the entire product by building all of the components. You will also need a dedicated hardware setup to run this script. Generally, this will take a couple of forms. First, you will want to build the entire product at least once a day. This is your nightly build. In many organizations, you will also desire to build more frequently than that, perhaps with hourly development builds in between. With systems increasing in size and numbers of supported platforms, these big builds can take too long— that is, the build time exceeds the time between builds. In this case, you need to parallelize the builds and fortunately, there are commercial tools that can help you do this. Note that doing this forces strict standard for the component builds the developers do to ensure that they can be safely run in a parallel environment. Also notice that with these frequent parallel processes, maintaining the reliability of the environment becomes crucial, unlike keeping a large web site going.

Automated Tests

As soon as one of your builds is finished, it should be passed to an automated test. Good automated tests for this purpose have a couple of parts. You need a scheduler that notices a build is done and runs the test. You need a test distribution mechanism that identifies and provisions the target hardware, installs the build, copies the test to it, runs the test, and reports back the result. You should also have a standard way of constructing automated tests, which typically amounts to some scripting system and a standard API exposed to the tests. Nowadays, depending on your environment, many of the infrastructure components listed here are available either as commercial or open source products.

Besides the framework, you need to pick a plausible set of test cases to put into the suite. The key points are picking tests that offer reasonably broad coverage and run both reliably and not too slowly.

Also notice that you can have different tiers of tests: a short test run hourly; a long test run daily; and a long test run weekly.

Execution and Triage

Typically, you have four main groups collaborating on the entire setup. First, your tools group will build the infrastructure. Second, your QA team will provide automated tests. Since both builds and tests will fail all too often in a fast moving organization, the third thing you need is a triage group that analyzes both build and test failures. If these are infrastructure failures, the tools and QA teams can fix them. If these are product failures, the issues need to be escalated to Development. And here is where you come in! The fourth role is for Senior Management. As the head of Engineering, you need to create a culture around demanding that builds succeed, tests pass, and fixes failures promptly. You need to demand metrics to show that the processes are both healthy and effective.

Feedback to the Developer

The daily build process has a crucial feedback loop to the developer. The developers always need to know when it is safe to merge their personal tree with the latest sources. The daily build process, especially when augmented with hourly builds and tests, provides immediate feedback regarding the state of the source code. A good trick is to label any change level that passes the automated tests. The developers can then always sync to the last point that passed the tests. Likewise, QA groups can use the results from the automation to determine which builds are good.

For large systems, another good practice is to make the binaries of daily or hourly builds available to developers to allow them to build only those parts of the system they have changed. This can be done by checking in binaries, using symbolic links, or utilizing virtualized storage. Despite being complicated, this can save a lot of time. This technique though depends on a very stable build process.

Branch Management

As long as you have no more than 100 developers working on a system simultaneously and that other processes are working well, you can have everyone check into the same main code stream. However, as you get into many hundreds of developers working on the same area of code, there will be so much churn in the code line that even given low error rates, the code line will be broken almost all the time. The cure for this is to organize a series of branches from the main code line and have developers work in their associated branch. One would then need a dedicated staff who will manage merging changes from the branches into the main line in an orderly way to make sure automated tests keep passing and the integrity of the main code line is preserved. For large organizations, these mechanisms can become complicated and bureaucratic. Whenever possible, it is much preferable to keep the system as modular as possible, so that one never gets an unreasonable number of people modifying the same piece of code at the same time.

Automated Defect Detection

An important area in Release Engineering that many organizations fail to take full advantage of are the tools that automatically locate bugs in the code. The idea here is to go beyond automated tests that exercise compiled code to doing automated analysis of source code to find defects. There are different approaches to this in different programming languages. Coverity and Lint are among the common tools in this space. In most cases, these tools are integrated into the build process. They produce detailed reports of errors and warnings found. While the output requires some triage, these tools are surprisingly effective in detecting real issues and in preventing customer escapes. Development groups are sometimes afraid of using these tools because of the apparently daunting nature of going through thousands of messages generated by the tools. However, an intern or two can easily chip away at these reports, leaving a more manageable flow of real defects to the developers. Again, controlled experiments show these tools work and save a lot of money over allowing QA or customers to find the same issues.

3.8 Quality Management

Introduction

Quality is all about ensuring that the products we build meet the customers' intended needs. In the race to bring new products and technologies to market, the hi-tech world has a reputation for playing fast and loose with quality. Struggles with quality dominate many development efforts. The fact that we have to do so many patches, escalations, and maintenance releases and that people joke so much about the blue screen of death shows that the quality issue remains incompletely resolved. In this chapter, we will take a look at QA's management implications in an engineering organization.

Quality vs. Quality Assurance

First, we need to make a crucial distinction between quality and quality assurance. They are intimately related yet very different. Quality is an attribute of a system while QA is the activity in Engineering that verifies the sufficient quality of a system. Note that it is the developers who put the quality into the system but it is the QA team that determines its presence or absence. Before we spend too much time on QA, we need to first understand what we mean by quality.

Kinds of Quality

There are many kinds of quality in any engineering system that needs to be investigated, measured, and verified separately.

Requirements for Quality

As mentioned earlier, quality is an attribute and not simply an activity. In fact, one can extend this and say that quality is both a value and an attitude for the entire company. Quality decisions are a form of risk management— a balance of the costs and consequences. This thinking should be explicit during product planning and requirements creation. One way to make this more concrete especially to the Business team is to consider the customers' views of quality.

Customer Perceived Quality

Does the product do what the customer wants? This is all about studying the quality of the specification. This is the most important part of quality but is barely touched by many QA organizations. Because of the technology-centric worldview of many engineering organizations, this kind of quality is frequently ignored which often cause unexpected product failures. There are many activities in this space. These are:

- Doing usability testing
- Understanding reliability and performance profiles
- Determining total cost of ownership
- Determining support costs
- Validating customer solutions scenarios
- Interviewing customers, sales engineers, professional services, and support

Design for Quality

The design of the product can greatly affect quality, especially for products that have any form of manufacturing. Generally, designs that are difficult to build (i.e. those that have extremely tight tolerances or many manual adjustments) will have problems with quality. Software designs do not have the same kind of manufacturing problems but they can also cause issues with quality. Examples for this include: software that is very fragile to user inputs and database values or network response times.

Process Quality

Is the stated development process being followed and does it work? This is all about assessing the discipline of the development organization. If the process is followed correctly, the work will be done faster and will be more accurate. The mindset of a team that properly follows its process will also bode well for maintaining an equal discipline in building the product. For instance, modern Agile methodology demands daily builds and automated tests as well as keeping both builds and tests passing every day. A good example of a process quality measure is to track the ability to build and successfully test the product.

Implementation Quality

Does the product do what its specification says it should do? Much classical QA falls in this area- testing software to see if it matches its specification and filing bugs if it does not. Implementation quality can take many forms from measuring if functionality works as advertised to checking performance and reliability.

Manufacturing Quality

For products that are physically constructed and distributed, this is a measurement of how well the product has been built. Improvement in manufacturing quality was the original goal of "Six-Sigma" approaches but which have since expanded in scope. Manufacturing quality is not simply how well the production line works as it also involves the selection of suppliers, vendors, and outsourcing contractors.

Anecdote

In my first position out of school, I was a hardware developer. One of my first circuits was an audio alarm circuit. There was no discussion of what was required so I designed a circuit whose volume could be adjusted widely for maximum flexibility. This turned out to be a big mistake since the manual adjustment of volume was the slowest part of the manufacturing process backing up the production line. The customers were often annoyed by the volume. This led to many complaints about the product despite the fact it was adjustable.

This incident demonstrates many types of quality problems. There was no understanding of the customer and the usability. In fact, the wide range of adjustable volume was a big part of the problem since some users would turn it up and some would turn it down and they would argue about it. Future versions of the product gave the customer less flexibility, enforcing a compromise between users. There was also a breakdown between design engineering and manufacturing. The adjustment step was not recognized as an expensive process in either the design reviews or the manufacturing reviews. No one recognized that there was no easy metric for what volume the system should be adjusted to. Variations of components and operators led to a wide variation in the volume of the final product. Finally, no one actually realized this issue was happening for a long time. It was not recognized until the product was successful enough to requiring scaling up and there were enough units then in the field for the customer service issues to become evident.

Staffing for Quality

The QA Organization

Typically, every development organization has a counterpart QA organization. Each QA organization needs the following different skill sets:

- Good programmers to write automation
- Skillful testers to do high level manual testing
- Experienced QA engineers to do test planning
- System administrator types to help run the automation

It is a giant mistake to leave the development of the automation to second-class programmers because the automation will be a huge piece of software that has to be maintained for the long run. The low quality of much QA automation—often written by poorly trained amateur programmers—is one of the main drags on QA quality due to its high maintenance costs. It is important to hire sufficiently technical people in this area!

While QA positions are regularly paid 90 percent of their development counterparts, it is crucial to recruit and retain enough talented QA engineers to effectively implement modern development methodologies that require adequately compensating the more skilled QA engineers.

Notice that QA divides into different areas. The parts of QA that work with the developers usually need to be collocated with the developers. With adequate process, system and automated test can be located in another possibly less expensive location.

QA and Agile

The transition to Agile development is still happening in many organizations and is causing many dislocations for QA groups. A few years ago, many relatively non-technical people could easily find entry-level jobs in QA. However, QA is becoming ever more of a pure Engineering function nowadays. The focus in Agile on automated tests is requiring the employment of more pure programmers in QA groups. QA engineers are discovering that they spend more of their time working with developers early in the cycle during planning and test development. While this generally creates more job satisfaction, it does require more technical and thoughtful QA staff. Helping QA groups' transition into this new world is an important part of the engineering manager's job.

QA Leadership

One of the occupational hazards of QA organizations is that they tend to be highly tactical, myopic, and devoid of technical leadership. This comes from the less technical background of much of the staff, their tendency being at the back end of the schedule to bear the brunt of all schedule overruns, and the inherent pain of having to run all the project end games. This is an ongoing challenge for the engineering leader. While you will have to work extra hard to hire and develop real technical leaders within the QA organization, you will also need to work carefully with the organization as you undertake various process improvement efforts. This is because the QA teams will be often quite afraid of almost any change undertaken, especially those which increase the level of technical sophistication of the process.

QA teams are also very sensitive to the admittedly often-real threat of having their jobs moved elsewhere. This is especially relevant in the common scenario where a manual test effort gets automated, the regression testing is sent offshore, and the domestic QA force is retargeted at test planning, developer collaboration, and solutions testing. In this case, you need to spend extra time reassuring the team that you value them and that their new assignments will be more challenging and interesting than their old ones. In general, QA teams are second only to technical publications (tech pubs) teams in terms of their level of anxiety in response to proposed changes. It is something you will get to spend lots of time on.

Quality in Development

As we said earlier, QA can check for quality but only Development can put the quality in! This manifests itself in a couple of practical ways. First of all, the development process is always marked by the contrast between QA's ability to find problems and Development's ability to fix problems. It is critical that Development be able to keep up with the QA find rate. Otherwise, the advantage of having QA is largely lost. This requires having enough resources devoted to fixing these problems! Secondly, Development is responsible for writing and executing unit tests and pre-checking smoke tests. Most studies show that having developers write and run appropriate unit tests on each module they create is crucial for quickly producing high quality code.

The main challenge with unit testing is that the tests need to be developed religiously from the beginning. They can be discouragingly hard to add retroactively to large systems.

QA in the Software Development Process

General Approach

The following are the three principles that underlie a good QA:

- QA needs to work side by side with Development from the beginning of the project.
- All tests should be automated to the greatest extent possible.
- Many parts of the automation should be run daily using the current build and these need to be kept passing as a very high management priority.

Manual vs. Automated Testing

Experienced manual testers can often do a very effective job in testing a product and this may be totally adequate in the startup stage. But in the long run, this approach does not scale. Test runs will never be repeatable because they are all in someone's head and not transferable to anyone else's. There is no clarity about how long the activity takes, how much of it is done, or how much of the system works. One of the important cultural transforms in an organization is to systematize both test plans and coverage and automate as much as possible.

Automation is very different from manual testing. Automated testing only verifies that known conditions still work. In contrast, manual testing by its nature discovers new conditions that might or might not work. This explains why automated testing is best for regression purposes, whereas manual testing is more appropriate for brand new features. In a mature organization, new test cases are discovered manually and are quickly incorporated into automated test suites. Thus, such an organization will have both gifted testers who can discover new test cases and programmers who can code the resulting cases.

Nonetheless, the shift from the first paradigm to the second is often hard because the test engineers will not be used to being explicit about what and how they do things. Teaching them how to write formal test plans and to stick to them can be a challenge. In many cases, it is necessary to replace at least some of the staff, adding more technical engineers to the less technical QA engineers. Either you or your QA director will have to spend much energy on such cultural shifts as the organization grows.

QA Activities

The following are some of the distinctive activities in a QA organization.

Test Planning

Test planning involves understanding use cases for new projects and features and defining realistic and comprehensive test cases for these use cases. These test plans should be reviewed with developers and inventoried in a database such as Quality Center where they can be prioritized and grouped into test sets.

Test Development

Test development is the activity where automated tests for test plans are implemented. Building these tests is a regular programming task and should be staffed and executed as such. It also implies the presence of an appropriate environment. This environment must provide a repository of automated tests, a scheduler for deploying them, a means of installing the build on a given hardware platform together with the tests and data, a way to run the software on the target system, and a method of trapping errors and reporting results back to a central results database.

Test Monitoring

If most tests are automated, then test execution is mostly about monitoring the automation to make it work properly. Note that if sufficient quantities of configurations are targeted by the automation, simply setting up and keeping all the automation machines running become a time-consuming project.

Manual Testing

The main use of manual testing is for explicitly trying out new user interfaces to break them or find scenarios that developers had not considered. This relates closely to usability testing as well. It is also important in reproducing customer escalations where it is not obvious why there was a test escape.

Defect Verification

Another very manual task is to make sure that defects, which developers have indicated as being fixed, are indeed truly fixed. Before a product is shipped, all fixed defects should be verified.

Kinds of Tests

Unit tests

Unit tests should be done, written, and executed by developers. These should genuinely focus on testing units of code, stubbing out irrelevant functionality. These are frequently formalized into pre-checking tests that have to be run to ensure that check-ins will not break the next build.

System tests

In traditional QA testing, much of QA was concerned with manually verifying the behavior of the system. Nowadays, these tests should be automated and be ran daily as part of the build cycle to prove that there is a functioning system at all times.

Platform testing

Platform testing is a specialized form of system testing focusing on validating new hardware and software configurations with a given release.

Performance testing

Do not forget to verify the performance and reliability of the system under realistic load with realistic scenarios over a realistic timeframe. Too much QA is often focused on testing lightly loaded systems with minimal data and fragmentary scenarios. Note that there are two distinct cases here: (1) performance concentrating on the ability of the system to run fast enough and (2) scalability, which verifies that at a given performance level, adequate quantities of users can be supported. Also remember that reliability is implicit in both of these since we are measuring the maximum performance and scalability that can be achieved with compromising reliability.

Usability testing

Usability testing is the process of verifying if the system is easy to use daily and if the set of customer use cases is covered. Ease of use is best done with a specialized usability team that performs controlled observations of users. More general verification of the specification requires reaching out to customers and collecting feedback on how well a given specification matches their expectations.

Installation and upgrade testing

Installation and upgrade testing need to be called out separately simply because it is such a large problem for many products. On one hand, installation code is tedious and viewed as an after thought by many engineers so a junior programmer cobbles it together at the last minute. On the other hand, it is often both the customer's first experience with the product and it is very complex and error prone. Therefore, it is an area that both serves to initially define the customer's experience with the product and has the potential to cause many problems. Testing this area very thoroughly pays off in spades in both customer satisfaction and support costs.

Fitting into Process

The successful QA organization has to be intimately involved in all phases of the development process.

Planning Phase

QA needs to be involved very early on to be able to plan for the kinds of automation and platforms needed to test a given system. This will in turn drive both resource and schedule needs. Starting early is a key to avoiding last minute crunches that affect so many QA organizations. The output of this phase is a master test plan that should be reviewed with Development.

Development Phase

During the development phase, system tests should be run continuously. Also, QA should work with developers on test plans as well as on trying out new modules as they become available. Automation should also be built as practical, recognizing that it will often lag the new features.

Test Phase

Once all features are built and integrated, there should be some quiet time to do extended system and platform testing as well as verifying all fixed defects. No matter how much testing happens during the development phase, one needs to stop changing the system long enough to produce some stable and repeatable test results. In many organizations, the test phase is ruined because Development is not done yet and many phases in the integration work are still going on, invalidating the results of the executing tests. Having strict entry criteria into test and a good program of iterative build and test in the development phase can prevent this problem.

End Game

In the end game, QA needs to focus on controlling change and making sure that what gets released is what got tested and that it actually works with all fixed bugs verified. This is almost always the most stressful period for QA. Notice that during this phase, developers are often being pulled off the project already and are starting the next release. They will then want QA to help on the next project, only to find QA unable to engage because the QA team is running at peak level on the previous release. Ensuring adequate resources to prevent this problem is a key management challenge.

The Deferral Danger

Most organizations near the end of a release start deferring defects out of a release to avoid destabilizing it. While this is theoretically reasonable, it has a big danger. Resolving defects by just taking them off the list without actually fixing them opens up the possibility of lowering quality. This is very insidious because many teams immediately jump from one release to the next and often forget to deal with the deferred issues. It is up to both the QA director and the engineering leader to act in good conscience and not allow customer quality compromises simply to meet schedules. Generally, the best mitigation for this danger is to have a pattern of regular releases so that if a defect misses one release, it can make it into the next one. This is often called the "release train" approach. Also, one needs to actively reprioritize the defects to make sure that the most important ones always bubble to the top.

Post Release Activities

Here are typical activities for QA to pursue after a release:

- Help diagnose customer escalations
- Validate new hardware configurations
- Spend time with customers and understand the things they look for in the product
- Improve test plans based on the perceived weaknesses during the previous runs

Metrics

You will want to collect many metrics about your QA process. At first, people will wonder why you bother. But you will see soon that for most organizations, the metrics are stable and repeatable. In fact, the main problem with the metrics is that they tell stories that people do not want to hear. If a project is going to be late, the metrics will usually tell you far in advance. You just have to be willing to listen. Maturity in an organization is not about creating metrics. It is about obeying them!

It is worthwhile to set up an automated mechanism to generate and render these metrics.

Process Quality

- Percentage of successful builds
- Percentage of successful automated tests

These metrics tell you the extent to which your developers can make progress. Without working builds, your developers rapidly get stuck. For a build to work, it has to both compile and pass basic automated tests. This is a fundamental measure of coherency in your development process.

Schedule Check

- Percentage of tests run
- Percentage of tests passed
- Bug find rate
- Bug fix rate

These metrics tell you to what extent you are tracking your schedule. Obviously, any area that has not been tested is an unknown. You just do not know how many defects are left to be found. If too many defects are found, then there will be extra unplanned work. If the bug find rate exceeds the fix rate—which is a common problem in many organizations—you are likely to fall behind on your schedule.

Test Coverage

A basic question about all testing is how much of the system is covered. You can do qualitative surveys of your test coverage but you will always be faced with nagging doubts afterwards. A better way to answer this question is to measure the coverage of the tests. This entails recompiling the system with instrumentation using a tool like gcov or its relatives. Then, while running tests, you should also obtain a trace to show how much of the source code gets exercised by the test suite. This lets you identify both where you have gaps in your coverage and where you have redundancies for which you can reduce coverage.

Customer Quality

- Time required to fix customer reported defects
- Trend in backlog of unfixed customer reported defects over time

This and similar metrics give you an indication of how responsive the organization is to field encountered defects. Since many organizations tend to defer many defects from one release to the next, these metrics will indicate the impact on the users of this process. A refinement of these metrics is to indicate which defects get fixed in a patch to the same version—as opposed to a later version— because this will indicate the extent to which fixes force major upgrades on the customer.

QA Tools

Test Planning and Result Tracking Systems

Any QA organization of sufficient scope will need a tool to organize test cases and test results. If you do not know what you are testing or what you learned, you know you have no control over your quality process. Formerly from Mercury Interactive and now owned by Hewlett-Packard, Quality Center is the industry standard for this task. Quality Center should integrate to your bug database and requirements tracking system so that you can tell for a given product what tests you want to execute at what phase, how these tests cover your features, how many of them you have executed, how many of them pass, and finally, which bugs go with which features. A good Quality Center implementation makes it easy to outsource routine manual regression test. It also interfaces effectively to your automated tools.

An important warning about Quality Center though is that most QA engineers hate it. The purpose of Quality Center is to systematize the assessment and measurement of test coverage, test execution, test productivity, and test pass or fail rates and distributions. Notice that managers—and not QA engineers—are the ones interested on these. For the QA engineers, this is a giant hassle. QA engineers who are not familiar with Quality Center will despise you for introducing it. You need to listen to them but you have to be firm. The greater control you have over the QA process will save you a lot of grief in the long run. Your staff will eventually see the benefits of a more scientific and less impressionistic approach to testing.

Automation Control Harnesses

To automate everything, one usually needs a meta-framework of some kind. Consider what is required to run automated tests after a fresh build. First, a set of servers has to be provisioned for running the tests and collecting results. Appropriate third party software has to be copied on to these machines. The product then has to be installed on one of them. The latest build of the automation has to be installed next. Then, the data has to be loaded. After that, the automation needs to be run and the results have to be collected. This problem is complicated to solve because normally, clusters of servers are only easily manageable if they are highly symmetrical. However, QA hardware is decisively irregular because of the need to support a broad platform matrix. The trick is to use a robust framework for managing these irregular clusters. IBM's Software Testing Automation Framework (STAF) open source framework5 is a great example of how to do this.

Automation Frameworks

Just as your developers create libraries of architectural components, your QA team will develop collections of automation frameworks and libraries on top of which the actual automation gets developed. You should view these as development artifacts just like the architectures and components created in Development.

Metrics Portal

You will also want a metrics portal to allow easy communication of metrics from your automation, test and build systems. These are often home built using various standard reporting tools or, depending on your development environment, you may already have one supplied by one of your tools.

---

5 See http://staf.sourceforge.net/index.php.

3.9 Technical Publications

Introduction

One of the stepchildren in many technical organizations is often the technical documentation effort. In startups, the focus is on creating new technology. How that technology is communicated is frequently a secondary concern. However, as the organization gets larger, the installed base grows and the costs of Support and Sales increases. In this case, a greater focus is required on documentation.

In this chapter, we will look at the common requirements for tech pubs as well as the standard ways of meeting those requirements. Then, we will discuss the management issues involved in running a tech pubs effort.

Do You Even Need Documents?

It is true that many simple web applications are fairly self-explanatory. They should not need a lot of documentation. The same goes for well-designed hardware appliances. (Who has ever read an iPod manual?)

Also, for many popular applications, there is a great deal of public documentation. Google becomes a front-end in searching through other peoples' web sites, web logs, and message boards. For applications with a very large installed base, this can become a significant expansion of the total amount of documentation available.

When do you need your own documents then? For more complex systems especially those involving significant training or configuration overhead, you will need to produce definitive information for your users. This becomes a simple economic matter of controlling your pre- and post-sales costs as well as removing all possible barriers to sales and adoption. Generally, organizations that worry about these costs and barriers take their documentation seriously.

Requirements

Kinds of Documentation

Ideally, there are different kinds of documents for a given product. These can involve:

- Solution Guide
- Compatibility matrix guide
- Quick start manual
- Installation manual
- Reference manual
- Troubleshooting manual
- Best practices
- Knowledge-based (KB) articles
- Safety notices

Notice that these manuals have very different audiences. Solution and Compatibility Guides are typically used as pre-sales documentation to guide configuration. Troubleshooting and KB articles are used by Support in problem resolution. Installation and Best Practice Guides are used by Professional Services at install time. All classes of users use the reference and quick start guides. Note that the actual end users may use only a small fraction of the total documentation. In thinking about documentation, you have to keep in mind all the different kinds of users you have and their often varying needs. For example, your Support staff may be more technical than the third party folks who do the install, which in turn are more technical than your end users.

User Experience

Traditionally, documentation meant big expensive books. More recently, the books were shipped on a CD as PDF files to save paper. Presently though, there are many different ways of deploying documentation. They include:

- Books
- Online help (i.e. Windows help)
- Web sites

Note that the move from books to online help and web sites has been accompanied by a basic shift to allow the user more control since these allow a user to search for results. But one can go much further than this.

The most modern view of documentation is to allow the user to define their own documentation. This means letting them define what they are interested in as well as to generate dynamically connected documents based on those preferences reflecting the user's interests. We will talk below as to how you can achieve this.

Rebranding

The moment you enter into OEM deals, your documentation task becomes harder since you will have to rebrand your documents. This means each time you update your own documents, you also need to update the OEM version. OEM agreements often contain SLAs for how quickly the OEM receives new products. This can be complex to manage in a timely way in your Documentation group.

Localization

Once you start selling internationally, you have to worry about translating the documentation. Your distributor may be willing to do this for you when you start out. As you do it on a larger scale, this becomes more expensive. There are many issues here and these are:

- Just as with an OEM, you have to maintain multiple versions.
- You have to be concerned about cultural differences.
- You have to worry about UI issues with length of phrases in different languages (this is particularly an issue for online help).
- Here is the kicker: Translation houses charge by the word. Unless you can decompose your text into phrases, you will be grossly overpaying for translation. Translating by the document is a worse deal than by the phrase, particularly, for retranslating new versions!

Reuse

After a while, your company may find itself with families of products sharing many parts. You will begin to ask yourself, "Why can't we reuse more of the documentation?" Accomplishing reuse in the documentation can save large amounts of money.

Production

Publishing documents can be complex, depending on your needs. For hardware products, documents become part of the Bill of Materials. They need to go through an appropriate change order/part # process and be integrated into the manufacturing process that can get more interesting with outsourced manufacturing. For online publishing, you have to work with your web site team for the appropriate workflow.

Technical Architecture

Framemaker

Traditionally, documents are written in Adobe Framemaker and compiled from there into PDF, HTML, or other formats. This is an easy approach because of its low infrastructure overhead. Furthermore, finding people who can do this is easy. The problem though is that you are producing monolithic documents with no reuse, which are hard to internationalize or customize for OEMs.

Darwin Information Typing Architecture (DITA) and Content Management

The more modern approach in building documentation is to think of documentation not in terms of books, but in information. Think of your documentation as a set of information tagged with certain attributes that

exist in a certain relationship. This is the world of DITA[6], the great innovation brought to the tech pubs world by IBM.

In DITA, the writers create topics. A topic is a piece of prose stored
in an XML file that contains tags describing its attributes. There also exist
XML documents called DITA maps that define the relationship between
topics. A document then is a map identifying a certain selection of topics
arranged in a certain way. Documents are published by applying XSL
transforms to their map to produce different kinds of output.

This totally changes how you work. Instantly, you have to reuse
since many maps can draw from the same topics. OEM versions are trivial;
they are just different XSLs applied to the same map. Localization is cheap
because you just send your new topic files to the translation house that
charges less for XML input than for random text.

It also allows a totally different kind of user interface. If you expose
the maps directly to the search engine, you can allow a user to pick what
kinds of things they want and dynamically generate a document from the
resulting dynamic map.

Most fascinatingly, it alters the psychology of a writer. Instead of
writing a "book", they are writing "topics" which most naturally map to "use
cases". This causes a writer to unsurprisingly shift from describing "the
system" to describing "how people use the system". This almost inevitably
creates clearer and easier to use documentation.   Schedule tracking also
becomes easier, because rather than measuring subjective percentages of a
large document, one can schedule a certain quantity of topics per a given
time period. This allows a more Agile approach to writing, as opposed to the
more waterfall-oriented technique common to traditional "big book"
approaches.

Making this transition also requires the organization to get serious
about information architecture, to think about how different pieces of
knowledge will get tagged, and to discover how to assemble them into

---

[6] See http://www.ibm.com/developerworks/xml/library/x-dita1/.

finished books. Note that these efforts can dovetail nicely with general corporate initiatives around content management and information tagging. These efforts will all require attention from some more senior staff that is not completely pre-occupied with routine writing tasks.

Another challenge in using DITA is that instead of a few books, you now have thousands of topics lying around. You will probably want to invest in a DITA-compliant content management system to handle all these pieces and their relationships. These content management systems, in many cases, directly interface to the translation houses automated systems as well as to your web site publishing infrastructure, thus, further simplifying your life.

However, all of these require more technology than most tech pub groups have had historically. In many cases, this implies your need to have some engineers help writers in getting the infrastructure going. Fancy dynamic UIs are also reasonably challenging technical projects but organizations that do it love the results.

Documentation Portal

Documentation is typically published to a documentation portal. Since a company will produce various kinds of documents from formal product documents to marketing brochures to support bulletins, the portal is crucial for bringing information together. It is important to make sure that different kinds of information are consistent and do not contradict with one another, which is often a problem because they come from different parts of a company. It is also crucial that metadata is setup correctly so that users can find what they are looking for.

Nowadays, another interesting possibility is opening documentation to users by adding Wiki and web log components to the portal. In this way, users can both comment on the published documentation as well as add their own materials. This is an excellent way of growing and involving the community of interested users.

Online Help

Online help is generally built using a Software Development Kit (SDK) and compiled directly with the application. Ideally it is context sensitive, but that depends on the complexity of the product. The main challenge is to keep writers integrated into the development schedule and to make sure that developers remember to put in the right hooks for the online help, particularly for context sensitive help. Harried teams often forget such details but they make a lot of difference for ease of use. If you are working in an XML-based environment, online help can also be generated as an output from your XML.

Single Sourcing

Single Sourcing is the process of organizing the documentation structure in order to maximize re-use for other products or for online help and training purposes. Documentation is organized into modules and tagged with keywords or matadata for easy re-use. This provides a greater efficiency in the authoring process, but requires the writer think in a broader context during the writing phase.

Management Considerations

Process

Your first management problem with tech pubs is the inevitable inferiority complex many writers have. It is not for nothing that *Dilbert* features the world's angriest technical writer. They are used to getting insufficient recognition, less pay, being forced to make up at the last minute for the delays in the development schedule, and generally, getting ignored by managers who do not understand their needs. The best way to counteract this is by paying proper attention to tech pubs, making sure they are properly integrated into the development process, and giving them some recognition!

Some key points as follows:

- Involve the writers early in the process so they can plan effectively.
- Consider their schedule needs in your planning process.
- Understand their issues; think about their career development too!

In fact, the move to DITA changes many of this. With the focus on topics as use cases, the documentation is more aligned to the requirements gathering effort and brought into focus more clearly during the early phases of the project. This allows for better planning. The more technical nature of the XML-based work also tends to integrate the writing with the engineering effort better. It makes for a more harmonious organizational environment with everyone producing code, rather than some producing code and others writing novels. Interestingly the move to reuse also creates peer pressure in the team for higher quality, as people will definitely say oh I can't reuse this topic – it's not written well enough.

Naturally, some writers will not make this transition equally well but it is something to work on! One of the harder parts of this transition is that by tradition, writers work alone on their books. The topic model fosters more of a collaborative team approach both among writers as well as with developers, which ultimately is good for morale but, in the short run, represents a big change of attitude.

Organization

Generally, a tech pub organization should be comprised of the following:

- Writers
- An artist for the illustrations
- Tools people especially for DITA to manage the production chain
- Editors

Editors are an interesting function but not all teams use them. Their traditional role of proofreading documents is being increasingly supplanted by automated proofing tools— some of which are becoming highly effective. However, a more interesting role for editors is to help define standards for look-and-feel and content-design. They then have the same role as an architect does in a software project. With DITA, someone needs to decide which tags to use, how to build maps, and how the finished document should look. All these standards are the responsibility of a content architecture effort that can be done by a team of writers. But in a large organization, it is often the province of dedicated editors who are talented in this area.

Staffing

Junior technical writers generally have few skills beyond being able to write MS Word documents. A typical well-trained technical writer is conversant with Frame and general editorial practices. Knowledge of DITA and other modern skills is a higher order skill set that one needs to hunt down. In particular, more senior writers who can help with UI design, requirements analysis, and information design are harder to find than their more junior brethren. Your typical recruiting channels often will not find these people since they are more setup for finding engineers. However, a good tech pubs manager can use other channels, notably some of the tech pubs professional groups to locate people.

Writing does lend itself to offshore work. As long as one is willing to do some training, completely serviceable writers can be hired in India and, more recently, in China as well. The main issue is that in some countries, this profession is not that popular and one has to dig harder to find people.

4. People Stuff

Leading an engineering organization is fundamentally about people or, as one of our bosses likes to say, "Managing would be easy if you didn't have to deal with people." In order to achieve your organization's goals, you need to understand every aspect of planning, recruiting, training, motivating, retaining, growing, and reorganizing teams.

Since you are hiring creative and talented people, you will also deal with a host of complex personalities. Since many of the issues that you will discuss with your team will be complex and ambiguous, there will be strong differences in opinion, accentuated by differences in style. A crucial part of your job is working with different personalities and styles on your team, while maintaining overall harmony and productive cooperation. In this section, we will look at all the human factors involved in creating and leading successful teams.

4.1 Leadership, Management, and Integrity

Leadership is a much more complicated topic than simply being the "boss". Engineering managers generally start off as technical leads, a role that emphasizes technical competence. As the Engineering manager advances in title, the job becomes less about being the technical authority and more about becoming a leader. This can be a difficult transition for engineers because it emphasizes "soft" interpersonal skills that are less a part of their training and career to date.

For the aspiring Engineering leader the bookshelves provide a dizzying array of texts on leadership and management. Because this topic is important in all industries and across many fields, there are an amazing number of books on the topic, taking a wide variety of approaches. Some books attempt to learn lessons from famous people, not all of who were business people or even real humans. Others books emphasize fads or catchy sounding new acronyms, or pseudo-psychological theories. While these approaches must be helpful to some people, they generally do not appeal to people with technical backgrounds

The authors we have found the most helpful are Barry Z. Posner, who is the dean of the Leavey School of Business and professor of leadership at Santa Clara University and James M. Kouzes, chairman emeritus of the Tom Peters Company and an executive fellow at the Center of Innovation and Entrepreneurship at the Leavy School of Business, Santa Clara University. Their groundbreaking book "The Leadership Challenge" and their Leadership Practices Inventory tools have been used worldwide, across multiple cultures and industries. Rather than being a cookbook of catch phrases or management exercise, Posner & Kouzes' work identifies the fundamental qualities of leadership through their own research and that of other academics. We find this gives the work a grounded timeless quality that makes the principles more useful, although it does take effort to apply them.

Posner & Kouzes have found that across cultures, industries and their decades of research, the characteristics people find most important have stayed consistent. These traits of honesty, being forward-looking, inspiring and competent when viewed in the context of communication research lead to the conclusion that "Credibility is the foundation of leadership". [Posner & Kouzes Pg 21]. As we describe the job of senior management in engineering, we'll make reference to how these leadership principles are vital to being successful. The topic of leadership is very broad, so we'll give some advice specific to the Engineering roles we're focusing on. We encourage you to continue researching and studying this topic as your career progresses.

Role of Senior Engineering Management

Engineering Management has the two following essential tasks:

- To build and direct an efficient organization that can do the work and perform operational responsibilities
- To manage the complex web of communications between Engineering and all the other interested parties including other peers, superiors and individual contributors, customers, board members, venture capitalists (VCs), and customers

The exact nature of these tasks evolves as companies grow. This means that engineering leaders have to grow along with the changes in the company. In this chapter, we will introduce three concepts that define a successful relationship between an engineering leader and the people he or she deals with. These are:

- Integrity
- Leadership
- Management

We will also look at how the management role evolves as the company grows.

Integrity

In "Credibility", Posner & Kouzes cited large studies where integrity was the most frequent characteristic managers chose as crucial to leadership. Integrity, defined as being truthful, trustworthy, having character and having convictions, is critical to leaders having credibility. The first rule to become a successful manager is to always maintain your integrity at all times. This means being honest with your staff, superiors, customers, and community. There will be times when it is tempting to take the easy way and try to hide bad news or overstate good news. In the short run, it may be painful to be honest. But in the long run, honesty and integrity can create a tremendous amount of credibility. There will be times when one must hide confidential information, or allow someone to believe something that was never stated: the real world is filled with grey areas. But any job that requires you to compromise your integrity is ultimately bad for you as a person and bad for your career. We can illustrate the power of integrity with a couple of stories from our professional lives:

Story #1: Competitive Bids

Our company did well with competitive bids. There was a case where a competitor came in with a lower bid that is 40 to 45 percent less to try to buy their way into the business. I told the customer he just could not build it for this price. The customer had to go to another vendor because of internal regulation but six months later, the vendor was kicked out and we got the job.

Story #2: Coming Clean with the Customer

My company had a long history of quality problems. We got a huge OEM contract from a bigger firm. I admitted to them that contrary to what was implied during the contract negotiation, our bug database was misleading and we had a huge backlog of about 3,000 issues. I explained our action plan for correcting these. Over the last couple of months, we have corrected most of these problems. Initially, Senior Management was very nervous about admitting this. However, in the meantime, the customer greatly respects us for being honest as well as acting on our promises. The engineering morale is way up for management because of the team's honesty about the quality situation.

Story #3: Integrity is a character issue

At an early stage startup, the founders got many of their initial contracts by lying to clients and telling them that they had experience with that kind of work. Their rationale was that they ended up doing good work and there was no harm, the client was never the wiser. However the staff of the company was aware of this practice, and even though they understood the rationale, it affected their view of the founders and the company. Nothing was said overtly, but when an anonymous feedback system was implemented, the founders were shocked to find that they rated poorly on perceptions of honesty and acting fairly. The true cost of the lying was their credibility and the price they paid was a company culture that didn't value integrity.

Leadership and Management

As head of Engineering, your job is to lead and manage the organization. This implies both setting direction and ensuring execution. Finding the right balance of effort between these two critical areas is very important. The nature of that balance will be different between a small 6-12-engineer startup and a 300-person organization. The choices you make will also affect your career development in the long run.

Be a Leader

Being a manager is a bureaucratic exercise unless grounded in good leadership. A good definition of being a leader is "someone whom people follow". There are two aspects to this. First, there are the characteristics of a leader that cause people to follow them and second, there are the characteristics of a leader that cause them to lead in the right direction toward success.

The good leader

As we mentioned earlier, credibility is the fundamental characteristic of leadership. This makes sense since it is hard to follow someone who is not trustworthy and is apparently dishonest or incompetent. Since leadership requires a leap of faith to accomplish difficult goals, a leader needs to be able to inspire people to work towards a common goal.

Urgency

Once you have got people following you, a sense of urgency is vital. "Time is money" is the old adage. A key role of the leader is to continually manage, coach, and motivate the team to produce at the highest level possible. While keeping the pressure up will not make you more popular, it will keep you delivering on your roadmap.

Critical thinking

Another important attribute of a successful leader is critical thinking. The bigger your organization is, the more people will "manage up" and tell you what they think you want to hear. You have to relentlessly probe to get at the core issues, which often involves careful listening to understand if people have thought the issues through and if they are presenting information in an honest and unbiased manner. Acting rashly without hearing all sides of an issue or obviously favoring some staff over others leads to the belief that "spin" is more important than the facts. Addressing issues in an unbiased and factual manner helps to set the expectation that critical thinking is valued.

Direction

Finally, and this is clearly part of the inspirational and forward-looking part of being a leader, you need to be able to communicate a clear vision to the team. This does not require clairvoyance on your part although that helps. It requires guiding the team into spending enough time on long-term planning and making sure your development efforts are well-aligned with the general business vision of the executive team. Much of this pertains to the communication with other stakeholders and ensuring that enough time is left for both strategic and tactical planning. Make sure you can tell both your long-term and short-term story and that the short-term story logically leads to the long-term story. Enforce that with your team too.

Good leadership is simply modeling the right values for your team and getting them to follow your example.

Be a Manager

A good manager sets and effectively communicates the direction for the team, energizes and motivates, and removes obstacles so that the team can be as productive as possible. It is management's job to ensure that the team has sufficient resources and that the responsibilities are correctly defined and distributed. Once implemented, the manager's job is to identify and eliminate obstacles to progress, which can include people, ambiguous goals, and resources. Managers cannot create the product by themselves but they can help build the right team and create the right climate to allow the staff to succeed. As they say:

- When it is done right, it is the team.
- When it is not done right, it is the manager.

Management has many aspects. It includes setting the culture, creating an organizational structure, dealing with transitions in the group and hard people, and simply adjusting to the effects of growth. We will look at all of these in this and the following chapters. We will start by examining the basics of managing an organization effectively.

Managing Organizations and Scale

Small and Growing Organization

Management characteristics

The VPE in a technology startup is usually the executive, with the largest number of subordinates. Other departments will not be staffed-up until there is a product to sell. This means the VPE has the largest number of individuals to work with since the company, in its formative stage does not have a layer of managers dedicated to the Engineering staff. At the same time, the executive team is going full-speed on market positioning, fund-raising, product specification, and messaging. The VPE must represent Engineering in all of these discussions and wear many hats, which can include HR, Purchasing, IT, Program manager, Technical lead, QA manager, and Documentation.

The main task of an engineering leader is to advance the product as quickly as possible while burning as little cash as possible. It is a very challenging role but despite being risky, it can be ultimately very rewarding. Normally, engineering leaders face resource limitations such as personnel shortage, equipment inadequacy, tight budget, and lack of specific expertise. Time-management and prioritization are very critical here, both the VPE and the team.

Staffing

A startup generally hires experienced engineers who can work with minimal supervision. Hiring has to focus on immediate short-term goals. Unless the first product is on time and successful, there will not be a second release. Startups also generally like to hire staff with startup experience since not everyone is comfortable in a smaller fast-paced environment.

One effective way of deciding what kinds of resources will be needed is to create a spreadsheet with the rows representing team members and the columns representing skills of each member. This matrix will help you see beyond the obvious and analyze the requirements for training and staffing.

Structure

At first, you will likely have a flat structure where you manage the entire staff directly. However, you should not equate a flat organization with being unstructured. Roles need to be defined— even if you only have a handful of people in the team— or you will risk overlapped efforts and worse, trampling of each other's work. Roles clarification also breeds stronger sense of ownership that in turn breeds good behaviors such as proactive drive for improvement. The role should fit the personnel and expertise area well. A database expert should own the database area although they may also work on programming in other fields. Since an engineering leader can have between 10 to 20 direct reports—some of them junior engineers— mentoring is a key role. Spreading the vision and clearly communicating the roadmap goals is paramount. Weekly 1:1 meetings with each direct report are important to ensure that less senior employees are "on-track". These 1:1 meetings are your chance to connect with your subordinates and discuss personal goals, reinforce values, and resolve any outstanding issues. One should use these meetings not only to address the points to be improved but also to comment and give positive feedback on the positive points.

Medium Organization

Management characteristics

In a medium-sized organization, there is a single engineering organization run by a VPE that encompasses a broad range of teams, which often include Development, QA, Technical Documentation, Lab Management, and sometimes, Product Management, focusing both on product and functional specialties. At this stage, the VPE has to focus on building independent effective teams to free up their time to work on planning, communication with other parts of the company, customer discussions, and other activities. The company has accrued an installed base of customers who need support and products that need maintenance. The development focus begins to shift generally from features alone to a balance of features and quality.

Staffing

As the organization starts to mature, the hiring process will become more structured and will require the leader to place new hires into an organization chart that would include well defined job levels. The engineering leader will still be able to directly influence the hires since he/she will be second-level manager and will be able to have some direct interactions with the new hires.

Structure

In a medium-sized organization, the VPE is a second-line manager, supervising a set of first-line managers. In this case, more time is spent on communication. The key to success here is having strong enough first-line managers the VPE can trust and delegate tasks to. However, engineering leaders should always know when to intervene and fix problems.

Even when relying on first level managers to execute the plan, it is prerequisite that the engineering leader first defines a clear set of guidelines and makes sure that managers are aligned with them. Although each person has their own style of translating guidelines into action, it is very important to have the original vision captured and conveyed in a clear faction.

Large Organization

Management characteristics

In very large companies, Engineering is no longer monolithic. The overall product development organization in this case is often run by pure Business people who may have their own P/L responsibilities. Here, engineering leadership is distributed and will be found in both vice-president and director level positions, running just a part of Engineering, and normally reporting to a general manager of some kind. The relationship to the general manager may be similar to that to the CEO in a smaller organization. However, the need to understand underlying business issues is emphasized because one may need to interact with and gain support from several layers of essentially non-technical management. As Development grows, the number of management layers also grows. There may be as many as three to five layers of organization composed of senior directors, directors, managers, and project leads. Unless communication is managed effectively, the leader can quickly get out of touch with the state of projects, releases, and the strengths and weaknesses of the hands-on team. Likewise, the team may not have an accurate and up-to-date understanding of the company directives. This explains why it is important to have skip-level and all-hands meetings to disseminate information in a timely manner.

Staffing

The engineering leader working in a large organization is often a fourth level manager, with directors, senior managers, and managers reporting to them. Typically, the distinction between the directors and senior managers at this level is that the directors can be trusted to work more independently, to set more of their own agenda, and to have a broader impact outside of their own organization whereas the senior managers are required to have more direction and to be more local in their scope.

Structure

With bigger teams, one can think about organizational design. This means one can classify workers into different groups by skill set, seniority and other criteria and plan abstractly what makeup of people one is looking for, what kinds of recruiting to do, or what kinds of career growth to encourage. So while a smaller team can only hire particular people for particular jobs, in a larger organization, you can hire 20 college hires and find roles for them afterwards. We can also ask the following questions: which people should we groom to become directors and what attributes should they have? Questions on how one can most economically grow their team and in which geography one can find the right talent for the right price also tends to be more practical in a larger organization.

The organization may be composed of multiple product groups, including teams of Development and QA engineers, as well as Product Management, Tool, and Infrastructure teams.

Vertical communication

In a large organization, there are normally a number of layers of management. Information tends to flow up and down very badly in most organizations. This requires special steps to make sure that everyone is communicated with. Skip level 1-1s and group meetings to align on strategy both become very important for keeping a large organization in sync. Connecting via 1:1s with the senior team members is a very good way to capture the read of what is going on without spending lots of time. These conversations will help you complement the information fed to the leader by their managers. One should make sure to not disclose the sources of information and be also tactful when probing other members about a particular item.

Time-management

In large organizations, it is easy to get stretched too thin because there are simply too many things to keep track of, too many meetings to go to, and too many people to meet. The key to success is a careful setting of priorities and delegation. A point that is often overlooked is the importance of a clear definition of how to escalate issues and report critical items back to you. Remember that changes in the escalation guidelines will change what items reach you and will impact the way you manage your time. Generally, one has to allow one's direct reports to run their teams on their own. One can then focus on setting the agenda for the team and on deep diving as required into the teams to investigate or help with particular issues. This model is flexible and highly scalable. This requires having managers working for one who can be trusted. It also obliges you to master an often very broad range of product and market issues without getting too bogged down in detail. There is a fine line between knowing enough to help set strategic plans and be able to spout trouble and trying to know too much that becomes futile in larger teams. Learning to quickly dive into things and then coming up quickly again for air is a useful skill at this level.

<u>Growing with the Organization</u>

Whatever size of organization you are with, you will need to learn to grow with that organization as it evolves and changes.

Learning to Delegate

The more you advance in management, the more you need to learn to effectively delegate. This involves identifying people you can trust and relying on them to reach the right outcome. This level of trust is a subtle thing. It is easy to become too trusting and get some nasty surprises and just as easy to micromanage. The balance between these is often tricky. The right level of trust can be built via effective mentoring. A good way of managing this trust is to allow people to operate independently and, occasionally, to dig deeply and spot check what is going on. Another good technique is to communicate your direct reports and interact with other people and find out what they are seeing.

Staying Technical

In many small companies, an engineering leader serves as the technical leader. As the company gets bigger, success is less about creating the technology itself and more about fostering an organization and environment that can create the technology and have it thrive. As the organization gets bigger, more success would mean finding, motivating, growing, retaining, and working with people.

Nonetheless, in Engineering, there is no substitute for having the technology knowledge to be able to drive the business itself forward. With one's time divided between competing demands and too many meetings, it is easy to lose the technical edge. Therefore, one always needs to spend some time keeping up with relevant business and technical trends. One key is to learn about those aspects of technology which are directly relevant to and that differentiate one's business while staying clear of many implementation details that others can take on.

Your early experience as a programmer, technical lead, and first line manager is never forgotten and often is still relevant. However, be cautioned that disruptive technology trends can make it hard to relate one's early experience with the new approaches. Many managers who grew up with assembler had a hard time switching to structured C code and, in turn, those C managers had an equally hard time understanding object-oriented design and design patterns. This is an important reason why you need to invest the effort to keep learning and expanding your knowledge.

This is important even in a large organization. While this requires careful time-management and prioritization, we have often been amazed at the technical depth of many of the senior executives we have worked with. While they may not know the details, they are aware of the technical essence of their companies' products and technologies very well, even engineering leaders and CEOs of very large public companies. The important lesson is the importance of abstraction and understanding what level of detail is relevant and necessary. Typically, the amount of technical detail required for identifying opportunity and assessing risk is independent of job title. Observing someone who is good at this is a great way of learning!

Career Implications

All our discussions show that there are considerable differences between managing a small startup and a large organization. As your career evolves—particularly as your startup grows into something big—you may get opportunities to experience both of these scenarios. Different people may choose different responses to this situation. Some may enjoy bouncing back and forth while others may take pleasure in specializing in one or the other.

In terms of your career progression and finding the next job, your resume after a while will start to tell a story of some kind. For many people, it will indicate that your preference is either to work only for small companies or to work mostly for bigger ones. If you want to jump back and forth, you will need to exert some effort to show that you are well-qualified and interested in working in both kinds of organizations. The practical challenge is to remember what an environment is like after working in the other. In a startup, one can get away with quick and dirty solutions that would never scale. Conversely in a large organization, you can do things that are inconceivable in a smaller organization. The small organization, for its part, will typically be capable of quick decisions and nimble moves not seen in their bigger counterpart. Each of these scenarios requires different skill sets to be successful in. If you want to move from one environment to another, the best thing to do is to show that you have been successful in both kinds of environments and that you are capable of succeeding in each.

Management vs. Leadership

In larger teams, it is easy to let the urgent dominate the important. There are so many meetings to go to that simply managing day-to-day tactical objectives can be a full-time job. But this is not generally sufficient for success at the senior management level. One needs to own one's business and be able to drive it strategically. This is the difference between management and leadership. Are you able to set the right objectives for your team? Do you understand how to make a difference for the business?

On the other hand, in smaller teams, this is even more crucial as there is no one else to fall back on. You are the technical leader and there will be no proper direction if you cannot provide one. This can lead to potentially disastrous consequences for the organization.

4.2 Company Culture

What is Culture?

Culture Defined

Culture is the personality of the organization. Formally, it can be defined as the collective values, behaviors, and expectations of a group of employees. It can refer to the following:

- Processes of decision making
- Rules around WHO gets to make decisions
- Rules about what behaviors will be rewarded and what are going to be rejected
- The values that guide conduct, actions, and decisions

Culture tells employees how to behave: how to dress, what hours to work, and when and how to speak up or voice opinions. Culture ultimately defines the types of employees who will be successful and satisfied in an organization. Creating the culture in an engineering organization is challenging mainly because the initial members will have more impact in shaping the organization. Bringing the wrong people to a small team can disrupt and sometimes prevent you to create the organization you have planned. This is like getting the right people on the bus and then driving to your destination.

During change, one of the most common mistakes of engineering managers is not recognizing that there is a culture in place and that either you compromise and adjust to it or you plan to replace a substantial part of your team with new people who would be more aligned with the new order.

Moral Setting of Culture

No matter how explicit or implicit standards of conduct or values are within an organization, it is only as good as the leadership of the organization. Organization members can see hypocrisy from miles away. It is incumbent on leadership and management to "walk the talk" at all times. This includes personal life, if their personal lives are publicly known.

Moral culture is the foundation for company culture. If the leadership does not have high moral values, it does not matter if you have the right people doing right things. It will be just a matter of time until the system disintegrates.

Culture relates directly how employees are going to be rewarded based on their behavior. A culture based on the wrong values foster bad behavior. Despite producing some good results in the short term, this kind of culture will still hurt the company in the long run. An inadequate culture will also attract the wrong people who will worsen the dysfunction and the level of cynicism of the good team members.

Why Culture Matters

Humans are highly socialized animals and are excellent at fitting in or adapting to different social contexts. People generally behave according to others' expectations of them and, in the absence of explicit rules; this behavior is defined implicitly by culture. Obviously, it is impossible— and insulting to your engineers— to establish a rule for every behavior you would like or expect from them. Therefore, to get the kind of behavior you want, you need to establish a culture that fosters it.

A good company culture can result in improved productivity and lowered costs. Productivity gains result from engaged and empowered employees. If your engineers are disconnected and unmotivated, your organization's productivity will immediately reflect that.

Lowered costs result from improved retention and recruiting. Happy engineers will stay with you longer. Interview candidates will quickly sense happy engineers and a strong culture. If the culture is right for them, they will desire to be part of it and if otherwise, then you will not want them anyway.

Culture: An Alternative to Process

Companies require a number of people who will collaborate effectively to achieve difficult goals. These partnerships are governed by social habits— some of which are informal and some, formal. Formal social habits are a company's documented processes. Informal habits, on the other hand, are the ones that define a company's culture. Because informal habits are more flexible and easier to learn and follow than the formal ones, it has been said that culture is what keeps a company from degenerating into bureaucracy. Trying to compensate for defective culture with processes is often a hallmark of dysfunctional organizations.

The Role of the Leader

Establishing Culture

Every department's culture exists within the culture of the whole company. It would then be very hard to create an engineering culture that is at odds with the overall corporate culture. For example, if a company values shipping quickly over quality, every group from Marketing to Customer Support expects this behavior. It is very difficult for one department or one executive to be the lone holdout. One of the signs of a good company is having its entire department's culture evolve together in a complementary way. This is a challenge especially for startups whose culture often changes and evolves very quickly.

Your department's culture will be a reflection of your leadership style. Employees take cues on how to behave from the leaders. If you are open and engaged, so then will your engineers. You will not succeed in trying to establish a culture that you do not adhere to. If you do not respect your engineers, it is unlikely they will respect you. As we covered in the section on leadership, credibility is the most important quality in a leader. If you have established credibility, you are already well on your way to building your department's culture.

In addition to setting the example, you can also help establish culture through other means. You can help foster communication with an open office space and low walled cubicles. Similarly, having regular team outings will give you and your engineers the groundwork for communication beyond work related issues. The more you communicate with your engineers, the more you establish the culture you want.

Maintaining Culture

Rewarding work that is "above and beyond" can build employee enthusiasm but it will backfire if this is not done right. "Fair is not the same as equal" and if you reward everyone, you are not rewarding people who go "above and beyond". This is even worse if you reward "the favorites" rather than those who deserve it. If you cannot do this right, it is better not to do anything!

When there is fast growth in staffing, it is important that existing employees are not trapped in doing maintenance just because they know the product. Since working on new products is generally viewed as more enjoyable to do, there will be resentment if only new hires get to do this.

If you are undergoing rapid growth, it will become difficult to maintain the culture you have worked hard to establish. In any hiring decision, you should consider the candidate's fit to the established culture. You should also include a culture section into your new hire training program with many "what-if" scenarios describing different situations and the expected behavior. Anonymous employee surveys provide early warnings of cultural problems or at least, employee perceptions. One way to help new hires to learn about your culture is to pair them with engineers who have been in the organization for some time who can orient them during their first days.

Good Culture

Traits of a Good Culture

- People run towards problems, not away
- People work for company's gain, not their team's

Developing a Good Culture

Build a meritocracy. When employees believe their accomplishments will be recognized and rewarded, they will worry more about the overall company success than their own situation. This entails dedicating time and attention to managing employees, no matter how busy things are. Sometimes, employees will be in a position where they cannot realize their full potential due to them being too valuable, "maintaining" a legacy module, or supporting critical customers. In situations like that, the engineering leader must develop a partnership with these employees and develop a "project" to take them from the current situation to one that they feel is developing their career. These adjustments help to compensate for situations where some team members cannot benefit from the meritocracy model.

Innovative Culture

As problems and solutions become more sophisticated, more value is produced from collaboration of several individuals than from the individual contributions alone. Successful innovative companies create some form of structure that foster collaboration and also allow reward for individual contributions. This combination can be seen in innovative companies of different sizes.

Another key indicator of an innovative company culture is the level of knowledge shared by individuals from different groups. This can be measured by the quality of technical Wikis or any other form of content sharing tool maintained by Engineering.

How Size can Influence Culture

Engineering groups in smaller organizations tend to tackle the critical tasks earlier. On the other hand, it is more common in large organizations to address the less complex tasks first and postpone the resolution of the most critical tasks. Nowadays, most of the leading Silicon Valley companies have a flat organizational chart and many are designed to be self-organizing entities with smaller fairly autonomous groups.

Depending on the size of each autonomous group, the level of both formality and bureaucracy increases. This slows down the pace of development. The key metric is not necessarily the size of an organization but the size of each of the autonomous groups in that organization.

Diversity and Culture

Typically, when a company starts, its founders normally share some common social and cultural context. As the company grows, this can cause challenges as newcomers who do not share this background arrive. A good example is a company two of us worked for. Most of the early employees in this company were Russian. Thus, most conversations in the break room would be in Russian, until a non-Russian walked in, at which point people would start speaking English. Normally, this is fairly harmless but as a leader, one has to make sure that people do not feel excluded because they do not belong to the existing culture.

What should one do about this? There are a couple of approaches. Some east coast financial companies find that golf is so much a part of their culture that in making sure no one is left out, they provide golf classes for everyone. This is not so common in Silicon Valley. A more common approach is simply to ensure that all-important activities are open to and comfortable for all employees. In fact, as the company grows, particularly to different locations in different regions, it becomes all the more important to figure out how to separate company culture from specific habits of specific groups of people. For example, one of the authors' companies has a beer bash every Friday. However, in India, some people do not drink and are uncomfortable with that. Since the building has multiple floors, the solution was to have the party with beer on one floor and without beer on the other floor. This is the kind of creative compromise needed to keep everyone happy.

Another interesting issue is the differing needs of both younger and older employees. The younger folks— newly out of college— tend to view work as a major part of their social life. They like to do things in groups; they love to hang out. Older employees, for their part, are likely to have family obligations. They want to do their job and then go home. This, sometimes, causes issues in planning events because not everyone will be equally excited. Again, the trick is flexibility and compromise. What matters in situations like this is listening carefully and being in touch with what the employees feel. One needs to particularly watch out for the common phenomenon: senior management may come from a different cultural group as many of the employees and may become out of touch with what some of the more newly hired people are thinking.

Another angle on diversity are the sheer cultural differences in how people approach work— ranging from attitudes towards hierarchy— in how much they speak up and how ready they are to admit bad news or to contradict the boss. For example, some newly hired employees may be uncertain in their English skills and as a result, they may become reluctant to speak up. Since you hired these folks, you need to make sure they are getting properly integrated! The key lesson in all this is to be aware and sensitive. You cannot always predict what will go wrong but if you stay in touch and listen carefully, you can often get pointers on what you need to adjust.

Confrontation and Tension

Some managers thrive on being extremely confrontational, as they like to exploit tensions within a group. In the short run, charismatic and intense leaders can move teams to accomplish amazing things while in the long run, if they are too abrasive, they can also burn so many bridges that they self-destruct. There is a broad continuum here. Some leaders who are very confrontational are also excellent at creating loyalty. They vigorously lead their organization forward. At their best, such leaders tend to get a long fine with those who are capable and those who understand them and reserve their venom for the inept. Many famous CEOs like Larry Ellison or even Steve Jobs fall in this camp. At their worst, such people can exercise a corrosive effect on the organization. A good example come from the Customer Relationship Management (CRM) business where a well-known company, in spite of great products and a great team, was ultimately undone by the irascible personality of its president who could not resist interjecting arbitrary changes of direction, displays of favoritism, and general fits of meanness that raised the tension level in the organization tremendously and greatly lowered morale.

The lesson of the story is that having a strong and intense personality can be fine as long as a sufficiently bold and correct vision as well as a decent level of judgment about people accompany it. Such person will be so effective as to routinely attract the right people. Nonetheless, there are many examples of highly effective leaders who— at least outwardly— are milder in character. However, it is hard to imagine being an effective leader without at least some measure of pushiness.

Dealing with Hard Times

When doing layoffs, it is important to openly communicate how the selections were made. The people you want to retain will see how you selected the people to layoff and if it appears arbitrary or unfair, you will lose them too. In some cases, you can approach layoffs by focusing on the positions instead of the people. By communicating that some positions were eliminated, you move away from the personal agenda and focus on executing a difficult but fair plan.

Bad Culture

Symptoms of Bad Culture

- When a company is not a meritocracy. Most people in that company believe it is who you are and not what you have done that counts.
- When the company does not value responsibility and accountability from everyone
- When a company is secretive and what is communicated differs between different executives and managers
- When a company drinks its own Kool-Aid it believes the product or business is more capable than it actually is.
- When team members are more concerned about other people roles than their own

Fixing Bad Culture

Culture starts at the top with executives holding themselves and management to the standards they ask of their employees.

When to Bring in Consultants

If a culture is weakened by a deep-seated conflict between factions, bringing in outside resources as neutral mediators can be very effective. Change management experts can also help an organization if they are trying to do some systematic transformation with many people involved by helping everyone become effective in this transition, particularly if not all the involved parties are experienced in change management. Trained facilitators can help the group reach good decisions, especially with engineers who are quick to jump from problem to implementation without a clear understanding of the question. Since such consultants are quite expensive, in a larger organization, you may want to have someone like this on staff in HR. Failing that, having them focus on training managers in how to do change management can also be effective.

If cultural weakness stems from weak corporate management, then no consultants can help. However, consultants love this last case because they can make a lot of money from it! We have seen a number of costly sessions run by consultants to try to create culture and vision and it produced nothing except very large invoices for the consultants.

When to Run like Hell

- When executives do not acknowledge cultural problems that a sizable number of employees bring up in anonymous employee surveys
- When the company culture starts having you behave in ways you find uncomfortable or forces you to explain a behavior that you cannot explain

Anecdote

I worked for a company once solely focused on Initial Placement Offering (IPO) or acquisition. As a result, there was a culture of pretending. Everyone knew the product did not work but no one wanted to talk about it. Everything became a matter of pretense. Also, whom you hung out with counted for more than one's results. The company quickly fell apart the moment it was acquired because in fact, no one liked anyone else and the "mafia" surrounding the founders was incensed when the new owners took them to task for building something that was so broken. They did not want to hear that message.

How to Assess a Culture

You may only spend a few hours interviewing for a position where you will spend years of effort. It is important to get a sense of whether the culture is compatible with your beliefs or styles. When you interview with a company, it is significant to get a sense of the company's culture by asking the following questions to the CEO, executives, and the team you will manage:

- How are employees rewarded or recognized?
- Is the CEO a dictator type?
- Is a particular department (i.e. Marketing or Sales) favored over others? (How did the CEO rise through the ranks?)
- Is the culture one that accepts an adequate amount of risk, but not too much?
- What do ex-employees of the company say about the culture? Do they think it is good or bad? (It is worth trying to track down a few.)
- Ethics and culture are entwined. Does the company make the right ethical decisions for the employees, stockholders, and customers?
- What are the company communication mechanisms? Is having "fun" encouraged?
- How do decisions get made?
- How do promotions or advancement decisions get made?
- How does the culture recognize performance? What achievements draw recognition and accolades?
- What kind of humor is tolerated and encouraged? What kinds are discouraged?
- What standards are applied for time-management? Is it meeting start times, agendas, or action item closure?

- What do people do in their free time? Do they spend free time together? Do they like each other? Do these activities cross management levels and vertical department lines?
- How are mistakes punished and rewarded?
- Is there evidence of NIH? How strong is it?
- How does the company position and describe the competition, customers, partners, analysts, investors, and board members?
- What does the CEO like to do in their spare time?
- Has the management team ever been sued or levied restraining orders?
- How much authority is pushed into the lowest levels of the organization? Budget authority? Representation authority? Customer handling? Employee recognition?
- Are technical specialists respected as much as line managers?
- Are there many titles in the company? What are the levels of titles?
- Are there very wide spans of control per manager?
- What level of management has authority to provide employees monetary recognition and bonuses?
- How often are stock options and grants given subsequent to initial onboarding?
- When hiring packages are proposed and approved, how do compensation package targets get set?
- What does the competition say about the company?
- What do customers say about the company?
- What do non-customers or ex-prospects say about the company?
- What does the investment community say about the company?
- What kinds of stories are repeated to new employees or interviewees when being introduced to the company?
- Does the company support regular training and conference attendance?
- Do people smile and frown? Do they crack smiles ever?
- Do people gather around common areas to spend moments to talk with each other?
- What does the refrigerator look like? Is there lots of beer and ice cream?
- How long into the life of the company did the soft drinks stay free?

4.3 Communication

Introduction

In this chapter, we will look at the range of communication problems faced in an engineering organization, from company-wide general communication, meeting management, to one-on-one communication techniques.

What is Communication?

Communication is often viewed as a soft word that is not susceptible to rational analysis. We believe communication is best understood in terms of expectation management. We can start with the easier case: the absence of good communication. Miscommunication occurs when:

- Expectations are not met because they are not clear and agreed upon. This is the common case.
- Unstated personal agendas are at work and at odds— or at least not aligned— with the team's objectives. This is the "bad apple" case.
- Terms of discussion are not clearly defined a commonly shared definition. This is the easy case.

In contrast, the key to skilled and excellent communications is:

- A clear sincere regard for having all team members aligned with common objectives
- An environment where ambiguity can be addressed with clear and nonjudgmental question-answer discourse
- An environment where disagreement can be registered but with clear alignment of tasks committed. For example, if someone disagrees and their issues have been addressed and duly noted, they will either still pull the boat with the rest of the team or they can depart—vote with their feet— if the disagreement is so severe.

Organizations adopting Agile values have an even more critical emphasis on timely and candid communication. Agile is fundamentally about shortening the cycle between action and feedback. Thus, pushing Agile principles to interpersonal communication recommends that feedback does not wait. This requires proactive and courageous initiative on all parties. Encouraging candid feedback is as important as formulating constructive and timely feedback. Both practices must be active in order for such feedback to be efficiently and effectively incorporated into future business practices.

In general, delays in communication rarely improve the overall consequences or results intended.

Components of Communication

Communication is a complex phenomenon. It involves an awareness of others and what others "know". In an actual interaction, there is:

- An initiator
- A recipient (In an active dialogue, these roles often switch between two communicating parties. In larger groups, the switches happen among a larger number of participants.)
- A "world state" or representation in the "mind" of the initiator
- A "world state" or representation in the "mind" of the recipient
- A key "message" or state change the initiator wants to transmit to the recipient
- A representation of the message— the actual delivered artifact— that is transmitted from the initiator to the recipient.

The various issues of communication can be partially understood in this model. A more sophisticated awareness of the recipient's world model is the key to the initiator's success in the communication.

- This includes language of discourse.
- Are terms understood?
- Connotations and implications. Triggers that might fire misunderstandings or misconceptions.

Receptivity on the part of the recipient is also a key to the success of the communication.

- Is the recipient attempting to map the message to their world model?
- Is there already an active "response" or "rebuttal" instinct working while the message is still being transmitted by the initiator?

Company- or Organization- wide Communication

At each level of the organization, it is important that people are not only aware of the "big picture" but they also have more details at the level in which they are operating.

A leader should keep their team informed on how the technical roadmap gets integrated with Business. During substantial changes made to the roadmap, it is important that a leader give some information about the rational that motivated the change. This will keep the team owning the roadmap instead of being victims of it.

Regular Meetings

In order to increase trust and transparency, the leader should have regular meetings where managers of other departments are invited to give a short presentation about progress in their respective departments. One important tool for team building and communication is the weekly team brown bag lunch. With minimum planning effort, the management team can propose the points to be presented by these leaders in order to keep it short and interesting. These meetings help everybody understand the major challenges and also be informed of progress in several areas. The level of detail of these meetings can be managed in order to keep the confidential information protected.

Keeping people informed of developments at a certain level reduces the damage to morale that rumors can create. When people feel that they are on the same page, they understand that some things need to be confidential for the good of the company.

At the same time, sometimes it is also important not to over communicate. If you focus on a message, people will assume it is important. This can sometimes create unfounded worries in a team. People will ask, "Why are they talking about this so much?" or "Is there a problem?" You have to think hard in planning communication if you want your folks to worry more or less about a problem.

Also, as companies get bigger, you should not count on information trickling down vertically through the organization on a reliable basis. In larger organizations, you may need to put messages out in many different media outlets repeatedly until you have succeeded in reaching a sufficiently large proportion of the population.

Hard Times

During hard times, it is crucial that the management take the initiative of communicating the news. There are very few situations where it is better to postpone the release of bad news. On the other hand, it is important that the people communicating are prepared to answer questions and concerns and not only relay information.

Public Companies

Public companies add another level of complexity since the legal department should review any information presented during these meetings.

After a public presentation to investors and analysts, it is sometimes helpful to prepare a summary with the key points stated. Present this to the company in order to keep everybody on the same page. When the management takes the initiative of having everybody on board, there is less space for rumors and misunderstanding.

Transparency

Some companies view communication as a way of creating transparency so that all employees understand the goals of their company. Other companies view it as a way of presenting a desired viewpoint to employees, which they feel will benefit the company but which may not be consistent with the viewpoint presented to other employees or management. Technical managers, who have generally been trained with the idea of an "objective reality", will often find communication for transparency more natural. Business managers who have more training in negotiations and debate will often have a "subjective reality" view of communications and may find it natural to present the same information differently, depending on the audience.

Effective communication is something in between. There is no such thing as 100 percent transparency since that would mean everyone's salaries and medical histories would be open to viewing. Employees generally understand that some information will be withheld. While it is common to emphasize different viewpoints depending on the audience, it is deceptive if it goes to the extent that each group is left with a different message. While this may look like a clever way of dealing with difficult messages in the short-term, it will completely undermine the management's credibility in the long run.

One of us was the VPE at a startup services company that was roughly equally split between Technical teams and client-facing Business teams. The company was just beginning to scale up in business and the CEO and founder was concerned about the risk of increasing staff too quickly. He wanted to tell everyone to work harder, put in the extra effort, and grow the company without increasing staff. However, the co-founder, who represented the Business teams, did not want their teams to hear this. He felt they were already working hard enough, although this was based only on his intuition. So, the co-founders agreed that the Technical VPs should communicate to their teams to work harder, while the Business teams would only hear positive messages. Since they did not want to be unpopular, the Technical VPs were instructed to deliver the message as if it came from them, rather than from the founders. The result was a complete disaster.

The Technical teams were highly offended since they could legitimately argue that they were already working harder than the Business teams.

It was impossible to deliver the message as if it were from a single executive since the employees immediately wanted to know if the founders agreed. Thus, the best that could be done was to represent this as a message from "the executive team". The founders were mad at the Technical VPs because they heard the backlash from the employees and they would never acknowledge their role in creating the message. This led to confusion, divisiveness, and lack of trust and the credibility of the executive team was never restored. The lesson is that it is important to be as transparent as possible as well as to deliver the same essential message throughout the company because once the employees believe the messages they hear are spun and manipulated, you will lose credibility and may never recover it.

Meeting Management

Meetings can be a nuisance and a waste of time. But, if used sparingly and appropriately, meetings can be an effective tool to:

- Get everyone on the same page
- Apply peer pressure
- Coordinate actions that need tight management
- Keep things moving more effectively than otherwise in a team environment

The following are some good ideas around meetings:

- Do not make them longer than necessary. Try 30 minutes instead of one hour.
- Do not invite more people than you need.
- Do not have them more often than you need.
- Be clear on the purpose of the meeting: informational, status, or decision-making. Make sure everyone knows that.
- If any topic requires too much discussion on the part of some of the participants to resolve quickly in the meeting, ask them to take it offline.

- Be sure that everyone is speaking clearly when meetings have many remote participants.
- Review and optimize the meeting format with participants to align it with its objective.

The following is a general process for running an efficient recurring meeting that tracks issues. Such meetings are governed by an agenda:

- The agenda is a spreadsheet, ideally checked into a versioned repository like SharePoint.
- The agenda is best projected with a laptop— and optionally WebEx— during the meeting.
- An agenda is made up of items. Each item has a name, creator, an owner and a due date, notes field, resolution field, and status.
- Anyone can add agenda items any time.

Such a meeting is governed by rules of order:

- We do not move from one item to the next until we are done with it.
- Each item is either open or closed.
- When we are done talking about an item, we decide if it can be closed.
- Once the item is closed, the resolution field is filled in.
- If an item is closed between meetings, it will stay on the agenda with status closed and the team can confirm the resolution.
- After the meeting, closed items get moved to a separate archive tab to avoid clutter.
- If an item remains open, an owner has to be assigned with a due date.
- We do not bug people about items with future due dates, unless something new has come up.
- If there is an owner, there shall be action items described in the notes column.
- If there are new developments, even without a change in action items, those are recorded in the notes field too.
- If an item requires additional discussion with parties not in the room or outside investigation or simply communication of a resolu-

tion to others, we assign an action item and move on to the next item.

- At EVERY meeting, we go through ALL open items.
- If after a couple of weeks it appears that an item does not lend itself to action, the team can elect to close it as being futile. (Sometimes no action is a reasonable resolution.)
- Freeform discussion is great as long as at the end of each conversation, these rules have been observed.

Following these simple rules will cause the meeting to become quite orderly.

Other Kinds of Communication

1-1s

Having regular 1-1s with your staff is important to ensure that everyone has an opportunity to voice their needs and concerns to you. Besides your immediate staff, in a bigger organization, you should regularly meet with people further down in the hierarchy (skip level meetings), including a sampling of individual contributors. This will help you understand their reality and not just the management's.

These are also good opportunities to give almost real-time feedback or coaching to team members. In our experience, team members who care about both the company and the team or those who just care about improving themselves tend to like 1-1s most. They give suggestions and ask for feedback. They use such meetings as opportunities to improve their performance. If the leader provides valuable feedback and helps the team members improve, then they will earn a great deal of respect and loyalty from the team.

A challenge arises when your organization gets to have more than 100 people. At that point, you will increasingly have a hard time meeting with everyone and indeed, you may not even always remember who are in your organization and who are not. There are a couple of strategies for dealing with this. First, focus your 1-1s on the key contributors. Ask your managers who those are. Secondly, wander around and randomly talk with people. Then you can meet with groups. Take the team out to lunch and take signups for lunch. Many of this comes naturally when you visit branch offices so make sure you do not shortchange the folks at headquarters.

Motivational Speech

Good motivational speech is an art. If you are good at Jedi mind skills and can easily create a reality distortion field (Steven Jobs is the prime example!), you can make people follow you through anything. Not all of us have that much charisma. Generally, if you make an honest and sincere effort to keep everyone in the organization aligned with the company's goals as well as how their personal work ties into those goals, this can be very motivational. For this to be effective, the goals have to be sensible. The management needs to have a good track record for executing on those goals and you need to be scrupulous about being honest and clear about what you cannot say and why. Engineers are very logical and skeptical of hypocrisy so make sure you walk the talk. If you say what you do and do what you say, then what you say will be quite motivational. If not, well, it won't.

Applying Pressure

As leaders, we often hope self-motivation is sufficient to get the team moving. Unfortunately, not all team members are self-motivated or sufficiently motivated under certain circumstances. In such a situation, a leader has to apply pressure sufficiently to get their team moving.

You have to apply pressure sparingly and only when necessary. A team that is constantly under pressure is an unhappy team and if it is necessary to constantly use pressure, the team may be dysfunctional.

The following are some situations that warrant pressure treatment:

• Extraordinarily tight schedule, hopefully for important reasons like a large contract, the company's survival being at stake, or preparing for a convention at a specific date

- Team is at risk of missing committed deadline or has missed deadline already

One of the techniques in applying pressure effectively is to use intermediate milestones— also known as deadlines— to keep the team moving. This is applicable for a longer project. If necessary, especially when delivery date is very tight, consider using tighter and more frequent milestones. An important point in increasing pressure is to increase the frequency with which any delay gets formally communicated from management to the team. This helps the team to really pay attention to what is happening. If you are using Agile processes, it will only require that the top engineering manager send an email pointing out any delay and remembering how much more is needed to complete the job. Giving this level of clarity to the team often will translate into added commitment to finish the project.

Giving Praise

There is an old guideline that tells you to "give positive feedback publicly and negative feedback in private". In most cases, that rule holds true. However, there are some situations where it is important to make it clear that some types of behavior are not going to be tolerated. These situations include cases where there is a clear direction and team agreement and one member decides that it is going to sabotage the process and poison the environment.

If you reach to a point where you have to fire somebody for these reasons, it is better to make the real reasons clear as to why the employee is leaving. Statements like, "He needed to spend more time with his family" or "He left because his daily commute was too hard" are not productive since they create deception instead of reinforcing the direction that the manager is trying to convey.

Giving Feedback

Managers are so often busy that they often forget the impact of feedback. When a job is well done, recognize and notify Senior Management publicly. That is totally motivating! And if you see something not quite right, do give feedback. Praise is easy to give and often overlooked. Constructive feedback for mistakes is more time-consuming but is often an excellent investment in your human capital that yields rich rewards, both for your organization and for yourself, in knowing you have made someone's life better.

Rewards

Spot bonuses are a great way of rewarding people for extraordinary achievements. If someone sacrifices their Christmas to save an important customer's business, you owe them some generosity! Do note though that you should not use bonuses to cover up for deficient compensation policies. If someone needs a promotion or raise, then do that. Also, be careful of the tax implications of the bonus. Company-wide reward programs, such as public recognition plus stock for an accepted patent, can also be very positive for morale.

Fun and Games

Parties are good to celebrate good news but they will be met with cynicism if they are viewed as a diversion. Using parties to distract people from bad news is a total morale killer. After the completion of a project with a tight schedule, it is more than fair to take your team out to do something together and commemorate. It does not need to be fancy. You would be amazed how people enjoy a couple of hours outside the office for a pizza and just hanging out. It is a mental break that reinforces the message that the team is always moving together.

Formal Performance Review

Performance reviews are a unique opportunity to make corrections and adjustments. It is important to make this part of the culture by per-forming them regularly, at least semi-annually. This process not only sends a message to the team related with performance assessment but it also allows a more productive engagement between the manager and the employee since everybody feels that the conversation is part of the project.

It is crucial to bear in mind that performance review needs to be part of a continuous process of mentoring and feedback. What you do in the review process should never be a surprise to anyone. Generally, the review cycle starts at the beginning of the year in the previous year's review process by setting both organizational and employee goals. Within the year, you will give feedback to your staff. When it becomes time for the review, your employees will give you a self-review for what they accomplished vis-à-vis their goals. Typically, each company will have some taxonomy for describing performance in various categories, normally stressing both values and execution. You then need to write the reviews. At the same time, you will assign some formal score to the review that is used as a basis for compensation decisions— may it be for promotion, pay raise, or bonus. The best performers will usually need to be disproportionately rewarded. Once it is all settled, you have to communicate the review to the employee and agree on goals and action plans for the next year. Part of this act needs to be the understanding of the employee's ambitions and working out an improvement plan to help the employee meet those goals.

Typically, the hardest parts of the review process are dealing with people whose personal view on their performance is at odds with your view as well as the corresponding disagreements about raises and the like. This is where you need to draw from the written record the feedback you have given throughout the year. Again, the record should never be a surprise, even if the employee does not grasp its significance right away.

As the head of Engineering, you have a couple of roles to play. First, you need to make sure your managers follow the process. Generally, they should be properly trained in the review process, employee development, and performance management. You should read the reviews written by your managers to make sure they are doing it well! Secondly, you need to coordinate the distribution of performance ratings, raises, and bonuses across the organization. The company will usually assign you a certain total budget and expected distribution of ratings and raise or bonus percentages. You need to work with your staff to make sure these guidelines are met. Part of the challenge is doing good leveling and making sure that everyone assess people in the same way. This is particularly tricky if you preside over multiple skill sets that are not readily comparable. Above all, your job is to ensure that the entire process is executed fairly across your whole organization.

Peer Review

Peer review is an important part of the overall performance management process. One of the challenges of any organization is that people interact with others in many different ways. Some people manage up very differently than they manage down. For example, they may be very polite and attentive with you or with another director or VP but they may become rude, overbearing, and dictatorial if they are with their peers or subordinates. Thus, it is dangerous to review people based only on your view of them. The best way to get accurate performance readings is to understand what kind of people a person interacts with up, down, and sideways, and poll all of them as to their views on the person. Done formally, this becomes a 360-degree review. Otherwise, you will also find it quite surprising as to the range of views a given person provokes on the people around them.

Another aspect of peer review is to create a buddy system where people are formally paired with buddies who can mentor them. This is particularly useful with new employees. It can also be utilized as part of an employee's development plan to help them develop particular skills.

Peer Communication

Regular peer communication is useful for addressing and resolving issues that cross-organizational boundaries. Some parts of this will happen naturally at your CEO's regular senior staff meeting. However, you will find it easier to get help from a peer if you have regular 1-1 communication with him. You want to have these at a neutral place like over coffee and held regular enough to ensure ongoing transparency of your respective organizations. This is especially effective with peer organizations that have demands on Engineering like Sales or Services.

4.4 Engineering Organization

Introduction

In this chapter, we will look at how both the roles and the organization of a company evolve during different phases of the company, as well as at different size levels.

How an Engineering Organization Changes as a Product or Company Matures

Startup with a Vision

While you are building prototype and raising money, you will likely have two or three dedicated senior engineers building a prototype usually with their own money. There will typically be one business visionary with the VC contacts to eventually get funding.

At this stage, it is easy to create a shared vision and since the whole team fits in the room, communication can be very informal. Typically, there will be no disruptive forces influencing the group, granted that the founders are close friends. Work is intense but focused with few distractions.

Post-Financing

Now comes the race to complete 1.0. Many companies progress beyond the post funding stage a few months before a VPE is hired. However, most of them have the equivalent of a CTO appointed by this stage. Normally, there is no Engineering Management, HR, and CFO. There is only a part-time accountant.

A VPE may be hired at the direction of the VCs within a few months of funding to actively drive the product strategy and to communicate effectively with the board on matters related to budget, scheduling, issues, and risks.

The transition to post-financing could be challenging particularly if the CTO or the founder cannot handle the management side of the engineering organization and the VCs are trying to bring a VPE.

The VPE has to be able to communicate with the founders the rationale for the existence of their position. It is also important to negotiate upfront who is in charge of what. During these meetings, the VPE has the chance to detect points of tension and areas where there will be some intersection on the decision- making process.

It is critical for the VPE to be able to negotiate and communicate each point in order to gain trust. During the day-to-day operations, if an issue comes up and is not clearly completely a part of the VPE role negotiated, they should resolve the matter with either the CTO or founder. These simple rules will help build a strong management team and dissipate resentment.

During the negotiation about who does what, it is important to make sure that there is enough clarity on the final configuration. Simplicity is a key factor here. Elaborating configurations without resolving some immediate conflicts can create confusion as the company grows.

Post-1.0 Ship

After the initial shipment, the emphasis shifts t o building revenues, building support, and responding to early customers. At this point, Customer Support and sustaining Engineering become more important. Many companies either build a separate sustaining Engineering team— either on a rotating or dedicated basis— or they offshore sustaining engineering to save cost.

Also, at this stage, the engineering management structure begins to form, either with one or two directors or managers of Engineering. It is still generally too early to consider adding QA management. Most VCs encourage the engineering structure of an early stage startup to be very flat—

ideally one VPE and up to 14 to 15 direct reports— until the product validation stage with early adopters is complete and sales start to ramp up. A flat
organization means that the VPE has a better pulse on issues, risks, and
schedules and there is lower "latency" in the organization since issues are
uncovered earlier.

Engineering Organization at 1-5 Engineers - Founders and Friends

At this stage, the team is motivated to take the product as far as
possible—ideally to ship status— before going out to get VC funding. VC
funding is easier if the team has a handful of successful customer references
or at minimum identified prospects. The founders are likely to work without
pay.

Project Management

Project Management is normally done by one of the founders. One
who has the most engineering management experience usually gravitates to
this role. Project management, however, is informal and part-time basis and
may or may not be detailed in an official MS Project-like schedule. It is
typically driven in an ad-hoc fashion, either based on the vision of the
founder/s or ideally by an identified pool of prospects.

Requirements Management

If the company is using Agile practices, it documents a set of user
stories and drives the product architecture and design based on these core
requirements. There is usually no formal MRD; Product Marketing normally details this and that function likely does not exist at this stage.

Communication and Collaboration

Communication is broadcast–oriented. The team is small and has to
communicate quickly and effectively. There may be a daily "huddle" to
assign tasks based on interest or expertise, check status, and make sure the
product is evolving in the right direction.

Training

There is no training at an early stage startup. The founders are likely experts at software architecture, design, and implementation.

QA

QA is an extravagance. Engineering (or the founders) typically perform unit testing and ideally find customer prospects that have the time and patience to deal with a buggy and rapidly evolving product. They often do this testing in exchange for a discount on the forthcoming GA version.

Documentation

Documentation is limited and is done by the engineers in the form of simple online help or non-elegant PDF/HTML documentation.

Testing

Both the unit and automated integration tests are executed at some level. Normally, there is neither regression testing nor minimum automation on the UI level nor formal definition of test cases and test plans.

Support

Second tier support is mostly done by Engineering and/or the person responsible for coding the specific module.

Engineering Organization at 6-25 Engineers - Informal Group

Project Management

At this stage, the company may justify a dedicated Project Management role, closer to the 20-engineer level. You can think of an engineering organization as a living creature. It starts as a little pet and is light and flexible. As it grows, this creature gains weight, becomes less flexible and needs more coordination. Nowadays, most engineering organizations are configured with a number of fairly independent small groups. Each of these groups has its projects and goals. This configuration minimizes the need of a very formal communication protocol and keeps the workplace attractive for engineers with a more entrepreneurial spirit.

Requirements Management

Requirements management is now more formalized. The company has an installed base to "evolve" and Marketing takes more ownership for gathering customer or prospect requirements and formalizing these into either use cases or stories or an MRD.

This area suffers a great change since the requirements need to be part of a vision that cannot be validated by Engineering. People are in different rooms and should be focusing on solving specific problems. Technical requirement and architecture documents are the few artifacts that enable each member of the organization to learn more about the rest of the team.

Communication and Collaboration

The company institutes a weekly Program Review driven by the Project Management to track schedule or task status, risks, barriers, and process metrics.

Collaboration is another key area in an engineering organization that requires special attention. Weekly brown bag lunches, architecture reviews, and mentoring meetings enable exchange of ideas and experiences. This can be a valuable tool to keep a team more informed and also foster innovation as a byproduct.

Training

A this stage, customer and employee training becomes more important and the same person tasked to perform customer training— if there is— may also include training engineering new-hires about the company products including design and architecture as well as engineering processes or procedures. However, employee training is still informal and may be done with a series of recorded ad-hoc brown bag lunch seminars.

QA

QA is now more formalized. There are a handful of full-time QA engineers who may report directly to the VPE. As the company grows to 20 or more engineers, a QA manager or director is often hired. A general rule of thumb is one QA engineer for every two and a half developers. This ratio varies greatly, based on company culture, target market, product category, and product ancestry. At this stage the continuous integration is almost a must. Both the unit and automated integration tests are executed in real time. Some automation at the UI level is developed to execute automated regression tests. Also, formal definition of test cases and test plans help to reuse artifacts between QA and the rest of the team.

Documentation

Tech pubs are now more formalized, with at least one dedicated senior technical writer who manages the input from Engineering, has expertise in Frame, Word, Acrobat, and Open Office (depending on company), and who also generates most of the on-line help. Ideally, there should be one technical writer for every four or five developers. But rations vary greatly.

Support

Second tier support is mostly done by Engineering and/or the person responsible for coding the specific module.

Engineering IT

Depending on the kind of product being built, it will become necessary to hire system administrators to procure, install, and support the hardware used by the group. General rules of thumb are about one system administrator for every $2-$3 million in capital equipment as well as one for every 30 developers.

Maintenance

There are no formal divisions between new development and maintenance and work gets assigned normally to the same person who originally developed the code.

Engineering Organization at 26-50 Engineers - Formal Group

Project Management

At this stage, there is normally a dedicated Project Management function with one or two dedicated project managers.

Requirement Management

Requirements Management at this point is more formalized with documented use cases or MRDs. These are reviewed and prioritized by a company roadmap committed by and are comprised of the executive staff. A company roadmap is formalized as well. This, in turn, drives high-level requirements for subsequent product releases.

Communication and Collaboration

Communication is now more hierarchical. The VPE has a weekly staff meeting to communicate the status from the executive staff and to get the status from their direct reports. In turn, each respective engineering manager has their own weekly team status meeting. The entire company may have a weekly or monthly meeting to relay news such as company successes, objectives, or announcement of new hires.

Training

It is large enough to justify a dedicated trainer for Engineering approximately for a team composed of 40 to 50 engineers. Training includes new-hire sessions regarding product usage, architecture, design, development processes, and procedures.

QA

At this size of organization, there is a dedicated director of QA position. The outsourcing strategy is in full swing, with a large percentage of the testing organization managed remotely. Also, performance testing is being performed as a normal part of the release process instead of being driven by an ad hoc process executed by engineers.

Documentation

Using the rule of thumb of one technical writer for every five or more engineers, there are now five or more technical writers. This ratio varies drastically, however, as many companies rely on the developers to write the draft technical documentation.

Support

A support group composed of a few people is formed and processes to track customer issues and bugs are in place.

Engineering IT

As the organization gets bigger, you will also need about one build engineer for every 60 or so developers, in addition to scaling your system administrators. You may also need specialized staffs like DBA's and network specialists, depending on the work.

Maintenance

Once the number of customers reaches a critical mass, customer service issues start to take resources from Development and Operations. Cases begin to be formally scheduled during planning.

Engineering Organization at 50+ Engineers

Project Management

At this stage, there is typically a dedicated Project Management function with two ore more dedicated project managers. While at XXXX Corporation, as the engineering organization grew from 30 staff to 400, including developers, QA, and documentation, and other professions, the number of dedicated project managers went from one to five. So the ratio was roughly one project manager for every 40 to 50 engineers. With an Engineering team of 400, one senior project manager— typically, director level— is dedicated full-time to manage the overall company roadmap. The others serve the role of creating and maintaining the tactical formal project and release schedules.

Requirements Management

At this stage, Requirements Management is very formalized with documented use cases or MRDs. Requirements are validated with a customer advisory board and via surveys. In-depth user stories or use cases are reviewed in a cross-functional team with representation from Engineering, Marketing, Support, Professional Services, and in some cases, Sales Engineering. The company roadmap representing several products is reviewed and prioritized by the executive staff and Senior Management. A company long-term roadmap at least two years out is formalized as well. This in turn drives high-level requirements for subsequent product releases.

Communication and Collaboration

Communication is now more hierarchical. The leader has a weekly staff meeting to communicate the status from the executive staff and to get the status from their direct reports. In turn, each respective engineering manager has their own weekly team status meeting. The entire company may have a weekly or monthly meeting to relay news such as company successes, objectives, and announcement of new hires. A formalized Wiki repository is employed to facilitate communication at a project or product level.

Training

With an over 50-engineer team size, there is justification to dedicate a training function for Engineering. Training includes new-hire sessions regarding product usage, architecture, design, development processes, and procedures. Formalized new-hire tools like Wiki training pages are created to bring staff up to speed faster.

QA

At this size of the organization, there is often a dedicated director of QA position. The outsourcing strategy is in full swing with a large percentage of the testing organization managed offshore.

Release Engineering

At companies of 50+ engineers, there will likely be a separate team of developers focused on the entire infrastructure. This group often goes by names like "Release Engineering" or "Engineering Tools". You will usually need a couple of different sub teams within this group. They are:

- Tools developers
- Build architects
- Database Administrators (DBA)
- Source Code Management (SCM) experts
- System administrators (to run build environment)
- Director or manager of Release Engineering (for large Release Engineering groups of six or more)

You may also want to differentiate between the developers and the operational team that monitors the build or tests and triage the results.

Documentation

At XXXX, we used the rule of thumb of one technical writer for every five engineers. This ratio varies drastically, however, as many companies, especially in their earlier stages rely on the developers to write the draft technical documentation. The product category also has a big impact on documentation effort. On-demand products, for example, live or die on their simplicity or usability and should not warrant a large documentation effort.

Engineering IT

As the organization becomes very large, you will want dedicated staff for source control, configuration management, and general tools support. You will also need properly trained procurement specialists as well as budget planners who can keep track of and manage capital equipment and leases.

Process Group

In a large organization, you will also want a process team whose focus is ensuring that the overall product development methodology is agreed upon and correctly documented, new hires are properly trained on it, and that collects metrics on compliance.

Benchmarking Team

At companies where product performance is critical, a dedicated team of experts in measuring performance and suggesting improvements to Engineering is created. When one of us worked at RRRR, the development organization included a team of four experts (one for every approximately 50 engineers and most of whom have PhDs in CS) who perform the following tasks:

- Establishes customer use profiles
- Creates environments and simulations of customer profiles
- Executes performance, scalability, and latency benchmarks

- Documents results and provides suggestions to development for resolution of bottlenecks in some cases

Complexities in a Growing Organization

Rapid growth requires frequent re-factoring of an organization, mainly because individual managers are winding up with too many people reporting to them. In building aggressive hiring plans, one should, as much as possible, construct management plans to show how the management hierarchy will evolve. This involves thinking about whether to add more levels of management or to grow horizontally. It also involves closely examining managers and potential future managers for their capacity for growth. Team lead, first line manager, and second line manager are all different jobs and not everyone is ready for promotion simply because their team is growing. Thus, as you plan to hire people, you should think about which managers you can grow, which you can promote, and where you want to hire externally. You may also find that certain monolithic organizations are no longer scale and need to be broken up or redistributed.

Inflection Points

As an organization grows, there are a number of changes that can occur which can radically affect its shape and composition. You should look for the initial signs that a particular organizational model or process is reaching its limits and plans to reorganization with training, staffing, etc.

Multiple Product Lines

Having multiple product lines certainly complicates the management structure. If you had only one Development team before, you will now have multiple independent ones. This already creates the management task of arbitrating and prioritizing between them. A subtler problem is that you and the other Senior Management team may be very used to thinking in terms of whatever single product you started out with. All of a sudden, there are now other products that you will also have to pay attention to and you will need to delegate some of your oversight and authority to the people running those products. Often, organizations have a hard time with this with many people on team still thinking of themselves as the company that makes X, when in reality it is the company that makes X, Y, and Z. Enforcing and modeling is a key responsibility of Senior Management.

Multiple Sites

Communication gets harder at the square of distance. As your team grows, even filling up an entire large floor of a building can cause more communication problems. As you add multiple floors, buildings, and sites, these get progressively worse. The challenge is that as long as an organization is small and collocated, everybody can informally communicate and many things simply happen. As separations get wider, people will simply not bother to informally connect to others further away. Specifically, as geographic and time differences intervene, people will need to work with other people they have never met and who are inconvenient to talk to. This can cause enormous productivity and morale challenges.

To address these issues, you need to do the following:

- **Formalize communication processes**
  In a small team for example, if the build breaks, whoever notices will step in and help and maybe holler across the cubicles to get help. In a large team, on the other hand, you need to have a formalized escalation plan as well as clear definitions of ownership. As a manager, you have to notice when your team's informal communication processes are inadequate. You should help define new and more formal ones. At the same time, you should strive to localize work as much as possible to maximize the number of issues that can be handled informally. You should only resort to the more formal mechanisms, if forced to by the scale of the environment.

- **Create opportunities for people to meet one another by cross-site travel and activities**
  Neither of these have organizational consequences. In general, organizational structure does not need to be too tied to geography. Thus, if you have multiple sites, you might want to appoint a manager to be the site manager who will handle cross-department issues relevant to that site. In certain cases, if work is geographically de-

termined, you can also have a manager responsible for a given team for that site. Other than that, many different organizational structures can work with a larger and more distributed organization, provided that the communication issues are dealt with.

- **Try to create more self-contained teams**
  Self-contained teams reduce the amount of communication and can simplify the challenges of communication across sites. These are not easy to assemble and can present another challenge during execution. However, maximizing the amount of local communication and reducing remote communication requirements will increase overall team productivity.

Alternatives to the Simple Organization

Typically, a fast growing organization simply gets bigger without much consideration for its structure until one day people realize that things have become very inefficient. At this point, there will be discussions on centralizing shared functions and, at times, a desire to have different organizations cooperatively managing staff in matrix-style arrangement.

When to Centralize Functions

As an organization grows, there are economies of scale in hiring specialists to perform certain functions. At the same time, it may make sense to centralize those resources to achieve greater economies and better career paths. For example, if technical writers are scattered in an organization, consistent look and feel in documentation would be difficult to achieve. These writers will feel lost because they will be so outnumbered by the developers that they will often feel lost in the shuffle, especially as most of their managers will have little experience with them and have a hard time providing them enough guidance. In that sense, there are many things to gain by centralizing their work. However, what one needs to guard against is that the newly centralized organization starts becoming unresponsive. One good technique for solving this is by managing inside the centralized organization pools of resources assigned to the different client groups with regular sessions to rebalance those resources. This kind of centralization works well for infrastructure groups such as documentation, Engineering IT, builds and tools, and such.

A second kind of centralization is deeper and that concerns the unity of Engineering itself. In small organizations, Engineering is very much one thing— reporting to one Technical VP and creating all of a company's products. As the company grows, this model will become non-functional since it will become too hard to properly balance resources inside of a giant engineering organization from outside of it. At this point, it makes sense to divide the organization into multiple Business units, each with their own Profit/Loss (P/L), Product Management and Marketing, and Engineering teams. This approach is more scalable, although it encourages the different areas in Engineering to go their own way. If there are technical commonalities between the Business units, one can go with a hybrid model where certain technical and infrastructure functions are completely centralized and other functions spread out to the Business teams.

For the Engineering leader, the distribution of the organization into Business units opens new challenges. First, it offers new job opportunities. There is the possibility of graduating from running purely a Development team to becoming a general manager with P/L responsibilities over some product line. There are also risks, however, as the growing complexity in the organization can marginalize a once powerful leader who cannot grow their career attuned to changes. As a company makes changes like these, deciding clearly where you want to land afterwards is very important. You should also make sure that you have the right support to land in a useful spot in the organization.

When to Use Matrix Management

Matrix management is another approach to address centralizing and decentralizing tasks. This usually entails separating people management from project management. In this case, everyone has a direct manager who handles all their career issues and is then assigned to Product teams for the conduct of a project where they basically work for a second product specific manager. This approach can be useful if people often switch projects and there is insufficient continuity to keep them on one substantial project for a long time. In IT organizations where many relatively small— but separate— efforts are made, this can work well. This approach tends to lead to excessive management overhead in the case of pure development environments where deep expertise and continuity are valued. On the other hand, for aspects like technical writing, the approach can work quite well, with writers belonging to a home writing organization and being assigned to a Product team.

4.5 Leading through Transitions

Change

Changes are inevitable in any organization. But in a hi-tech environment, change IS constant. Unfortunately, as much as people try, most are naturally averse to too many changes. We will discuss in this chapter how to lead an organization through major changes and transitions with minimal interruptions and maximum results.

This is a popular quote attributed to Christina Baldwin: "Change is the constant, the signal for rebirth, the egg of the phoenix." How we deal with change in our leadership roles is crucial to our success and the company's as well. We will look at the three main kinds of change and these are:

- Change in the environment resulting from evolution of technologies, markets, and processes
- Quantitative change in an organization correlated with growth
- Qualitative change in an organization connected to evolving business models

A key concept that you need to understand is that change needs to be managed instead of just be executed. Planning helps you to see the actions that need to be made to reduce friction when the "real" change happens. Ask yourself, "What are the things that will position my team to be more aligned with this future scenario?" Doing this exercise will help you identify action items that could help you minimize disruption.

Monitor Industry Trends and Changes

The pace of technology trends and innovation within Silicon Valley is frenetic. In the last 25 years, there have been at least five mainstream or pervasive changes in: programming languages; software engineering methodologies or practices including Waterfall, ISO-9000, Six-Sigma,

CMM, Agile, and Scrum; and in management philosophy. The industry is littered with failed companies that were unable to adapt quickly to changing market conditions or competitive trends. Here are some of the things you need to track:

- Competition: Set Google alerts to monitor your competitors announcements. Also work closely with Product Marketing to understand competitive strengths and weaknesses
- Technology trends: Here the CTO and— to some extent— the engineering leader usually have a responsibility to keep a pulse on the latest technologies and models (i.e. Ajax, Spring, Dot Net, SaaS, and Flex) and to pick the best ones for the company's circumstances
- Process or methodology trends
- Hiring environment (i.e. Offshoring trends)
- Target market conditions
- Tools (i.e. SCM, collaboration, and QA automation)
- Invite engineers to present brown bags topics

In response to what you learn, you need to deploy processes that respond to changes:

- Consider a formalized "continuous improvement" process team to review, prioritize, and deploy changes in either the development or manufacturing process
- Consider forming an architecture committee to monitor and report on latest technology trends and assess impact to product architecture.

Rapid Growth and Its Effects

One of the unique aspects of the hi-tech world is how frequently one experiences organizations growing very rapidly through all these stages. This high rate of growth causes unique management changes in terms of the organization, processes, culture, and demands on a manager.

Obviously, as a company grows, management approaches have to evolve. But even in a smoothly growing organization, there will be events that will trigger some drastic changes. For example, the moment a company is too big to fit on a floor, building, or location, an immediate organizational adjustment to the new communication challenges should be in place. Part of managing successfully in a growing company is recognizing and anticipating these transitions and handling them smoothly.

Here are some examples of such transitions:

- Brainstorming new idea
- Commitment of founding team
- Founding
- First hires
- Management team complete
- "Can't remember who. . ." (It is important to know beyond which employee you cannot recall a name.)
- First financing - Angel? VC?
- First product release
- First partner
- First sale
- First million in sales
- First profitable quarter
- First profitable year
- Second product kickoff
- First change at executive level
- First remote site (Taking development overseas)
- Bring development back from overseas
- First acquisition
- First time organization requires a middle layer of Engineering Management (Not everyone can report to the VPE)
- Both the CTO and the VPE in the organization

Leading During Accelerated Growth

Humans naturally measure the present in terms of the past. In a fast growing organization, all organizations and processes always seem broken. This leads people to think that the company is somehow incompetent. This is a big mistake! When organizations and processes were created, they were just right for a smaller company. It is the fast pace of rapid growth that makes them always seem broken and they are just behind the times perpetually. One needs to reassure people that this is only a natural aspect of fast growth. If everything seems too perfect, it probably means the growth period is over.

One also has to reassure everyone that the continuous reorganization characteristic of fast growing companies is good since it allows the company to adapt to the fast growth. In the same way, one needs to show the employees that as new processes are instituted and old habits get changed, nonetheless, there is still continuity with and respect for the good things already achieved.

Mistakes Made by Fast-growing Companies

The following are some of the pitfalls in quickly growing which you, as the engineering leader, should strive not to emulate:

Arrogance (i.e. Netscape, Microsoft, Siebel, and Google)

Arrogance will hurt the organization during partnerships engagements and will also disrupt services to strategic clients. It's critical for the engineering leader to give a reality check about behavior and remind that the group should act in a professional way.

"We are the best" pride

Any statement that conveys the idea of an optimistic absolute inertial state will hurt your organization. Comments like these are normally uttered in commemorations of key milestones. As a general rule of thumb the engineering leader should recognize the accomplishment and at the same time remind the team that this is a temporary state. Comments like, "As of Today we are at the top "....", but let's make sure we continue to work hard to keep that way" will help you keep your team focused.

"We are inventing a new culture" hubris

These are comments normally made by CEO's in annual meetings. It's important for the engineering leader to translate that into a positive statement that conveys "opportunity" instead of entitlement. Reinstating this message as "We have a great opportunity to make a difference in a meaningful way" are more forward looking and communicate a "call for action".

"We hire only the best"

This message again assumes an inertial state. The engineering leader will be better served if they convey the idea that as an organization "We want to be a high performance team"

Lack of appreciation for the management's role

We've seen this in fast growing companies where engineers misbehave like kids and associate being immature to being brilliant. There is always space for humor and fun, but the engineering leader has to deliver a clear message that collaboration is a key factor in any high performance team. This kind of message uses the engineers' technical pride to self-regulate their own behavior.

VPE's Role in a High Growth Environment

There is also a tendency for certain managers to lose responsibilities over time. Consider the stories below:

Story #1

In my early startup, there was initially a one-man show in Product. That person ran everything from Product to UI to Engineering to IT. That is a boatload. Then, as the company grew, there appeared VPEs and VPs of IT and Operations, and others. It was not a reflection of the VP of Product, rather, early startup need to conserve cash so he had to take care of everything. But as the company grows, it is just not sustainable to have one person running too many departments, unless the VP of Product is now the president.

Story #2

At one of my last companies, there was initially one engineering manager and he was in charge of all Engineering with the staff of four. But as we grew, the team turned to 10 engineers and it no longer makes sense for the same engineering manager to manage everything. It was certainly possible that he grew to become director but he was not quite ready. Thus, his responsibilities were reduced to a few vertical areas and there was another engineering manager who covered the other vertical areas.

This all makes sense. The key point is to set the right expectation with the team, especially those holding the position of power, that this kind of situation will happen and it is a natural progression, not a reflection of one's capabilities. With the proper expectation, the morale will stay high when changes like this occur.

Sustaining High Growth

As a company gets reasonably large, new management challenges will arise if high growth is sustained. The principle one is that if there are new hires, the existing staff will literally lack the bandwidth to teach everyone. With the less junior being forced to tutor the more junior, there is a high risk of fatally diluting the culture. To address this problem, you have to make a plan that focuses on formal training programs to impart both knowledge and cultural continuity. Working on stringent and consistent employee appraisal and development mechanisms with HR is also imperative in this scenario. This holds true as the quick hiring will eventually cause a number of hiring mistakes even at the management level. This will tend to produce higher rate of HR issues relative to employee performance or the lack thereof.

Joining a New Organization

Starting a new job entails many challenges. Besides learning the new company's products, you also need to take stock of and start getting to know your new team. The following are some interesting cases to consider:

New Team is Incompetent

You will want to pay particular attention if managers reporting to you are inept. Individual contributors can be replaced but managers are more insidious because you are relying on them for information. If incompetent managers land in your team, you should get them out of your hierarchy as soon as possible! They will not make your life easier. You have to understand their situations and you either fix it quickly or get them out of there! The employees often know that their managers are fools and will respect you more if you get rid of the source of the problem. Moreover, you should also be wary of those people who are good at managing up and those who show a very different face to their subordinates.

New Team is in a State of Conflict

If your new team is divided and arguing, the challenge is to quickly determine the truth. The truth is often more flexible and harder to find than one might think. The best thing to do is to listen carefully with an open mind to everyone and while being supportive, avoid taking sides until you have heard all the issues. Be sure to reach out to individual contributors and work to reassure them that you are on their side. Once you figure out what is going on, you should move as quickly and decisively as possible to fix the problem and then communicate back to everyone. Interestingly, in many cases, even if an entire department features everyone fighting with everyone else, only one or two people are often the ultimate cause of all the problems. Removing those people may make all the difference in the new world. The key issue is to make a fast and fair determination and then show the team that you act decisively to fix it.

New Team is Very Demoralized

If people are demoralized, you should find out why! Making sure you talk to all the individual contributors is crucial for this purpose. You will not only get to the truth faster but you will also gain their respect. Unhappiness and conflict are often associated with each other. If people are merely unhappy about a business strategy, the problem is usually in a conflict with some manager, possibly in other groups. Sometimes, there are people in a group who simply seem to cause conflict a lot. You should try to push them out of your team. What works for Steve Jobs or Larry Ellison does not translate well for a local software team.

New Boss Wants You to Make Some Changes Quickly

If you arrive in a troubled situation, you will be pressured to deliver changes quickly. Yet all the issues outlined above require patience to figure out what is going on. The trick to getting the time to solve these problems is to consciously look for low hanging fruit and go for some quick successes early to show everyone that you are on top of things. After that, you should work on clearly communicating both your findings and strategy to those above and below you.

Qualitative Change in the Business

Companies almost never grow in a strictly linear way. There are various events that cause sudden drastic changes in their operation. These are often associated with periods of: fast growth or shrinkage; acquiring or being acquired by another company; or major changes in the company's business plan.

Startups

Startups are prone to a great deal of transition. The small size of a company means that each additional hire can strongly change the culture and politics. Since startups must often change strategies overnight, departments and individuals can find their priorities and even their relative status changing. Both success and failures can cause startups to make radical changes. Failure can cause the investors to lose confidence and, at times, they will install their own advisers or managers. Success can lead to inflated expectations and corporate arrogance as people begin to build empires. It is a virtual guarantee that the early years of a startup will experience frequent and drastic transitions. Being able to manage through transitions and provide some stability for Engineering is critical for a VPE in a startup.

Being Acquired by Another Company

Being acquired by another company can generate a fair amount of disruption, depending on the motivation for the acquisition. Understanding the acquiring company plan allows you to align your efforts and reposition yourself in the new organization. Among the main reasons that motivate an acquisition are the following:

- Acquire a technology to integrate in another product
- Acquire the company or service to leverage other services or products
- Increase market share by expanding the product line
- Increase market share by acquiring customers
- Combine services and reduce cost
- Reduce the acquisition targets of competitors

During times of high growth, the effects of the acquisition's motivation are minimized since talent is scarce and that any disruption during the acquisition can slow down the company's pace. However, during stable periods or a downturn, it is very important to understand as much as possible what rationale the acquiring company is operating under.

Acquiring Another Company

Typically, this is an exciting stage of growth for a company. In most cases, your company fundamentals are likely strong and growing if you are in a position to acquire another company. At the same time, it is also likely that if you are growing, there is little time to take on the additional effort required to perform the due diligence effort of an acquisition. You should not underestimate the time and effort required to perform an adequate evaluation of the acquisition candidate and its impact to your daily responsibilities. In a perfect world, the process can take days or weeks, not including the possible post-acquisition efforts. Temporarily delegating a substantial component of your ongoing day-to-day responsibilities to your management team, if possible, is the best practice. It is also a great help to have a pre-existing company strategy guide in performing the due-diligence effort: a checklist or questionnaire ready in the event of an acquisition.

Considerations for an acquisition must be couched in terms of the primary motivation for the acquisition. Is it to add a new revenue stream or technical talent? Is it to create a new distribution channel? Depending on the motivation, the due diligence process can be simplified and focused on a more manageable set of criteria. Normally, with a technical evaluation of an Engineering function, issues like team size, organization, product technologies, third party licenses, patents, and cultural fit all matter in the decision. It is also tempting to follow the pack and not to be the only naysayer. Trust your gut and make sure that both risks and issues are adequately documented and openly discussed with the other evaluators.

Leading During Major Reorganizations

During a protracted and disruptive change such as a reorganization, the best thing for you to do as a manager is to communicate openly and honestly with the organization as much as you can. You should tell folks what you do and do not know and stress that you care about them by looking after their interests and by keeping them posted as you learn more or are able to tell more. At the same time, it is good not to over communicate because dwelling on something— especially those that has not been decided yet— is not productive. One does not want to emphasize something to the extent that everyone starts to worry about it. Usually, if you keep people informed and show that you care, things will be fine. Obviously, if the changes affect people's jobs and lives (i.e. positions disappearing, being moved), then one has to be extra-sensitive to the communication used. In such cases, one should not try to sugar coat hard news but simply try to be direct, honest, and fair as possible. With such difficult cases, one needs to closely coordinate with HR and Senior Management to establish a correct and consistent communications posture. Again, try to avoid being inconsistent— patronizing or hypocritical. If you show yourself to be transparent and fair, these communications become easier.

In many large companies, reorganizations are a frequent occurrence and most people will be used to them. In this case, you want to reach out especially to the more junior team members to whom this will come more of a shock.

Leading During Layoffs

Unfortunately, there are times when a company must do layoffs to survive. The role of management is to ease the exit of those who are leaving and to reassure those who remain that at least for now, they are not part of the current "reduction in force". It is important to help those who are laid off to leave with dignity not only because it is the right thing to do, but also because they are the friends and confidants of those who remain. How they are treated will also affect the morale of the remaining staff.

Layoffs also require some transparency into the decision-making. While it is a bad idea to denigrate those who are laid off, it is still important to explain the rationale behind the choices. When layoff decisions appear political, irrational, or uninformed, the remaining staff will lose their remaining confidence in their company. They are likely to spend their efforts in worrying about their future or seeking new jobs, rather than trying to help the company recover. While it can be tempting to side with the employees against the founders, the board of directors or the investors or VCs, it is the VPE's role as an executive to help explain and implement corporate decisions. This means that the VPE will often face the brunt of the questioning from the engineering staff and it is up to the VPE to show leadership and to keep Engineering running. Tactically, managing the entire process is critical from the selection process to the communications with those affected, those remaining, and the follow-up communications.

Selection Process

Depending on the specifics of the company reduction, the factors used in selecting those for the layoff may vary. One specific example is when a company cuts a specific technology or product line. In this case, employees with unique skills sets or specific product line experience are more likely candidates than others for cuts. Other factors include adaptability, compensation, performance, seniority, and unique skill sets (i.e. this is the only person who knows ABCD). In the end, managers will likely perform a stack ranking of their respective organizations and then Senior Management must merge these into an integrated ranked list. This all assumes that the culture permits the engineering managers to make these ranking decisions for their own departments (strongly recommended).

In a perfect world, each department has a specific profit target to meet and the manager has the freedom up to a certain degree on where to make cuts. It is the role of the head of Engineering to ensure that the management team understands the "new" company focus or vision and to oversee the reduction process, making sure fairness is taken into account when it comes to rankings and interdepartmental tradeoff decisions. It is also a responsibility of the head of Engineering to make sure that Engineering as a whole is represented fairly in the discussion about percentage cuts by department. Any implications of the cuts to product delivery and quality or content should be communicated ideally to the rest of the executive team in advance of the cuts. It is a rare opportunity for the Engineering leader to reset any company expectations.

Communication

As mentioned above, communication of layoffs is an extremely delicate process. When talking to those being let go, the person performing the layoff must adhere to the following guidelines:

- Provide a simple "high level" explanation for the reduction, (i.e. Sales will not or did not meet their number).
- Be careful not to denigrate others for placing the company in the position.
- Be careful not to compare the employee to others.
- Do not give specifics of numbers of staff or $$.
- Ensure the employee is dealt with in a professional manner.
- Ensure that specific factors involved in the decision process such as performance and seniority are not discussed.
- Depending on the employees' mindset, permit a quick departure and opportunity to pack-up after hours.

- Be careful not to commit to providing a reference. Many companies prohibit this.
- Carefully explain the benefits provided to those affected such as severance pay and benefits. Ask the employee to reiterate back at the end of the session, if necessary.

For those being retained, it is important to convey a realistic sense of stability. Not leaving the company open to future legal liabilities such as wrongful termination is crucial as well. It is important to be open and honest about the cause for the layoff, the measures that will be done to minimize the potential for a future layoff, and the effect of the layoff to the company vision and product focus, if at all. It is best to use terms such as, "I don't have a crystal ball but..." when dealing with questions regarding additional rounds of cuts and job stability.

4.6 Recruiting

Introduction

Recruiting is about the process of finding new employees. The problem has two parts. First, "sourcing" is about identifying the candidates you might want to hire. Second, "hiring" is about interviewing candidates and choosing one among them to make an offer to.

Sourcing Techniques

There are a variety of ways for finding candidates. Each method has advantages and disadvantages. At a small startup company where cash is critical, it is often best to take a stepwise approach in recruiting that minimizes the use of expensive external recruiters. This process may start with the lowest cost approach of using internal referrals, possibly with the use of referral fees. The next least expensive approach is the use of low-cost job boards like Craig's List. If the search is still unsuccessful after one to two weeks, then it is recommended to use more expensive job posting services like HotJobs and Monster. As a last resort, you can use retained recruiters (see below). One factor that affects the timing of these stepwise approaches is the urgency of filling the position.

Personal Network

Very few sources will beat your personal network. It is your job to actively network with engineers you have worked with successfully in prior engagements and to stay in touch with their career growth.

It is also incumbent on VP-level management to network in professional circles. In Silicon Valley, this would likely include SDForum SIGs, VPE COP, CSPA, TiE or others based on interest, and others that can easily be found with modest effort.

Employee Referral

Offer your employees a finder's fee for each referral that gets hired. This is by far the cheapest and most effective way of finding people. You get better people faster and with less cost than with any other technique.

Job Boards

If you do not have great internal referrals, this is the next cheapest option for finding good candidates. Monster, Craig's List, and other sites are frequently used to find key engineering talent. In recent years, however, as the job market has tightened again, jobs boards are not as timely as they were after the bubble burst.

Recruiters

A recruiter is someone whom you hire to help you find employees. They come in three types: contingent recruiters who get paid when they find someone; retained recruiters who are paid to find someone; and internal recruiters who are paid employees who do recruiting.

A good recruiter has the following attributes:

- Listens carefully and asks questions not only about the job description, but also about company culture and trends
- Is willing to negotiate rates (range typically from 15 to 25 percent of one year salary)
- Pre-sells the company to the employee
- Presents a variety of candidates all within the "mandatory requirements" listed in the job description
- Will pre-screen employees in person

The best way to find a good recruiter is by word of mouth. Tip: if you find a good one, they can find you your next job too!

Contingent Recruiters

Tips for working with contingent recruiters:

- Make sure you negotiate your fee up front. Fifteen percent of the first year salary can be negotiated if the recruiter is hungry enough. Twenty percent is normal and any more than that, the position must have unique skills to warrant the higher rate.
- Some recruiters are ruthless so be careful if you invite them onsite. Guard your phone lists.
- Make sure you do the reference checking, not the recruiter.
- Some contingent recruiters will take a combination of money and stock. If you are an early stage company watching cash, this is a great option.

Retained Recruiters

Retained recruiters are those compensated for the search rather than for the particular candidate. While commonly used for senior staff, it is rare an engineering manager will use one for an engineering position.

Internal Recruiters

If you find yourself spending too much money on external recruiters, you may want to hire your own. This is way cheaper. However, since the internal recruiters are paid more on salary than on commission, they also are often not quite as effective as the external recruiters.

Recruiting Different Categories of Candidates

Recruiting College Interns

Part-time college internships can make a positive impact on the productivity of a Development group. As we like to say, college students "do not know what they cannot do" as they will typically attack non-elegant problems with a fresh perspective. Most colleges have internship programs or job web sites open for posting by employers. Berkeley[7], Stanford[8], and other universities have excellent sites for hiring managers. The employer benefits of hiring college interns include flexible hours, cost effective rates, and the opportunity to convert to full-time at graduation, as well as tolerance for "less glamorous" work.

Recruiting New Graduates

Recruiting new graduates is usually done by internal recruiters by going on campus, although sometimes it can be successful to post on school job boards, especially for well-known companies like Google. Less known companies often find it helpful to go on campus job fairs. Since students graduate at specific times and new graduates need more training, this type of hiring requires more planning.

Recruiting Early Career

Employee referrals are always good.

Recruiting Senior Staff

Employee referrals are always good.

Recruiting Director Level and Above

Since it is more difficult to find people at this level, companies often use either contingent or retained recruiters, in addition to any internal recruiting. It is important to keep good records of the applications, since there can be dispute over whether anyone deserves to be compensated for a hire or not.

---

[7] For more information on Berkeley's job website, go to
http://www.berkeley.edu/students/jobs/
[8] For more information on Stanford's job website, go to
http://cardinalcareers.stanford.edu/communities/softwared/

Hiring Process

Job Description

This is where the recruiting process can either get off to a great start or be doomed. The job description is in essence the specification for the skills and experience you need to fill in the position. The job description has to clearly delineate what is mandatory (i.e. years of experience, college education level, and programming skills) versus "nice to have".

It is very important to have a clear definition of the "real" job duties during the interview process. Sometimes, recruiters will embellish the job responsibilities in order to attract talent. In some cases, this process will generate leads but will most likely produce employees who are not a good fit. Before the interview, a manager should visualize an imaginary new employee performing their duties daily, during crises and conflicts, or during good times. This exercise helps you to envision what kind of person would be ideal for a certain position.

Interview Process

Formalizing the hiring process is important. You should decide up front who should interview a set of candidates and what kinds of questions to ask. You do not want everyone to ask the same questions. Each interviewer must understand their individual role in the interview process. Who is testing technical ability? Who is checking skill and talent level? Who is looking for team fit? Who is selling the candidate on the company? You also want different candidates to get similar questions so you can compare them. There should be a standard form used to collect feedback on candidates. This is important not only to ensure top notch hiring, but also in many cases, it is required for legal reasons such as affirmative action.

You have to make sure you have a broad set of interviewers who will evaluate a candidate from all relevant perspectives. Remember, if this candidate has to interface with other departments, have the representatives from those departments involve themselves in the process.

Interview Questions

During the interview, your goal is to find answers for four main questions. These are:

- Are they capable of doing the job?
- Are they willing to do the job?
- Will they be happy doing the job?
- Will they fit well with the team?

You still have to derive the answers to these questions even if a candidate cannot answer them. Having a list of "goals" in mind helps conduct more focused and shorter interviews.

To answer these broad questions, the team needs to ask a number of more specific questions, particularly when dealing with highly technical positions. The choice of questions matters. The following are the guidelines that your team can use when conducting technical recruiting interviews:

- Can the candidate think on their feet or butt?
- Will the candidate engage openly and honestly about an area they don't understand well?
- Does the candidate resort to BS or generalities?
- Does the candidate get nervous and flustered?
- Does the candidate have the specific background you are probing for?
- Will the candidate take a stand on an issue, even though it may not be a politically correct?

For calibration, it is useful to have a very good problem-solving question where even though a solution can be simply achieved, a more elegant answer can be derived if further thought is invested. It helps if the problem has more than one acceptable solution. These can be used to discuss tradeoffs and what comes to mind as the "obvious" choice. Awareness of solutions or the ability to map known solutions can be an indicator of the strength of a candidate's formal education.

A controversial issue is the use of weird puzzle questions. Some companies like Microsoft enjoy using this technique. Thus, it could be said that the odd complexities of many Microsoft technologies stem from hiring many people good at solving weird puzzles.

Decision-Making Process

In general, a team needs to hire for TALENT, not SKILLS. If you need a particular skill, engage an expert contractor. Engineers tend to look directly for skills and skip over the talent part. Furthermore, many developers get too critical and have the tendency to reject all candidates. This is not productive. For specialized jobs, you have to look for potential more than the current skill-set. This is obviously harder to interview for but you have to do it anyway.

Negotiating Compensation

You should understand the components of the offer that motivate the candidate. You have to ask them if they prefer stock options or money. Also, is a bonus plan a must for them? If the candidate has or expects multiple offers, there are some strategies for improving your odds such as making an initial offer that can be sweetened if necessary. Tell the candidate openly to give you last right of refusal. The following are strategies in startups for negotiating compensation:

If you are looking for top-level talent, expect to pay more than "average" for your engineer. They have access to Salary.com and other resources, so do not insult your candidate by saying, "We only hire the best" and not make a competitive offer. Use Salary.com or other resources to establish a 70 to 75th percentile cash computation for the job, company size, and geography. Be careful for printed resources because they can easily become out-of-date. On top of that, also add a good equity offer. Make sure the candidate is not motivated by the cash component of the offer, but by the equity. (Remember, this is startup we are talking about).

For establishing a good equity component of an offer, the company has to plan early on how much investment is (still) required as well as how much dilution is therefore anticipated. At each round of funding beginning with the creation of the company, the founders need to plan the financing and equity dilution scenarios carefully. In each round, you have to designate what title will be offered in the option package. It is reasonable to graduate the packages within the "round", reflecting the sequence in which employees are hired. Note the total shares allocated per title-range and account for the number of individuals likely to be hired into that range in each time frame. If you do not do this with each additional round of financing, your overall "fairness" target is likely to be missed and there will be offers outside acceptable deviations from an ideal plan. This will create problems later on, guaranteed.

Prepare three offer packages. The first package is what you will offer to a candidate in a face-to-face presentation. The second one will have lower salary but more stock. Finally, the third will have higher salary but less stock. The third is the least ideal. You want the candidate to go for either the first or second offer. The third one should be presented only if the candidate is particularly key to plugging a hole in the team and is sensitive to cash.

Closing the Deal

In some countries especially in India, once your candidate accepted an offer, you have to keep selling him/her to make sure they will show up, rather than him/her taking some other competing offer. Get the "soon-to-be-employee" involved earlier than the start date by sending them non-proprietary reading or invite them to company events if possible (minimized the chance of competing offer taking hold). You should tell the candidate the following:

- Upsides for the company
- Upsides for the candidate and their career
- Positive feedback from interviewers
- They have the skills to make a real difference.

4.7 Talent, Compensation, Growth, and Retention

Introduction

Even in the best of times, hiring and training new staff requires a lot of work. The more senior position you are trying to fill, the harder it is to find the right person. Hiring and training someone the first time is difficult enough; having to hire replacements after you have had attrition makes it that much worse. In many circumstances, you will not find it practical to hire all the necessary people at the skill levels you need. In fact, to meet your targets, the only economically viable approach in many cases is to hire enough junior folks, train them, and then make sure they stay with you. This brings us to the topic of growing and retaining talent. We will discuss more about how you can keep a healthy distribution of talent while both maximizing skill levels and minimizing turnover and recruiting costs.

The Distributions of Levels

Different people have different levels of experience and talent. Naturally, more senior people are more productive and capable of independent action than their junior counterparts but they are also more expensive. Top-notch senior people are also hard to find and the good ones are doubly expensive. A company, therefore, has to make decisions about the mix of talents it wants. In a startup, you may want a small number of very senior people who are versatile and productive and those who can work with minimum supervision. But to scale, tapping only the senior people will be prohibitively expensive for a company and, in fact, it will not be a good use of their time because much of the work required in a large organization does not need such high-powered talent. The first challenge then is to decide on an appropriate distribution of the levels of experience.

A good HR team can help create an appropriate system of levels for employees, capturing different degrees of experience and capability. There will obviously be different salary bands associated with these. You can then decide on an appropriate mix of people at different levels. In a typical organization, one might use five levels of engineers, ranging from new college graduates (coming at level 1), through normal individual contributors (levels 2 to 3). At higher levels, you would find senior engineers who exercise technical leadership across teams and divisions or even company-wide (levels 4-5).

The actual distribution of levels is subject to a number of factors. The big tradeoff is the fact that the junior people cost less and the senior ones charge more. The ability to absorb cheaper junior staff will have to do with how well you can factor work and give out precise enough task descriptions to allow more junior personnel to be productive. Depending on the kind of work involved, there will be some useful mix of junior and senior personnel that is minimally expensive and maximally productive.

Career Growth

Your staff will want their careers to advance. If you do not provide them career growth opportunities, they will seek growth elsewhere. Thus, turnover will increase. Therefore, you need to create opportunities for your employees to gain new skills and advance. This requires setting up clear expectations about requirements to be promoted to a new level as well as providing adequate training and mentoring possibilities to help people in their careers. In some countries like India and China, people are very ambitious and seek very fast advancement. In such cases, in addition to genuine career growth, one may need to increase the number of job levels simply to allow for more frequent promotion without diluting the overall leveling.

Economics of Levels

In certain geographies, there may be different availabilities of talent at different levels. In one location, for example, you may then be able to find many people who belong to levels 1 to 3 but only few who fit in levels 4 to 5. On the other hand, another site might be top-heavy in upper level people. This may have to do with both cultural and historical reasons. As a result, you may have a hard time achieving your ideal distribution of people at a location using recruiting alone. If you cannot hire the talent, you need to grow the talent.

Investing in the Future

If you have a sufficiently long time horizon and are good both at employing junior people and at growing their talent, then you can create your own pool of senior talent easier than you could ever recruit it.

Individual Performance Management

The most basic tool for developing talent is the performance measurement mechanisms provided by HR. While the details vary from one company to another, the basic principle is that every employee should understand the expectations and objectives they need to fulfill in their job level. Each year, they should get assessed to determine how well they meet these expectations and objectives, with suggestions for how to improve these and what they would need to do to get to the next level. The resulting focal assessment is a document to be signed by both the employee and the manager delivered annually. This provides a formal rating of the employee's performance in the last year and a plan for professional growth for the next year. Since these ratings are used to determine pay increases in many companies, this is a sensitive topic for many employees. However, if you are serious about developing talent, this is more important than just handing out the grades. For one thing, you need to be very clear about setting out objectives for the next year and providing constructive development plans. After that, you have to give continuous feedback to the employee about meeting those objectives. If they are significant deviations from those objectives, either because of changes in company direction or because of the employee's performance, then this needs to be documented. Providing this feedback on an ongoing basis not only helps employees grow faster in their careers, but it also makes it easier to deal with employees with real performance issues. As the head of Engineering, you also need to work with your management team to make sure they are implementing this process thoroughly and consistently. This is often harder than it looks because engineering managers are often basically engineers at heart and they do not like dealing with the more difficult aspects of people management.

Part of the assessment process is also providing appropriate promotions and helping talented staff understand what they need to do for them to be considered for promotion. Having clearly defined job levels and expectations for those levels is an important tool there. The development plans written as part of the annual evaluations should include required steps for promotion. Effective promotion processes are critical for retention, especially in countries like India where fast promotion is an expectation. One needs to address the problem wherein organizations tend to have an easier time hiring people into a job rather than promoting, because they know all the faults of an internal candidate and none of the faults of an outsider. This is bad and you should stomp on it! Developing your talent requires you to recognize and promote promising folks in your organization.

Compensation

In most companies, compensation is closely tied to the annual performance review process. You need to work closely with HR to make sure that compensation is set appropriately. You will have to consider base salary, bonuses, and stock options or stock grants. You will always need to understand the current salary survey comparing distribution of salaries in your organization with those in peer companies. This needs to be done both country-by-country and region-by-region. Typically, HR provides the guidelines for this and the individual managers can then propose the annual adjustments.

Your role as an engineering leader is to make sure your organization does this fairly and in accord with HR policies. This can get quite tricky if you have a geographically spread organization or if different groups have different cultures. You need to make sure that a manager is not too cheap, one is too generous, or that someone else is playing favorites with some group. A good way of checking this is to download all the data into a spreadsheet and sort it to look for odd patterns. Getting this right is crucial to keeping your employees at least reasonably happy.

You should also consider individual preferences as part of this. While base pay is generally adjusted based on performance, bonuses and options are more about retention. In this area, you need to know your staff well enough to determine if they are more interested in money or stock. After all, it does not hurt to ask.

Training

Training is often a luxury that can often be ill–afforded for a small company. Instead, early hires are chosen to be fairly self-sufficient as they learn largely by osmosis. As the company gets larger, two things happen. First, as the product itself grows, more company specific knowledge needs to be mastered before a new employee can be productive. Second, as the pace of hiring increases, there are so many new hires that osmosis ceases to be that effective simply because the experienced people are outnumbered.

This causes the creation of training programs. After a while, the existence of training programs for new employees causes a new problem. The new people get the latest training. But the oldest employees, having started before the creation of these programs, are missing out on surprising numbers of materials covered in current training, especially when they have been focused on some particular part of the product set. This, in turn, encourages retraining programs for existing staff.

We will describe some basic training techniques below. These are not mutually exclusive and, in fact, may all be employed at once.

Buddies

As long as there are only few new hires, a good technique is to assign each new hire to an existing employee who will serve as their buddy as they start their new job. This starts to break down if there is a large new team where everyone is new.

Knowledge Transfer

When a number of people need to be trained at once, it is likely more economical to delegate an experienced person to spend some scheduled time with the new staff to conduct a formal knowledge transfer program. This particularly makes sense with transfers of work from one location to another. If the trainees are far away, you may want to think how to best structure this. Since there are usually less trainers than trainees, you may find it cheaper to send the trainer over to other location to work with everyone. This can involve intense short visits or even sending one or the other person to spend a whole year at the other location. A challenge with this technique is that the most senior members of your team you depend on for key innovation are also the ones you need to do this training. Thus, it is crucial not to overuse their time to avoid burnout or to simply make them unproductive.

Live Taught Classes

Classes handled by instructors are an effective and intensive way of delivering material. They are, however, expensive to put on especially when the employees are geographically distributed.

Video on Demand (VOD)

VOD is a way of lessening the cost of delivering classes and knowledge transfer sessions. Using relatively inexpensive hardware, one can film a knowledge transfer or live class and sync the video with the computer display. The result is a video that can readily be streamed across the network and delivered to the employees at any time and any place. However, having an instructor who is not that dynamic is the main challenge with this technique. Such videos can also be extremely dull to watch, reducing their effectiveness. Experience shows though that once folks make and watch a couple of these things, they actually improve in their ability to make good videos. At one of our companies, the CEO even celebrates engineers whose videos are especially popular.

Online Training Materials

A well setup web site that organizes reference materials and new employee instruction programs is certainly one of the cheapest and most versatile training strategies.

Career Path and Growth

Transfers and Rotation

Giving promising folks a chance to try different kinds of jobs is also a great way of growing talent. The main challenge with this is that most organizations are always overloaded tactically and will be afraid of losing key individuals for fear they will not come back. This can be mitigated by having a formal transfer and rotation process as well as having very heavy executive pressure to make sure the process happens. The benefits of cross-pollination and greater satisfaction and retention for key staff though are tremendous.

Reorganization

Many hi-tech companies frequently reorganize because of growth and changing business conditions. These reorganizations can open up new opportunities for the staff as well. Normally, this is more relevant for more Senior Management and Technical staff because in most reorganizations, the lower level teams are shuffled around intact. The major exception is when new business groups are formed or folded and in such case, many individual contributors will get moved around. In these situations, the staff will be quite concerned and you will need to spend extra time reassuring them that you have their best interests in mind.

What about Startups?

Realistically, there is little room for career development discussions in a small startup. An engineer working for a startup (pre-profit) and worried about career development is at the wrong place. A small company cannot afford such niceties. It must be single-mindedly focused on producing enough revenue to go cash-positive (i.e. for the week, month, quarter, or year). After the company achieved these milestones, raising this concern is appropriate but most likely in the context of "if we hit, then we can talk about career tracks".

But at the same time, if a startup is successful, there will be growth. As a company grows from 10 employees to 40, the roles and responsibilities of existing staff will change as the company's needs change. It is common for an initial engineer with some leadership potential to move into management as the company advances. Growing one's career as the organization grows is one of the attractions of a startup. The management challenge, however, is that much of this career growth will be relatively unsupervised in the initial mad dash. Thus, it is important to hire fairly self-sufficient people who can both do the work on their own and grow with the business on their own in an early stage startup. As the organization gets bigger and more stable, then the more formal mechanisms described above start to become more applicable.

Technical vs. Management Tracks

Another interesting challenge is how to accommodate individual ambition as well as how to provide appropriate leadership in the organization. In a startup, both the people and the technical management are usually combined. In a large organization, on the other hand, these skills do not always blend well. Managing a large group of people is tedious that it does not leave enough time to be deeply technical and, in any case, requires skills technologists often lack. Conversely, well-done technical leadership is not compatible with spending all day in meetings.

As a result, having separate but equal management and technical leadership tracks is very important. Once these are implemented, individuals need to be coached as to the way they want their careers to develop. Do they want to be technical directors or people management directors? An additional challenge is that outside of the US, technical leadership is not so popular. In India, for example, everyone wants to become a people manager, irrespective of his or her aptitude for the position: ("Every weekend my mother asks me when I am going to be a manager." – a true quote from one of our engineers.) Accordingly, you may need to do some training to simply instill an understanding of the different roles and their relationships.

Remember to Say "Thank You"

Do not forget that one of the most cost-effective ways to motivate and recognize performance is by saying "thank you" during a company or department all-hands events or by giving small spot-bonuses, such as movie ticket or gift cards. While the cost of these is low, the impact is usually quite high.

4.8 Firing

Introduction

One of the least enjoyable tasks of a manager is terminating an employee. However, it should not be avoided once determined necessary. Firing is a business decision since it is better for a business to eliminate or replace a position than to keep an employee. Your goal then is to minimize the company's exposure to discrimination and wrongful termination lawsuit. This requires that you:

- Have sound reasons for terminating the employee
- Have documented everything relevant to those reasons
- Choose the most appropriate technique for termination
- Treat the employee as fairly as circumstances allow

Firing people in a legally reasonable way is time-consuming and often emotionally draining. Thus, it is important to have the courage to undertake it when it is required. Bear in mind that your staff is usually as aware of the need to terminate someone as you are. If such a circumstance exists and you do not act, it will cause huge morale problems. In reality, it can open up to additional legal exposure if you are seen as being negligent in not stopping an abusive situation as soon as you became aware of it.

Anecdote

I had the experience of a director in another city that had a serious drinking problem and used intimidation to keep his problem in silence. When his behavior escalated to sexual harassment, action had to be taken. By the time he was finally removed, there was a huge sigh of relief from the team since the great weight his presence caused had been lifted off their back. They were so relieved that someone had finally broken through the veil of intimidation he created around himself.

When to Fire Someone

Partner with HR

If you ever find yourself in a situation wherein you are contemplating on firing someone, you definitely need to seek help. If you have an HR department, always consult with them first. Their advice is invaluable and it can save you from the blame and trouble if things go bad. If you are in a startup that has no HR department, then you need to act on your own understanding of the company procedures and ideally seek legal advice on behalf of the company.

Smaller companies cannot afford to have a full-time HR person. In such cases, there are specialized companies that provide HR management services. Before taking any action, you should present the situation to an HR professional.

Laws vary widely by state and country, with firing being harder in many foreign countries. You definitely need local advice on how to handle such matters in accordance to the existing laws in a specific region.

Causes for Termination

The most common reason for termination is poor performance. However, there are also rare times when an event such as an illegal activity or egregious violation of company policy caused an employee's termination. Extreme subordination can also fall in this category. While these conditions sometimes have a specific trigger, more often than not, they evolve gradually. Once you become aware of them, you need to investigate them carefully.

Questions of poor performance may not always be clear-cut. You may have an employee who performs well but is a poor team player and a disturbance to the team or an employee who may perform well only on tasks that motivate them or those that fall squarely in their experience. In these cases, you can convince yourself that it is easier to live with the pain than to take care of it permanently. A simple test is to ask yourself if you would welcome the employee's voluntary resignation. If the answer is yes, then you probably have a performance problem.

Avoiding Termination

Firing people is always a hard and unpleasant work. Therefore, you should find out if you can find ways to avoid it. These typically involve removing the person from the situation that caused the problem.

During this phase, you should revise the employee situation and try to identify what is the reason for the poor performance. It is because of the lack of skill or talent? As a guideline, if an employee is disruptive by nature, the manager should recognize that in some cases, the best solution is termination. You also have to account the resentment factor that an employee is going to incur during the change. Consider the following:

- Can you find them another job within the company?
- Reorganization (Sometimes a new organizational role can let people have a fresh start.)
- Is there another position for them within the department?
- Can they successfully complete a performance plan? Some people do learn.

All of the above not withstanding, we have had numerous cases where employees have been brought back from the brink. In these cases, a direct intervention by telling the employee, "You will change NOW or you will lose your job" did have an impact and the resulting positive discussion led to enormous changes in their effectiveness.

Documentation

What do you need to safely terminate an employee? In a written history of poor performance, the best practices should be described for keeping files on employees. The employee needs to be aware that a problem exists; it cannot be a surprise. Putting the employee on a performance plan before the termination is a good option. If the employee has been there long enough, then prior reviews should show some history of poor performance.

Methods of Termination

Performance Plans

The most common way of handling poorly performing employees is putting them on a performance plan. This is a document defining a set of tasks and expectations for the employee to be completed within a specific time period with the understanding that a failure to comply can result in termination. The given task must be reasonable and doable. It should be reviewed at regular intervals for success or failure. If at any time during the exercise it is agreed that the effort has failed, the employee can then be let go.

Egregious Cases

Employees who commit serious violations of company policy may be fired without any further performance plan, assuming the actions in question are properly documented.

Separation Agreements

In many cases, it may be easier to negotiate a separation agreement where an employee agrees to resign in exchange for some consideration or package. One needs to be careful though that proper protocol is followed because, otherwise, the company can still be exposed to liability. If there is a risk of litigation, such agreements can be very useful. If you are sure you want to terminate the employee and that the performance plan only serves as the way to get the proper documentation, you may offer the employee a choice of either going on the performance plan or choosing mutual separation agreement.

Giving the Papers

Timing: Normally, morning is better. HR will prefer not on a Friday in case the employee is unstable and has need of counseling.

Location: Somewhere discreet. Not at the employee's desk.

Who else should be there: HR

What to expect and what to say: During this process, you should present the historical facts that led you to make the decision to terminate the employee. If you have done your homework during the documentation phase, this should be a straightforward process. One mistake that some managers make is to let themselves be carried away by personal episodes instead of focusing on the fact that the employee is not doing their job.

Layoffs

If you are reorganizing or downsizing and if you can show you are eliminating a position, then you can let someone go without any performance plan. The only restriction is that one cannot then turn around and hire someone into that same position again. This only works if one is genuinely eliminating the position.

4.9 Personality Types

Why Bother?

There is a saying that tells us we see the world through our own eyes, through our own lenses. We can easily cite examples of colleagues who are too bossy, perfectionist, quiet, or weak, or something else. That, of course, is our own perception. From their perspective, they think they are just fine and we are the one who is too something or another.

These differences of perception exist because we all have different personalities. Depending on our personalities, we will tend to behave in certain manners and look at the world in certain ways. Understanding the different personalities will help you see the world from others' perspectives, hence, helping us build and maintain better understanding and relationships not only with our colleagues, but also with our friends and family.

You may ask, "Well, how can I possibly understand everyone around me?" Fortunately, as diverse as we all are, there are some broad categories of personalities as shorthand. Everyone's unique personality is essentially some combination of only four major personality types.

Different Personality Types

Characteristic of a driver or director:

- Fairly extrovert
- Likes to be in charge
- Careful about achieving goals or results
- Often make decision quickly, by gut feel if necessary
- Natural leader

Characteristic of a socializer or expressionist:

- Very extrovert
- Likes recognition, likes to be liked and to be a hero
- Naturally sociable
- Expressionist, generally loves to talk and tell stories
- Natural friend

Characteristic of a thinker or analyzer:

- Introvert
- Realistic and methodical, tends to take time to make decision and only after careful analysis
- Care a lot about being right and doing it the right way, can be perfectionist
- Generally care about result
- Natural recluse

Characteristic of a relater or amiable:

- Mostly introvert
- Care most about pleasing others
- Can easily empathize with others
- Often has difficulty making decisions
- Natural follower

Understanding these basic characteristics makes it easy to recognize the types. For example, you just meet someone at a party. By noticing if they are an extrovert or introvert (talkative, boisterous or quiet, or mellow) and by finding out if they talk about result or recognition, you can quickly determine if they are a driver or a socializer.

Does it sound too simple? Unfortunately, it is. Most people have some traits of multiple types and/or may put on different types depending on situations. Luckily, most people are also dominant or natural on one type. They can try to adopt other types but you can see through their dominant or natural type with a little work. This is especially true for a coworker with whom you work with regularly and will encounter various situations together.

How to Use this Knowledge in the Workplace

Understanding personality types at work gives you the edge on fostering good relationships with your colleagues. Note that as part of the characteristics, there is a brief description of what each personality cares most. Knowing what makes each personality type tick will give you many avenues to make them like you or, at least, like to work with you.

Story #1

Many engineers I worked with in a company happen to be thinkers or analyzers because it is a natural profession for them, although engineers do come with all other personality types as well. Thinker engineers like things to be done the right way, using the right process and methodology. This means they hate it when things are chaotic, say in a startup environment. The startup I joined was in such chaotic situation. They had eight engineers—most of whom I met. Most of them were thinkers, one was a driver, but the leader was not since he was a relater. By the time I joined, five of the eight engineers were so fed up so they left the company that was doing very well. The three who stayed were the relaters. The thinkers left because it was too chaotic and the team was not doing things the right way. The driver left because it was hard for an engineering team of eight to get good results without proper process. If the leader had known about the personality types, he would have set up a proper process and guiding principles and would likely have kept most of the engineers.

Story #2

In one company I worked at, my peers on the executive team were thinkers. For a span of time, there were no major idea that came out of the team and the company just sorted of muddling along. Why? Because thinkers need data to analyze. They need a lot of time and analysis to make a decision. When an entire team was just analyzing, no major decision was made. I was fed up with the non-decision so I tried to get things going. Fortunately, we had a relatively new boss, who was a socializer. A socializer does not drive so he did not make any decision, at least, during his first few months. I realized that to get the team to move on some major decision, I needed to get the new CEO to guide the team there or to make decision for them. But how will I do that? Again, this was where knowing the personality type came in handy. I told the CEO the idea I would like to push and asked him to feel free to take credit for it, which any socializer loves. As an extra kick, I made sure to tell him that if he did not do this, he would have nothing to be recognized for in his tenure at the company. Sure enough, this idea got through and became the company's new strategic initiative.

Management of Different Personality Types

When planning for possible difficult interactions, it is useful to assess the other party's tendencies or natural instincts. These could include the following:

- Do they take things personally or are they able to take objective feedback?
- Do they want specifics for new action or do they need to know why?
- Do they learn better by hearing or by seeing?
- Do they stay unruffled by surprises and direct feedback or do you have to "ease" into the discussion?

Anecdote

I was once a department manager of a team of 20 people composed of distinct four to six person teams. One team had a senior engineer who had a reputation of being very hard to get along with. I asked many people why they thought he was hard to get along with and they just said that he is too direct and critical without considering the feelings of the person receiving his input. In our next discussion, I discussed this feedback with the engineer who liked to take feedback directly as he thought others could. When he heard the feedback, he made an immediate abrupt change in his behavior and learned how to be more aware of the feelings of others when they were on the receiving end of his opinions. His team members saw an immediate improvement in their relationships with him. He himself thought the matter was handled effectively since the observation was delivered very directly to him.

With some other personality types, people will adopt and embrace plans with more commitment if they believe they initiated the plan. Perhaps, this applies to everyone. Thus, with these people, it may be very effective to discuss the data, present the evidence, and ask, "What can we do about this?" In the course of asking relevant questions, the conclusion could be very obvious to the other party and yet they "own" it, as they came up with the plan themselves while the conversation was taking place. All you need to do then is to support the plan, give credit, and help with plan execution.

We are always surprised when we encounter an engineer who just wants to be told what to do and what to build. We usually do not like hiring these engineers. Instead, we prefer those who want to understand the business reasons of the task at hand and how it fits into the overall plan of the company. These people can then adapt more readily if the specifics of the plan change— as they are likely to— in the course of adapting to new business or market needs.

In providing review, it is very useful to know whether the other is more receptive to lessons heard or to those seen. This can affect the preparation for the meeting and you can then choose the communications medium or channel the other party is most comfortable operating in. One engineer we know (very senior and very able) will speak for extended periods (up to 30 to 60 minutes at a time) using on spoken discourse. At no time, will he look for a piece of paper or a whiteboard to draw on in order to accentuate his ideas. Others will immediately gravitate to sketch out diagrams, circle key points, or draw relationships. When you see these different behaviors, note them, as you will benefit from this knowledge the next time you have a key discussion.

Interesting / Related links:

- Bad Boss–ology[9]
- Introduction to MBTI[10]
- Personality test center[11]
- Motivating different personality types[12]
- MBTI types at work[13]
- Temperament in the workplace[14]
- Seven basic styles of workplace behavior[15]

---

[9] http://www.badbossology.com/workplace-psychology
[10] http://www.teamtechnology.co.uk/mb-intro/mb-introc.htm
[11] http://www.personalitytest.net/cgi-bin/q.pl
[12] http://www.webgrrls.com/wfs.jhtml?/career/advice/motivating.phtml
[13] http://www.myersbriggs.org/type-use-for-everyday-life/mbti-type-at-work/
[14] http://www.advisorteam.com/newsletter/200412_teamanalysis.html
[15] http://news.thomasnet.com/IMT/archives/2005/02/7_basic_styles_1.html

4.10 Difficult People Situations

Introduction

A key role for engineering leaders is to build and manage their teams so they can effectively achieve the corporate goals. As one moves up in management and as the team grows, managing the individuals and teams becomes an increasingly dominant part of the job. Sooner or later, managing your team will eventually lead to difficult people situations and dealing with these is vital to your success. A single problem employee can undermine your entire organization and can distract from your team's achievements.

Difficult people situations can be broken down into team dysfunctions and difficult individuals. Team dysfunctions happen when an entire team is behaving badly and is not achieving. Newly hired managers often find this with their new teams since the dysfunction was the reason the previous management is gone. Since it is rare to completely build a team from scratch, it is important to develop the skills to recover teams that are not performing well.

The distinction between a team dysfunction and difficult individuals is that in the team dysfunction, the problems are not only centered on one or two individuals as they tend to be distributed throughout the team. This can be the result of the corporate environment such as anxiety over change or the perception that politics matters more than performance. The good news is that if the problem pertains to individuals reacting cultural or political situations, then addressing these can greatly improve the team.

Anecdote

During my first day at an Internet startup, I met the three current engineering team members. Each of the web developers told me how much they hated the other and how they were not capable at their job. The IT manager then told me how he could not stand to be in the office around them and that he has taken to working remotely. In an engineering office with only three people, two hated each other and the third was detaching himself. The team was obviously not performing well and it affected the rest of the company. It turns out the main problem was a total miscommunication of the roles and expectations of each team member. The senior member of the team had been told they were hiring someone to do QA and Customer Service and train into Development. He was under the impression the new hire did not have a technical background and that he would be the lead. However, they hired someone with a programming background who expected to have major Development responsibility and never made this clear. This led to immediate clashes that escalated to a poisonous environment. Working this out with all three team members and clarifying their roles and work assignments greatly relieved the tension and made the team more effective. While the team was never truly close or friendly with each other, they were productive and had, at least, a working relationship.

Difficult individual situations happen when it is a specific individual's behavior that causes most of the problems. There are many different ways people can be difficult in a work environment and we will categorize the behavior and resolution.

It is very important to deal with difficult individuals because their behavior affects their team members and can destroy an entire organization. Dealing fairly and openly with these individuals can also increase the managers' credibility in the eyes of the existing team members.

While firing may be eventually required, one reason to work with a difficult individual to try to improve the situation is that it sends the right message to the rest of the team. Team members want to believe that if they made mistakes without realizing it, they would get a chance to discuss things before a drastic event occurs. If they see that a difficult individual was given an ample opportunity to improve, they will feel that the management is fair to the employees. Besides, until you make the effort to work with a difficult individual, it is impossible to know why they behave the way they do. Distinguishing between bad behavior and bad people is crucial. Even good people can behave badly if they are put in a difficult situation. Thus, it is important to know why things occur before you take action.

Generally, all these situations require you to spend a lot of time on communication to make sure you properly understand the problem. Closely partnering with HR can be very useful in all these cases. Evidence will often be contradictory and not everyone will be completely forthcoming. Make sure you understand the right problem! What are the data points? What are the data sources of these problem reports?

In some situations, it is possible to spot rumormongers and saboteurs just by carefully analyzing these questions. If there remains credible evidence that there is a problem employee, you should plan a session where you can jointly explore the evidence and ask for explanation. We have seen an objective presentation of feedback become sufficient to turn around a "difficult" co-worker because such communication had never been attempted before.

Remembering that an ounce of prevention is worth a pound of cure, careful hiring can save you from most of these.

Team Dysfunction

Team dynamics are influenced by management, corporate culture, and the makeup of the team. When taking over a team, it is important to understand what the important drivers of their behavior are. Here are a few common scenarios:

Dealing with Change

This entails dealing with anxiety caused by a change in the organization such as a change in goals and offshoring. When anxiety is a problem, over-communication helps. You need to ensure that everyone, including the individual contributors, knows you care and that you are listening to them. This is definitely a time when you do not want to delegate but you need to make yourself accessible to the team. At the same time, you have to stress the importance of moving forward and not dwelling too much on anxiety.

Too much talk about anxiety can itself cause more anxiety. Keeping the team busy with new challenges is a good medicine.

Not Working toward Common Goals

When team members are not collaborating toward a common goal, the work is inefficient and the progress is slow. This can happen when the work is disorganized and the roles are unclear. When there is an organizational vacuum, aggressive team members will seek their own agenda while the introverted ones may withdraw. The key is to have a plan with clearly defined responsibilities that the team commits to. Behavior can be measured against agreed upon milestones and there should be no more working at cross-purposes.

Dealing with Group Incompetence

If you find a team with chronic group dysfunctions and that has a massive mismatch between abilities and needs, it may be easiest to just start over. One can waste a lot of time trying to fix such a team. This might be a great time to create a brand new team and reorganize the current team out of existence. This is a drastic medicine but, just as with a car, one has to decide when it is not worth fixing it anymore. This is sometimes true of organizations.

Team cannot Get Along with Manager

Sometimes, you will encounter a team that is completely alienated from its manager. The problem is often manifested by attrition, people's complaints to HR, or through other back channels. This is typically a pre-existing condition that you inherit or something you can accidentally cause by making a big mistake in promoting or hiring a new manager or through reorganization. To avoid mass attrition and morale problems, you need to immediately speak to all involved with the help of HR and find out what is going on. It may be the case that the manager needs to make some unpopular changes and needs help with the message or it may simply be a very bad fit. Either way, you need to act quickly and decisively.

On the other hand, it may be the case that the manager is right and that you simply need to manage through some major transition in the team. In any situation, you need to make sure you have heard from everyone in a non-threatening setting and have truly gotten to the bottom of people's feelings. A warning is that in some cases, people are intimidated by a manager and only if that manager is gone— say put on leave— will you find out the real truth of what is happening. This is particularly the case if the manager is in a remote location and has done a good job only telling you their view of the situation.

You can help prevent this kind of problem from occurring by spending plenty of time in skip level meetings so that people will feel comfortable about opening up with you. You can also avert it by involving people in hiring decisions concerning new managers for them.

Clash between Team Members

If two or more people have trouble getting along to the extent that it affects their and the team's performance, you need to intervene. A combination of talking with everyone separately and as a group, preferably with HR present, can help ferret out the true causes of the disagreements. In many cases, this kind of open discussion can resolve the issue. If one or more team members just will not change, then this is a matter of performance management.

Difficult Individuals

Arsonist or Firefighter

- Identifier: This person gets a thrill out of creating and exposing disasters— either intentionally or unintentionally— just to be the hero by stepping in to resolve the issue.

- Resolution: Do not reward the "heroic action" without first condemning the "arsonist" behavior at the same time. Find other healthy ways to recognize this person's contributions.

Cannot Say "No"

- Identifier: These people usually have good intentions but in trying to please everyone, this person rarely meets their commitments. They thrive on being the go-to person. Since they often work for long hours, these people are often victims of burnout and get negative feedback for missing some other commitments.

- Resolution: Explain to the person the negative impacts of the missed goals by their over-committing. Also, make it clear that it is alright to say NO— and in fact, reward them when they say NO— and that they need to provide better estimates.

The Flamer

- Identifier: These people normally humiliate or criticize "publicly" another person or team or others' opinions, either verbally or classically in email. Such behavior has a huge morale impact on their team and if not addressed quickly, other team members will be less reluctant to solicit important feedback.

- Resolution: Depending on the severity of the behavior, you should document the incident, meet with the person to explain the damage done, and place a corrective action note in the employee's file as well as mention the behavior at the person's next personnel review.

Frustrated People

- Identifier: These are usually the frustrated long-time employees. However, these can also pertain to the younger engineers who get so emotionally involved in their organization that after some years, they become very unhappy because of all the baggage they have accumulated. Their memories and history will color all interpretation of current events.

- Resolution: In cases like this, one needs to pull them out of their current situation and change it somehow by: giving them new assignment; making them try another job somewhere else; and spending enough time with them to listen to and work through their frustrations.

The "Future Architecture" Guy

- Identifier: An architect becomes obsessed with using only the latest and greatest technology, even if it is neither mature enough nor even directly applicable to the situation at hand.

- Resolution: This explains why you need to remain somewhat technical. You have to be able to recognize when people are going overboard being mesmerized by bright, shiny things. You need to bring them back down to earth. Creating a more broad-based technology board to review new technologies and figure out which ones are applicable to your current situation can help you address this.

The "Helping Manager"

- Identifier: This one is quite insidious. Another manager volunteers to help you in some enterprise but then, starts stabbing you in the back by using the knowledge they acquired from your situation to say bad things about you to others. This is definitely a kind of help you do not need.

- Resolution: Like all political problems, you need to maintain solid and open communication with both your boss and trusted colleagues who are clued into the gossip situation. This way, you will not be surprised by these kinds of things. Sometimes, if the manager in question is in fact genuinely helpful and merely feeling insecure, you can sometimes turn this around to your benefit if you proactively work with the person in question and show them that you are not their enemy. At the same time, you cannot let them get away with continuing the behavior either.

The Hidden Alliance (Good Guy / Bad Guy Scenarios)

- Identifier: Sometimes, when you join a new organization, you have to be careful about hidden connections. For example, let us say you discover that the facilities manager is completely incompetent. You complain to the CEO and then you discover that she is his girlfriend. This is not career enhancing.

- Resolution: This is tricky. You need to build up your informal communication network in the company and get the unofficial scoop on things. There is always someone you can befriend who will tell you the little secrets. This can save you from much embarrassment. Always be careful when you start a new job. Be very open to understanding the unspoken connections and be careful about saying negative things to anyone.

The Know-it-All

- Identifier: The know-it-all claims to be the authority on all matters, whether or not they have any real expertise. This is especially disruptive if they do not know everything about the topic at all.

- Resolution: This condition is usually caused by insecurity. This is one of these things that you need to be watchful for because these people can annoy your team even more than they annoy you. You need to proactively counsel them on appropriate kinds of discourse.

The Loner

- Identifier: Some engineers prefer computers over people. More specifically, some brilliant engineers are very good with computers but are very bad with people. They cannot delegate tasks, mentor other team members, and cooperate with others. All they want to do is to code. Sometimes, such people are insanely productive. One of us had such a person who single-handedly created over half of the organization's total code. The only downside was since he never interacted with anyone, he would often create new features without being asked or indeed notifying anyone.

- Resolution: Such people are easy to deal with. You can give them technical tasks they can do alone, plus plenty of darkness and pizza. However, as with the example noted, you will have to oversee them enough— whether they want it or not— to ensure that their work remains aligned to company goals. It is especially important with such folks to find someone who can intellectually connect with the individual, whether that is you, another manager, or another senior engineer. Establishing that intellectual connection often opens up a good channel for communication.

A special case to consider is that of distributed open source teams. In this case, many of your folks may be working alone because of their geographical location and not because of any inherent character trait. Note that you still need to bring them together face-to-face because in person, most people are nicer than their email messages suggest. The personal contact will ease the social interactions when they are apart.

The Malcontent

- Identifier: There is someone on the team who is always unhappy, critical, and cynical. They continually criticize you behind your back and the rest of Senior Management. The entire team will soon get unhappy. One of us had a guy who was the senior engineer on his team in Bangalore and was angry about being passed over for promotion to manager. As a result, he started openly criticizing the US team and created a rift between the two teams. This drastically lowered the team's morale and productivity.

- Resolution: Malcontents are quite a poisonous thing. As in the case listed, this can happen gradually and quietly. You need to act fast once you discover it. Talk to the person and understand what is bugging him/her. If it cannot be fixed and you cannot get them to change their attitude, remove them from the organization as quickly as possible. You will then need to do active damage control with the team to reassure them. Also, you should bring about a more positive attitude in the team and this can take months to do. You have to act aggressively on this because this is something hard to recover from.

The Marketing Consultant from the CEO's Old-Boy Network

- Identifier: When higher management suddenly brings in a consultant who is their golf buddy or something similar, it is usually a sign of trouble. In companies, as in nature, parasitic organisms such as management consultants tend to infect weaker hosts. The presence of consultants is often a strong indicator of insecure and/or incompetent management.

- Resolution: You need to assess if the infestation is basically harmless and will blow-over or if it is a prelude to problematic management changes. The example that provoked this entry soon led to a major change in corporate direction that ended in bankruptcy. As a result, even if the consultant is harmless, the causes for it might lead you to question the future of the organization or, at least, of the current management team.

New to Business

- Identifier: Sometimes, you will hire people right out of college who have never worked in an office environment before. They may be surprised that you expect them to take on every assignment given to them, without a break and without that much of a choice in the matter. They may have no idea how to talk properly on the phone or send a professional email.

- Resolution: This situation only becomes a problem if you do not realize you have someone very junior on your hands. It mostly becomes an issue when an organization that mostly hires fairly experienced people suddenly takes on some newbies. The solution is easy: Training!

Passive Aggressive

- Identifier: These kinds of people will normally say one thing to your face but complain later or behind your back.

- Resolution: You can address this by tactfully catching the person in the act and by acknowledging the behavior directly. Since this person often tries to avoid conflict, make it clear to them that it is safe to confront conflict without repercussions.

The Politician

- Identifier: These people will usually communicate the wrong information outside the group, either to business stakeholders or executives. They might have personal relationships with those people or are trying to cultivate those connections. They generally relish their perceived power in passing information to important people in the company, often by revealing information too early or by mixing opinion with fact. This can completely undermine management authority and can violate the team's privacy, making it harder for team members to be open and direct in team meetings.

- Resolution: It is important to explain to the company management why they should not act upon things they hear in the "back channels". Ask them where they heard the rumors and then explain that not only why the rumor is wrong, but also why it is bad for the company to react. Having more transparency in working with your fellow executives helps to remove their interest in rumors. Then, it is important to discuss with the "politician" why they act that way. Perhaps, they feel they need more recognition or they just enjoy chatting. Regardless of the reasons, they need to understand where the boundaries of good behavior are and you have to call their attention when they cross the line.

The Prima Donna

- Identifier: The prima donna is usually a senior engineer who— by virtue of their intelligence, productivity, and past history— claims to be exempt from following any usual processes and feels free to act exactly as they see fit. These people are quite annoying to deal with.

- Resolution: This can be tricky. This syndrome is often seen in engineers who indeed have made a great— although often past— contribution to the company and those who now have a somewhat inflated sense of their self-worth. With such folks, you have to make a judgment as to how much they actually contribute to their company today. If they are contributing a lot and not making too much of a disruption, you can look the other way, subject to a bit of cajoling now and then. But often, the truth is this person is resting on their laurels and is possibly more of a disruption than a benefit. You may want to look at finding this person a new assignment. Replacing them with some fresh eyes may bring a marked up tick to the organization.

Saboteur

- Identifier: This is the person who enjoys being "right" at the expense of the product or release and who can hold a release or product line hostage while debating an esoteric and non-critical technical decision.

- Resolution: This behavior has to be addressed quickly and severely before it affects the company bottom-line. Cases should be clearly documented and a performance plan must be put in place. If possible, technical decisions have to be "quantitatively objectified" and that decisions have to be made in a timely manner in an objective forum such as in architecture or technical committee.

The Sales Guy who Spends Thousands of Dollars on Lap Dances in Vegas

- Identifier: The issue here is someone who wastes huge amounts of company money. This, by itself, is bad. If an individual does this publicly and gets away with it, it can create a culture of misappropriating company resources. There are other similar kinds of lapses of judgment. An example is an engineer or team that creates product features that change the company's market position or exposes it to technical risks without approval from management or a senior leader who visits important customers and tells them that their product is obsolete, and thus, deeply offending them.

- Resolution: The key question in this case is not only the initial behavior, but also the pattern of it and the extent and at what level Senior Management is aware of such behavior and is tolerating it. If you discover that Senior Management is tolerating this, it is a very bad sign. It means that management is showing very poor judgment and it is unlikely that this is the only area where this is the case. In that situation, you have to run— and not walk— towards another job. You and your colleagues' integrity are one of your main assets in life. Do not squander it.

The Time-Drain Communication

- Identifier: This is someone whose communication problems waste a lot of peoples' time. There is a variety of species here. There are engineers who give lengthy technical discourses instead of simply getting to the point and stating their question. There are Support people who do not read the documentation and escalate everything. There are new employees straight out of school who simply have not mastered proper email etiquette and are either vague or too rude in their requests or who do not reply properly.

- Resolution: What all these people have in common is a failure to learn proper corporate communication skills. The following are some of the basic rules that one needs to teach everyone for good communication:

  - Be prepared, assemble your facts.
  - Concisely say what you are going to say, spell it out, then reiterate the topic. Try to avoid taking more than a page to say anything.
  - Understand the correct protocol for whom to ask what or when to escalate. Opt for having direct communications with the right people, rather than blasting them scatter-shot. Again, understanding who your audience is a part of being prepared.
  - Be careful with emails to keep them from being too rude. For difficult situations, a phone call or face-to-face interaction is always better.

> ➤ When running meetings, learn to do it well. As the leader of the organization, the key thing is that if you recognize these issues, you need to make sure your staff is being coached appropriately.

The Time-Drain Performance

- Identifier: A mediocre employee who is just bad enough to be a performance problem but not as to require immediate termination can often turn into a huge time-drain by forcing you to intervene in countless small problems they create.

- Resolution: One has to recognize that poor performance is not only a function of a few big failures but also a pattern of repeated small failures is just as bad. If you find your time being sucked out by such a persistent mediocrity, you need to notify HR and put this person on a performance plan NOW before they waste any more of your time.

The Title-God

- Identifier: This one occurs more in large organizations where there are people who worship titles. This comes in a couple of forms: the VP who is friendly to VPs and directors but not to mere managers; the executive assistant who will not work for less than a senior VP; and the product manager who acts differently to Senior Management than to fellow employees.

- Resolution: Being annoying, it is only treatable if the person either works for you or you have a good relationship with their boss and can offer some guidance. Again, if you see it happening many times, it is one of those warning signs of a deteriorating corporate culture. Depending on the sensitivity of Senior Management, they may or may not appreciate the significance of that.

The Whiz-Kid

- Identifier: A brilliant but somewhat inexperienced contributor suddenly becomes the pet of Senior Management. They get lots of attention for flawed but allegedly masterful efforts.

- Resolution: This is typically a sign of pointy-haired boss infestation. If this starts to happen many times— especially without you being consulted— it is usually a sign to run very fast.

The X-police (X = Whatever)

- Identifier: Sometimes, a person in an organization will become not only interested in process, but also obsessed with it and will drive relentlessly and dogmatically certain issues like coding standards, conformity to a specific product lifecycle process, and the like. While the general nature of this effort is useful, driving it to extremes can be distracting and a waste of time. Extreme debates about code formatting are good examples of this.

- Resolution: While most organizations benefit from an increase in process sophistication, you need to provide clear leadership and guidance on how far you want these efforts to be taken. You have to step in once the point of diminishing return is reached. Many engineers lack a real sense of proportion and as an engineering leader, you need to step in with some reasonable judgment.

Serious Issues

Substance Abuse, Mental Illness, and Related Problems

A complex and troubling issue we sometimes have to deal with is when employees show signs of mental illness or substance abuse. These will normally show up very indirectly. Usually, as managers, we may mostly notice a drop in performance and increased absenteeism. The more challenging part is that people who are not well sometimes rely on their co-workers to cover for them, which creates a double issue as someone else in the organization is now coerced into being an enabler. Frequently, we will start getting reports of erratic behavior at parties or complaints from fellow workers about an unusual behavior.

Catching these problems early requires you to have an open and trusting relationship with your organization, with everyone aware— based on your reminders— that they can ALWAYS come to you or to HR with either their own problems or their worries about a colleague. Once you hear of an issue, you have to immediately engage HR to take appropriate steps to understand the situation and provide whatever help is required, if any. The worst possible thing to do from a humanitarian, legal, and morale stand-point is to ignore one of these situations once you become aware of it even indirectly.

Sexual Harassment, Discrimination

Harassment— sexual or otherwise— and discriminatory behavior need to be managed very aggressively. Such problems can often be related to other situations such as substance abuse. If a manager is involved, the team can be surprisingly silent about these situations until there is some blow-up. This explains why it is very important to keep open communication at all levels of the organization so that "self-sealing" behavior can be detected.

Note that addressing this kind of problems raises significant legal challenges. You will need to work closely both with your company's HR and legal folks to address such situations. Both the failure to properly address known conditions as well as the failure to provide proper treatment can result in significant liability exposure to the company. If an employee requests help for a substance abuse issue, this generally puts them in a protected class, just as if they could not work because of some debilitating illness.

Anecdotes

Story #1

DL had the reputation of being very hard to work with, as he was very blunt and opinionated. Although people would not want to work with him, no one ever told him why. I had a very successful project that DL wanted to join. I took him in but I had a quick chat with him first regarding his reputation. He was surprised to hear the feedback but afterwards became very accommodating. He became very productive.

Story #2

JRD and KLG are two of the brightest and most productive engineers I have had the privilege to work with. On their own, they are very good and I have excellent relationships with both of them. For some reason, I still cannot understand why they have very different personalities and styles and why they never became truly comfortable with each other, though they each came to respect each other's contributions. Given their preference, they would not, however, seek to form a startup together.

My job was to ensure they were both productive in their given areas of responsibility and address the shortcomings or stylistic differences of one with the other. If not done, the startup would have caved, as both of them were two of my first three engineers at the startup.

4.11 Performance Management – Team

Introduction

Looking at your team's performance is an important and sensitive topic for a manager. At all times, you want to make sure your team is productive and is not facing obstacles in their workflow. You also want to ensure you have an appropriate distribution of skills and skill levels. You want your management team to be leading effectively and have sufficient bandwidth. While these are constant concerns, they tend to become particularly relevant in the face of change: the need for rapid growth; a change in market or technology direction; or changing economic concerns. At those times, you may want to specifically reassess the capabilities of the team.

Team Productivity

Team productivity can be measured in a variety of ways. In any system with formal project management techniques, it is fairly easy to naively compute productivity. In Agile development, for example, you can measure user stories per developer per iteration. You can measure the ratio of your team's schedule estimates to their actual performance. This is easy especially when doing either Agile or earned value management. If your QA teams use Quality Center, you can directly compute number of test cases handled per engineer per week.

You can truly measure these things but you need to be very careful. First of all, a cardinal principal of metrics is that metrics depending on honest answers from staff can never be used to measure individual productivity, only aggregate productivity. The reason for this is simple psychology: if the staff knows they are being evaluated in this fashion, they will never give you another honest answer. Thus, while you can compute these metrics on an individual basis for your own interest, you should keep the results quiet. Never publicly communicate that you are using these measurements for individual evaluation.

The other challenge is that different people often work on quite different domains and the numbers on an individual basis are often not directly comparable. What you can and should do is to use these metrics to understand if your group is facing obstacles. Thus, if one team consistently underperforms another team and there are no obvious technology differences, you should try to understand that. You can also use these metrics to measure the effectiveness of tool enhancements and other productivity improving measures.

In addition to these metrics, you can also rely on other kinds of measures. This can include direct measurements of how long individual operations done frequently by the staff take— for example, how long it takes to do a build. It can also include qualitative assessments by the staff as to how productive they feel. Again, you should take these measures as a way of improving the environment for the team rather than as a way of poking at particular individuals.

Team Performance

You need to stay keenly aware of the overall distribution of skills, skill levels, and performance levels of the team. Working with HR, each employee will be assigned to a particular level with a job category and will be assigned a rating as part of the annual focal review process. An important metric about the team is how many of each type of job do you have, at what levels are they, and what their performance is. There are two dimensions to this. First is the raw distribution of jobs, such as:

- Level 1: 5%
- Level 2: 25%
- Level 3: 45%
- Level 4: 20%
- Level 5: 15%

This kind of chart is useful for understanding the general capability level of a team. A team that is too junior cannot be entrusted with difficult assignments. A team that is too senior, on the other hand, lacks people to do simpler assignments and is not investing in their own future. Typically, this analysis is useful for deciding what kinds of people to hire and how to distribute work.

The second dimension is to understand where there are pockets of low performers. There is controversy about how to manage this situation. Some companies deal with this problem by automatically getting rid of the bottom 10 percent every year. This is often done by making a stack ranking of all the employees in a group. The problem with this approach is that if a team is already quite good, you are then forced to get rid of competent employees. This is especially true in smaller groups or groups that require small quantities of relatively specialized employees. Another problem is that it is often hard to compare employees especially across disparate teams resulting in artificial comparisons.

A more flexible approach is to always work with your managers to make sure that low performance is always detected and dealt with. Anyone who is not performing up to expectation needs to be coached to improve his or her work or be managed out. As a result, at focal review time there should be few people who are not performing based on what is expected of them because they will have either been managed up or out by then. A check on that situation is that if you see a group comprised of too many low performers, you need to work with their manager to aggressively deal with this problem because this will adversely affect the team's morale and productivity if left unchecked. Fixing these performance problems is also a good way of increasing effective capacity without hiring more staff.

Therefore, you do need to compare— as part of the focal review process— the assessment habits of your managers and make sure that they are using consistent approaches in assigning performance ratings. It is very bad for the team if one manager is a hard grader and another, an easy grader. Every one needs to be assessed the same way and the management needs a shared understanding on how to do this.

Management Performance

A special case of team performance is management performance. Here, you need to determine if your leaders are showing effective management and leadership as well as if they have sufficient bandwidth. This is especially important in fast growing organizations. Seemingly overnight, a manager can go from a few to a ton of direct reports and can go from being completely on top of their world to being close to burnout. Since new hires require a lot of attention for training, this is dangerous. Thus, you always need to monitor your managers to ensure they have the bandwidth to handle their team.

There are a couple of solutions to use if managers are running out of bandwidth. First, if they are a second or higher level manager, you can work on their time-management skills and get them to delegate more. Since managers in a fast growing company are often thrust into situations of greater authority than they are used to, they often need coaching in effective delegation. The second approach is to simply hire more managers. In this case, you need to decide if you want to split the team or make your manager a second level manager and give him/her manager/s below him/her. How you make this decision depends on your assessment of the manager's maturity. If they can handle being a second level manager, then give the person a manager underneath him/her. Otherwise, split the team. This is a non-trivial decision because being a second level manager is very different from being a first level one. It requires a higher degree of trust and detachment often hard for first-line managers who tend to be very hands-on.

Related to the bandwidth problem is the issue on leadership. In a growing organization, your own responsibilities often increase and you need to delegate more. In this case, the question is if you can trust a given group's management team with more independent authority. Often, the group is good at doing what you tell them to. However, will they set direction appropriately without you looking over their shoulders all the time? Part of managing your team's performance is working with your management leaders to help them grow in their planning, decision-making, and solution-driving skills.

5. Resourcing Strategies

In any engineering organization, one of the most basic investment decisions is finding out how new products should be developed. There exists a continuum of options, ranging from building a product entirely with employees, to working with contractors or outsourcing the project, all the way to partnerships and simply buying someone else's product. Open source projects provide another option. An engineering leader needs to understand all these approaches and learn how to decide between them.

In this chapter, we will start by examining what a company's core competencies are. In other words, we will determine which of its activities create the company's IP. With that, we will look at either building the given solution ourselves or obtaining it from a third party. The tradeoffs here largely concern how much one controls versus how other parties' expertise and energy are leveraged and how risk gets allocated between the various parties.

If we do all the work in-house, we have the maximum control and lowest risk but nominally the maximum possible return. The more of a product given to other parties, the more both control and risk are spread around. To that extent, return will be lower but, on the other hand, the other parties' superior expertise may more than compensate by allowing one to create better, cheaper, and faster products that greatly increase the ROI. The answers to these questions are often complex and one may make different decisions for different products, deciding to build one in house, acquiring another from a partner, and outsourcing a third.

If the decision is to make the product ourselves, another set of considerations is whether to use local employees, offshore employees, in-house contractors, or an off-premises outsourcing firm. Alternatively, the entire project can be outsourced to a vendor. If, on the other hand, the decision is to acquire the product, the question is whether to license it or to enter into a development partnership. Open source projects provide another option for blending internal and external resources.

5.1 Understanding Core Competencies

Core Competency Defined

At its simplest, core competencies are the things your company is good at. More formally, we can define a core competency as something that:

- Benefits your customers
- Can be used across a range of products
- Is hard to copy by others

We expect this competency to be something your company is "world-class" at that differentiates it from others. While the identification and nurturing of core competencies is crucial to your business planning, we are especially interested in core competencies in terms of how we make decisions about resourcing.

Identifying Core Competencies

Understanding which of your company's activities represent its core competencies is important. These competencies normally represent both skill sets and IP underlying your products, as opposed to being the products themselves. Again, a core competency is a world-class capability that a company has, is fundamental to its business, AND is something that provides competitive advantage. A common example of a fundamental capability that usually has no competitive advantage is payroll processing, so this is not a core competency. Some questions to help judge the competitive value of a capability are the following:

- Is it difficult to copy? Obviously, you want some barrier to entry, which can be time (12 months ahead of competition) or patents.
- Is it durable or will it quickly depreciate?
- Is there a competing technology or capability being developed that may beat it?

- How superior is it to the competition?
- Is it truly a part of the company or is it something that can go away such as an individual or a contract?

Utilizing Core Competencies

Core competencies drive business planning from two aspects: promoting differentiation and higher margins and driving choices in resourcing.

Creating Differentiation

A major goal of managing core competencies is to leverage the creation of differentiation. In areas where the company cannot create differentiation, the focus is on saving money. This process is generally called commoditization. On the other hand, we can try to realign the core competences to serve areas where the company can create differentiation factors. In these areas, we can obtain higher margins than in more commoditized areas.

Resourcing

The general rule in resourcing is that if a capability is a core competency, you should generally do it in-house. If a capability is not, then the task can be outsourced. We will explore this choice more in the next chapter on Build versus Buy Decisions.

Assessing Core Competencies

Here are some questions to ponder in terms of your company's approach to core competencies:

- Does the company know what its core competencies are?
- Does the company excel or is the company world-class in its core competencies?

- Does the company get distracted and diluted away from its core competencies?
- Is the company actively or proactively investing strategically in its core competencies?
- Is the company consciously evaluating and monitoring threats to its core competencies leadership?

5.2 Build vs. Buy Decisions

Introduction

In deciding how to resource a project, the first question you should consider is, "Should I build this myself or buy it from someone?" Answering this question requires understanding the four following issues:

- Core competencies and ownership
- Cost
- Time-to-market
- Risk

Depending on your answers to these questions, you will choose from the range of build options (hire onshore, offshore, insourcing or outsourcing) and a range of buy options (outsource project, licensing or development partnership). We will discuss these in the following chapters.

Core Competencies and Ownership

These guidelines will tell us if something is a candidate at all for buying as opposed to building.

- Is IP ownership important? IP ownership is difficult to negotiate in a "buy" decision and can be a limiting factor in a future M&A action by affecting the company valuation, especially if the "product" is considered a core competency.
- Is this a core competency? If not, then does it make sense to invest in building it yourself even if it is cheaper? Besides the opportunity cost of devoting engineering resources to the project, you will maintain it after and this may become a difficult cost to defend if this is not in the company's core competence.

- Are the licensing terms acceptable? (See Licensing section) This may be a factor even in build decisions when the build option includes open source software.

Cost

Let us say that this is not a core competency. Then the decision comes down to cost. The process mainly goes as:

- Evaluate vendors, select best offering, and calculate cost
- Calculate the cost of building it yourself, including opportunity cost
- Choose what is the most cost effective

Time-to-Market

How long will it take to build? Is this a delay that the organization can afford to absorb? Time-to-market is often a deciding factor in buying something, even if it costs more and has to be redone later. Time-to-market can be that important. This is especially true for peripheral pieces of large and strategic projects.

Risks

In reality, there are a number of other factors and risks that need to be considered. These are:

- Do you trust the vendor? Can they deliver what they promised? Are they familiar with your market vertical or are they breaking new ground with you?
- Is there a risk of vendor insolvency? If so, you should insist on source code escrow.
- Do you fully understand the requirements that the solution has to meet? If not, then a build decision is probably favored since you cannot evaluate a vendor against uncertain requirements. The exception

may be is if this technology is in an unfamiliar area and you are look-ing for a vendor to provide a full solution. However, you probably should not be considering a build option anyway.

- Do you trust your estimate of the build cost?
- Do you trust your or the vendor's estimate of the integration cost (if any)?
- If you "buy", who will maintain it? Who will take the first support call? Does your Engineering team have to fix bugs or will the out-source company maintain it and if so, under what conditions? Ide-ally, the outsourced development team will also maintain the product.
- Are the delivery deadlines tight or are the quality criteria critical for the task at-hand? If so, these are generally more difficult to manage with an external vendor, particularly one that:
  - ➢ Is based offshore
  - ➢ Does not speak fluent English
  - ➢ Does not use the same engineering development methodologies that you apply.

5.3 Staffing Models

Introduction

Suppose you have decided to develop a product yourself rather than acquiring it from an outside source. Obviously, as the head of Engineering, you are not going to build it yourself. You will need some people to do it! In this chapter, we will look at all the issues involved in finding the staff to develop and maintain products. We will assume that regardless of the case, you want to hire highly competent and motivated individuals who will do a good job for you while at the same time, minimizing your total expenditures. These two desires are at odds with one another because unless you pay market rates, you will not recruit or retain the best talent! In particular, we will look at the planning decisions you will make prior to hiring the first person.

Consider the following questions. Ask yourself:

- **In any given geography, can I even find enough of the right talent?**

  The availability of talent is a major reason why hi-tech firms cluster in particular areas like Silicon Valley. However, as companies get larger, their appetite for certain skill sets may become so large that they do not find enough of the right talent in one location and have to start looking elsewhere. Obviously, if you decide to look somewhere else, you will now face the complexities of having another location. We will look at that more later on.

- **Even if I can find enough of the right talent, is it affordable?**

  When you create your roadmap, you will often discover that you have a window of opportunity for a product but you just cannot afford enough engineers to get the job done with the available budget. At this point, you need to consider if you can find cheaper but equivalent talent elsewhere who can perform the total work within the given budget.

- **Can I hire all the people I need quickly enough?**
  If you have an urgent need of many people, it is impractical to recruit them one at a time. You should then look for an outsourcing company to supply staff with a defined skill set en masse.

- **Do I have room for all these people?**
  If you are doing a very fast growth with an outsourcer, you may want the outsourcer to supply the entire facility, rather than having the staff in your premises.

- **Do I have some non-core competency tasks that are relatively low-tech?**
  It may be more economical to hire these as contractors via a contracting company.

This set of questions will lead you into a complex set of decisions on the following topics:

- Should you do your development in one or several geographies?
- Can development in a cheaper geography significantly reduce your costs?
- Should you have an outsourcing company help to recruit in house staff (insourcing)?
- Should you hand entire projects to an external outsourced operation (outsourcing)?

How to Fail at Distributed Development in Three Easy Steps

Recipe for Failure

- Many companies acquire multiple sites through acquisition and do not integrate them afterwards. They wind up with a hodge podge of separate and overlapping teams with different cultures that are partially redundant and very hard to manage.

- When those same companies start to do badly, they develop a sudden urge to save money. Thus, they quickly hire a pile of engineers from a cheaper geography, hand them either just their maintenance work or simply everything and, after a short transition, lay off all their experienced staff.

- Soon, both productivity and quality are falling. To make matters worse, costs in the cheaper location escalate while turnover rises very high.

A Better Way

The three steps to failure mentioned above are very common in poorly managed businesses. All of us have seen these steps multiple times. But there is a better model, which has been practiced for years by the most successful multinational organizations:

- **Create a common corporate culture**
  - ➢ Understand the role of each site and how it fits into the whole
  - ➢ Understand the role of local and national culture at each site

- **Value all your employees equally**
  - ➢ Provide them with adequate training and meaningful career paths
  - ➢ Understand both the skill sets and the maturity levels at each site
  - ➢ Make sure every site has important projects to do that match with their skill profile

> ➤ Never give a site the notion that they just get the garbage work that no one else wants

If you follow this model, you will have motivated and effective employees at all your locations. We will elaborate on the requirements to make that happen later.

Distributed vs. Local Development

Going from having all your staff in one place to having multiple locations, particularly if some of those locations are in a different country, is a huge step. It forces you to think hard about your management systems. In this section, we will look at the different models for distributed development. We will bias this towards offshore work but the issues are the same whether your remote office is 600 or even 6,000 miles away.

Before the Internet boom in the late 1990s, when people talked about remote Engineering teams, the first image that came to mind was a group of engineers in India that would use a bulletin board system to download the source code at the close of the workday in the US, work on the project during daytime hours in India (overnight for the US), and then send it back to the US. This process created an illusion of parallelism. People worked regular hours in both offices and the organization could still produce code up to 24 hours per day.

Then, the Internet boom came along and the telecommunication companies created new capacity because they assumed that the demand for the Internet bandwidth would continue to accelerate indefinitely. At the same time, the need for engineering talent in technology companies increased rapidly. Companies initially addressed this need by importing talent and by the rapid creation of remote Engineering teams.

The remote Engineering teams offered access to engineering talent with promises of substantial cost savings. To take advantage of these savings, most organizations have their Engineering teams geographically distributed across the world. However, the old two work shift model is no longer effective, when the teams use software life cycle models based on

Agility. The time zone difference that allowed India to flourish as the center for remote teams became a serious limitation when real-time iteration is desired. Before starting either an offshoring or an outsourcing effort, you must understand the several ways that the local engineering organization can use remote resources.

Besides, the most obvious ways of breaking down the tasks is by module, component, risk level, or even technology. Other factors influence how the work should be allocated to each Engineering team.

Resource-Recycling Zones

The concept of "resource-recycling zones" proposed by Geoffrey Moore can be useful during the design phase of a remote Engineering organization. In this model, the work done in the company is classified by these three resource-recycling zones:

- **Invention zone** - Having an entrepreneurial emphasis, this zone is fast-paced and dynamic. It also has a large percentage of unpredictable processes. Employees working on this zone are motivated by the need to create an impact and then move on to the next challenge. When the innovation efforts have brought forth a viable solution, the work is ready to be moved to the deployment zone.

- **Deployment zone** - Focusing on service robustness and business scalability, this zone represents all the efforts that start at product launch and continue during several sale cycles. The typical profile on this zone is a manager with a more formal and disciplined approach in setting expectations and monitoring progress. When most of the improvements based on innovation are explored and the work becomes even more predictable, the effort is ready to move to the next zone. Processes are somewhat unpredictable.

- **Optimization zone** – This zone focuses on continuous improvement, cost reduction, and productivity. It represents the final phase on the life cycle and is led by people with process engineering and manufacturing mindset. Processes are very predictable.

The transition between zones represents a transformation on the job description of each person involved. In the past, technology organizations would nurture the same employee from the invention zone to the deployment zone and by the time the employee got to the optimization zone, they were ready for retirement. With the advent of more dynamic models and shorter product life cycles, the original model created a "death march" where people moved from one phase to the next until they were out of the company.

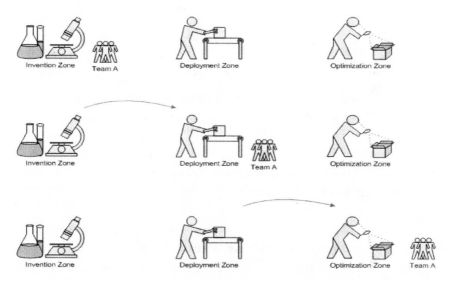

Teams "move" from zone to zone on a single project.

During the implementation of an offshore/outsource project it is important to allow employees to work on the zone that they are most productive at. In this way, when an innovation is complete it is ready to be "handed off" to the Deployment Zone. The same team then starts a new effort that is also strongly based on innovation. This model, aside from utilizing people in a more productive way, enables the company to create a more sustainable human resource model, since each employee has a cyclical contribution in taking efforts to the beginning of each zone and carrying them until the "hand off" to the next zone.

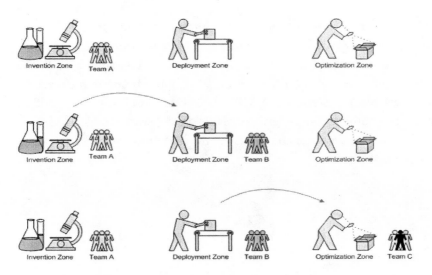

Each team continues to work on efforts that fit their skill set. Each effort is performed by different teams depending on the stage of the cycle.

Within this model, you should notice that there are risk considerations related with IP protection and turnover that must be addressed. Those will be explored in detail on the next section.

There is another dimension that needs to be considered when planning for an outsourced or offshore organization. What kind of culture will be nurtured at the remote offices? It is often impossible or unproductive to copy the culture that you have at your local office. There are often cases where cultural differences create challenges difficult to overcome.

One possible end scenario in people at the offshore office is having a hard time making decisions and expecting the "main" office to provide direction for all the details of the remote operation. Another possible environment can lead to developers feeling that the only progression of their careers is to move to management after few years.

These situations prevent the organization from creating a more experienced Engineering team and strong interaction between people and offices, both of which are critical to the success of the projects.

Assembly Line vs. Extended Teams

There are two classical approaches in communicating directions and goals with remote organizations. These are the "assembly line" and the "extended team".

Assembly Line

System requirements will be created in great detail and sent to the remote office that will assemble the software artifacts according to the specifications defined. This approach focuses on both risk control and consistency by creating a very formal and predictable communication channel with the remote team. Using objective metrics to assess performance, it is the easiest model to configure but is more time-consuming to maintain. It works better with less agile software life cycle models. Furthermore, it requires impeccable requirements prepared by experienced— and thus, expensive— professionals. It can also potentially create finger-pointing situations where the implementers will argue that the specification is wrong while the other side will assert that the requirements are not followed. This approach works well on projects where there is a high probability of turnover in the remote office.

Extended Team

Functional requirements are defined by the local team and sent to a remote team that is responsible for coming up with system requirement documents and/or prototypes to be approved by the main office.

This approach values collaboration and long-term relationship with the provider by changing the type of information that needs to flow through the communication channel. The key for success in this structure is to communicate guidelines instead of rules and let the remote team derive the rules and be more integrated to the other groups in the engineering organization.

If both the remote team and the local team have similar capabilities, having a backup organization operating remotely can reduce risk. On the other hand, IP risk needs to be managed closely in order to protect the interests of the organization.

While there are risks to an extended team structure, this approach creates a more sustainable model for the remote team, as there is a more integrated organization and career paths available for those members working on the remote side.

Offshoring

Offshoring defined

Offshoring, in its simplest form, means substituting nominally cheaper foreign labor for nominally more expensive domestic labor. Thus, it is a money-saving matter. The implication behind it is that the foreign labor is equivalent to the local labor but is only cheaper. Originally, offshoring always applied to labor in another country but it can also be extended to cover cheaper labor in other parts of the same country. However, this definition is far too simple to be useful. The first point is that offshoring generally means moving only some labor to another spot, not all of it. Therefore, it implies that work is done in at least two places. In offshoring, you need to be able to do geographically distributed work. The second point is that no work forces are completely fungible. Regardless of the country where you hired your remote employees, there will be cultural, political, financial, and skill-set differences.

Potential and Challenges of Offshoring

For some years, many companies were advised to save money by moving much of their development offshore. Indeed, most innovative and successful large hi-tech companies operate Development groups around the globe with great success and see high productivity across many of them. Other companies, especially the smaller ones, continue to struggle in achieving the hoped for productivity. Over time, those who have been successful at offshoring have approached the topic with a richer model. Part of it is about access to talent pools. While it may be very competitive and cost-prohibitive to compete for a senior engineer in Silicon Valley, you may find it easier to find someone equally— or at least 95 percent as good— in Vancouver, Toronto, St. Louis, Mumbai, or Shenzhen.

Another big advantage is from the support perspective. It is better to hand off either a level 3 or level 4 support case to someone near the customer's time zone and, thus, avoiding waking up the local engineer at odd hours. Additional benefits include the ability to ramp-up— and conversely, ramping-down— of sizable team quickly. An offshoring model works well when development staffing curves fluctuate drastically.

Investigating whether to do Offshore Development

The question of whether or not offshoring will work for you first requires you to address the following questions:

- Can my organization be productive in a geographically distributed environment?
- Do I understand that its implication for local workers is working either late night or early morning recurring phone calls, especially during ramp-up period?
- Do I need tools and policies for distributed source code management, test automation, and the like?
- Am I being realistic? Do I understand that the financial benefits typically occur at a minimum of six to nine months from launch?
- Am I aware that over the last few years, the rates for offshoring especially in India have gone up and average turnover rates are higher as well?
- Are my planning processes capable of comprehending and benefiting from the differences between the workforces in various geographies?
- Am I realistic regarding the minimum team size to maintain critical mass and keep thriving entity? Typically, eight or more employees in any outsourced location are considered a minimum.

Unless you have very good answers to these questions, naive attempts to offshore the work to other places in order to save money are doomed to failure. In addition, it is very important to realize that distributed work poses exactly the same challenges if the other group is 1,000 miles away in the same country or half way around the world!

Investigating Where to do Offshoring

Assuming you have decided to proceed, you can then ask how to choose the optimum locations to do work. Here are some of the factors you need to investigate:

- What skill sets do you need? Does a given location offer enough people with this skill set?
- Even if not enough people with a given skill set are available, are there a sufficient number of well-educated people who can be trained?
- Are other companies competing for the same talent pool? Is there enough to go around?
- What are the salary differences between areas such as entry level versus skilled workers? What is the rate of change of salaries over time?
- What are the political constraints? (i.e. IP protection, legal protection, or political stability)
- What are the strategic implications of a site? Does it tie into efforts to penetrate a given market?
- What are cultural factors in a site? (i.e. communication and learning style, work ethics)
- What are the real estate and bandwidth costs?
- What are the development methodologies used by the team and are they consistent with my local methodologies? (i.e. a CMM Level 5 outsource will likely be an overkill and will not work if you are a round A startup)
- Do you know how to split your work across sites to obtain maximum benefit from a site?

Economic Notes

Now that we have made you all nervous with hard questions, let us figure out how to succeed!

The most sophisticated approach in distributing development is to optimize the acquisition and utilization of talent across sites while minimizing expenditures. The real secret to effective offshore work is viewing it not as a matter of moving work to save money but as distributing work to get the best people in the best places for the least money.

If done properly, multisite development can dramatically increase your capacity and lower your costs. It is partially a matter of good management and good planning. Here are some useful considerations:

- **To accurately model development costs in a multisite world, you need to start by understanding the distribution of skills in your organization.**

  What kinds of skills do you need? What is the proportion of junior to senior staff? For example, you have five levels of Engineering from level 1 to 5. Determine what proportion of each do you have or need. After that, write down the local salary ranges for each level. Multiplying by the relative proportions of each job type and level, you can figure out the weighted cost to do work at each site. Many companies get this wrong! In many cheaper economies, you will be hiring more junior staff than in the US. Hence, your profile of the skill levels will be different. You cannot expect a group of people with two to five years of experience to do the exact work a similar group with 15 to 20 years does. Failing to consider that will cause a lot of headache! You need to be realistic about who you can hire and the work they can do.

- **In many low-cost geographies, you will hire very junior people and then train them.**

  In most countries, the spread in cost between entry-level and experienced workers is higher than in the US but people have an expectation of faster promotions. Thus, you can hire new entry-level workers very cheaply but once you have trained them and they are more capable, you will have to promote them to avoid creating turnover risk. This pattern of promotions is the main driver of the increasing labor costs in most places. As long as you keep growing, you will always have to add more junior workers that dilute this effect.

- **In a US software business, the main cost of development is labor.**
  If you go to a place where labor cost is one-third as much, your building, servers, and electricity, will suddenly dominate the costs. So, for example, if labor is 60 percent of your cost in the US, then it is only about 33 percent of your cost in India. As a result, a 10 percent increase in labor costs increases your total costs by six percent in the US, but only by three percent in India.

- **You need to include the travel cost, extra documentation, and training time in your planning.**
  Once your training systems are in place, their marginal costs become quite low. But both travel and communication costs will remain substantial expenses.

- **Currency fluctuations are also a planning risk.**
  If your company gets significant revenues abroad, you may be able to hedge against currency risk by paying foreign development costs using foreign revenue, sidestepping a certain amount of currency conversion.

Getting Started with Outsourcing

Let us suppose you have decided you need more flexibility in your hiring than just adding permanent staff at headquarters. How do you get started? The following are some of the approaches you can consider:

Insourcing

Insourcing is using an outsourcing or staffing vendor to provide people with a given skill set to work at your existing site. There are two common use cases. The first is if you need people with a well-defined, commonly available, and relatively non-technical skill set. Common examples are the rack-and-stack guys in a data center and front desk receptionists. These are all functions where you can save money and retain operational flexibility by having these functions staffed by a suitable provider. A second use case is with an existing and typically offshore facility where you want to quickly ramp up people with a commodity skill set, for example, manual QA or Oracle application consultants. In this case, one can contract with an outsource vendor to supply some suitable number of people (10, 20, or more) who can work as contractors. These contracts usually include a provision to buy out the contract and hire these folks as employees if it works out well. This approach is easy and flexible but should be understood mostly to be incremental to other approaches.

Outsourcing a Site

Another technique is to hire an outsourcing vendor to supply an entire self-contained site that is hosted at the vendor's facilities. Typically, the vendors manage the security such that each customer's operation is physically separated and only the staff assigned to that contract is allowed of physical access. This approach works well for commodity operations such as regression QA or call centers. Because of the physical separation of this staff, this arrangement lends itself neither to converting the staff into permanent employees nor even to creating the real corporate culture. As a result, this approach is best suited for fairly self-contained and non-strategic operations. Since turnover in such sites is often very high, the tasks need to be very well documented and require little training. Typically, this approach is used in cases where low cost and fast startup outweighs most other factors.

Build-To-Buy

If you want to have your own site, the easiest way is to go for a build-to-buy arrangement. In this case, you will contract with an outsourcing firm—and some that specialize in this kind of work—to set up an entire site for you and staff it. You will want to contribute a dedicated manager and some support staff. Then, you will work with the organization to set up your training, processes, and culture. This will require the same major involvement from your existing sites as if you built the site yourself. Since this approach is more expensive than having your own direct employee site, you will use this purely as a transition state and buy out the outsourcing firm as soon as it makes sense. The advantage of this approach is that it gets you running quickly without many legal and political hitches involved in starting completely from scratch.

This is also the best approach for very small companies that will not have the resources to set up an independent site of their own for some time.

Starting a Site Yourself

Finally, you can do it alone. This will require hiring a strong manager to run the site who will hire the bring-up team. This initial team needs to find an appropriate location, find a building, obtain government permits, and start the recruiting process. If you are new to the country, this can be surprisingly time-consuming. Unlike in the US where incorporation is a trivial process, in many countries this requires a lot of time and effort. Furthermore, you will want enough political connections to eliminate regulatory obstacles and obtain whatever government subsidies are available such as tax credits for hiring local college graduates. Once you are done with the permitting, you can then start recruiting your own team. You will want to start small and have the core group of people trained well. They can then help you recruit and train the next waves. Setting up a site like this is a multi-year endeavor.

Whether you start the site yourself or do build-to-buy, creating your own site is the hardest of all the approaches. But, in the long run, this is how you build a sustainable, happy, and productive site that is a worthy contributor to your organization. The effort is justified by its long-term contribution to your strategic goals.

Success Factors

Here are some of the key success factors for offshore, outsourced and insourced operations:

- Hire an excellent manager for your new site
- Have total executive support for your endeavor
- Make sure to spend a lot of time with the new site sharing your corporate culture with them and making them feel valued and included
- Make sure your existing staff does not feel threatened by these efforts and train them on actively supporting the new site

- Create publicity so that people will see that your company is a cool place to work at
- Many travel opportunities between the sites help bind people together. This is expensive but is worth it!

If you follow the best practices outlined here, you will not have major turnover problems. High turnover is almost always a consequence of shortsighted management practices!

Small Company vs. Large Company

The overhead of hiring an experienced manager to head the offshore organization creates an additional challenge for a small organization. Rather than opting to offshore, a good alternative is to outsource.

There is an inflexion point where the gains reached by offshoring compensate for the management overhead. For most small companies, offshoring is only recommended if one of the founders or a trusted party agrees to run the organization and live abroad.

Small organizations are more fragile and easier to disrupt. Consequently, the management of a small offshore operation has to be completely committed to the success and be rewarded with bonuses based on results. It is a common mistake to think that just by transferring an Engineering team faraway from the headquarters will automatically eliminate all the problems related with politics that naturally occur in these groups. In fact, it is considerable more difficult to deal with these issues remotely.

On the other hand, medium and large companies can justify the initial investment of rent, overhead, and so on because they benefit better from the economies of scale. Also, these companies are more likely to attract better talent since these are the companies recognized by the employee pool as good "resume builders".

Risk Management

Since having multiple sites increases the management complexity of an organization, business execution risk clearly increases. On the other hand, by having multiple sites, one mitigates the risk caused by drastic failure at any one of the sites.

In specific areas, one also needs to deal with political and IP risks. Political risks pertain to the government instability, war, and official corruption. You always need to do due diligence to understand the extent of these risks and your organization's appetite for them.

IP protection, on the other hand, is not managed well in many countries. You will need to work closely with your outsource vendor to properly indemnify you against risks and with your IT organization on physical protection. In certain environments, the final safeguard is to simply never allow the employees to know enough of the entire system to be able to pose a competitive threat in the future.

Metrics

- Cost per hour for local engineers versus offshore engineers at the same grade level
- Productivity of engineers
- Quality of code produced (i.e. bug density, local versus offshore)
- Turnover rates, local versus offshore
- Economic metrics - You need to continually measure the cost of work in a given site versus other sites. This needs to include total costs, including facility, communication, salary, and travel costs. Be careful to normalize salary costs to account relative experience levels and promotion rates of staffs in different areas.
- Productivity metrics - Measure both quantity (number of test cases executed per person) as well as quality (i.e. defect density)
- Innovation metrics - Patents filed

5.4 Outsourcing for Enterprise Software

Introduction

In the previous chapter, we discussed the different models for staffing an organization to build products, with outsourcing as an option for adding staff. In this chapter, we will look at outsourcing on a per product or per project basis. This model is most commonly encountered when acquiring enterprise software, which requires large-scale customization. In this case, one not only buys the software, but also contracts with an outsourcing firm to perform all the required customization and generally, to deliver the complete solution. The major advantage of this approach is that it allows you to acquire the exact quantity of specialized expertise you need to implement one of these products for just the time period you need. This allows you to more quickly, safely, and cheaply implement such a system than you could if your organization did it itself.

That is, at least, the theory. Such projects, particularly when done by IT on a large scale, are in fact often spectacular failures, costing millions of dollars and causing untold ruin to their company. For example, American La France, the famous maker of fire engines, filed for chapter 11 because their botched SAP implementation prevented them from delivering or supporting product in a timely way.

Why Enterprise Software Deployments are So Hard

Generally, any enterprise software package, whether it is a financial tool like SAP or a development tool like Quality Center, serves to automate some process in the organization. Since each organization has different processes, the applications need to be customized to match the local process. The challenge here is that most organizations do not explicitly understand their processes very well. Also, their processes in fact do not work very well either. If a company documents one process but in daily life follows another, then automating the documented process will fail. If the process followed is very inefficient, then automating it will simply automate the inefficiency. Thus, to be able to implement such a product, you need to first understand what your process is and decide if it is the right one. If it is the wrong one, you have to change the process because either having the wrong processes or choosing new ones without consensus are the usual reasons why so many enterprise software deployments fail. Thus, the first best practice is to understand that the outsourced project will create a major change management effort to systematize and optimize the target process. To succeed, you need to have a solid executive backing and make a real effort to carefully solicit requirements. This means understanding exactly who the key users are and what their use cases are. Of course, when talking to users, you cannot just take the current practice at face value. One has to understand what the new tool will enable. You also need to figure out what process would work well with the team and you have to work well with the tool in question. Only once the users (or a reasonable subset thereof), project team, and senior management agree that the process change proposed is reasonable will you have a real chance at success.

For some reason, many people try to do these projects in a strict Waterfall way: collecting requirements, then sending the outsourcing vendor off to implement, and then doing acceptance. This approach fails remarkably often because the users at the beginning did not understand the depths of process change required and did not state the right requirements. This argues strongly for doing an iterative approach where the system is built in phases with frequent user feedback to allow requirements to evolve as the shared understanding grows and to make sure the implementation stays is genuinely usable.

Choosing the Vendor

Let us suppose you have your mind set on solving some problem using a big fancy tool. The first thing you need to do is to scope out the scale of the process work involved. How many users and use cases are there? Are there any political obstacles? Do you have complex existing systems to interface as well as difficult training to do? Then, you need to ask how much of this you want to do and how much you want the vendor to do.

Now, you can go and solicit proposals from the vendors. When talking to the vendors, one needs to ensure that they have all the skill sets needed to succeed. You also have to ensure if the people they introduce to you are actually those who will actually do the work. Many consulting firms use the bait-and-switch approach, wowing you with senior staff only to replace them with junior staff after the sale is made. Generally, the outsourcers have an easier time with the actual coding: it is the process and requirements work that test their mettle. Make sure the outsourcer has solved a problem like this before and understands how hard your situation is. Come to think of it, you should understand how hard your situation is. Check their references. It is important that the vendor be able to provide the right quantity and quality of people to make this successful.

In negotiating the contract—which you are hopefully doing with your procurement and legal folks— make sure you divide the project into suitable phases with clear acceptance criteria. It is better to have many smaller milestones that you can definitively verify.

Monitoring the Project

Once the project gets going, make sure it is very actively program-managed. You need to make sure that the users make time for the consultants. If they get busy and avoid the consultants during the requirements gathering phases, the project will surely fail!

You also have to guarantee that the project makes consistent progress. If it gets stuck, you need to understand what the problem is. Is it vendor incompetency, the problem being harder than it looks, uncooperative users, political problems, or some other reason? Even if you outsource the whole thing, at the end of the day, it is still your responsibility to ensure that it keeps moving forward. You also have to look out for problems with the vendor, such as staff being supplied with the wrong skill set or experience or suddenly substituting one person for another of inferior quality.

If things get off the track in terms of missed deliverables, low quality, or unhappiness with the process, do not be afraid to pull the plug and bring in a different firm. If you decide to change vendors, figuring that out early on is a big win. That is the benefit of having many shorter milestones.

Accordingly, big projects tend to acquire an organizational complexity all their own. This is usually because they attack processes that cross business unit lines and generally the organization has a difficult time getting everyone to line up around a common tool. In this case, you need to supply extra management effort to achieve organizational alignment. This alignment may be so hard to achieve globally that you may want to split the project into multiple phases and bring one group of people into it at a time to the extent possible.

Another challenge is just dealing with change requests. In many cases, as the initial work progresses, the requirements change quite a bit. If a contract is written too stringently, you may wind up paying through the nose for these change orders. You need to protect yourself against this by making provisions in the contract for incremental development and requirements evolution.

As the product nears roll-out, you need to make sure that everyone relevant in the organization is lined up, ranging from training materials and program for all involved to necessary infrastructure upgrades.

In general, all these steps depend on supplying very strong program management. Even if the vendor provides much of the Program Management, you need your person involved at all times in monitoring the effort and properly escalating any issues promptly.

Three Simple Rules

Here are three simple rules for success in outsourcing an Enterprise development project:

- Understand and plan for the process change required
- Do all work incrementally with clear verification on iteration boundaries
- Your program manager needs to watch everything like a hawk

5.5 Development Partnerships

Introduction

Development partnerships occur whenever two or more organizations work together on a product. This is a common technique for spreading risk and optimizing for core competencies. For example, even if you build products in your core competency areas yourself, you may elect to form partnerships to address non-core areas.

Kinds of Partnerships

There are many different types of relationships, which vary in how closely the partners work together, the exclusivity of the relationship, and the balance of power. Some examples of development partnerships are the following:

Product Conforms to Government Standards and Regulations

All products conform to some level of standards, whether it is a software package that runs on a certain operating system or an electrical power requirement. However, many products are highly driven by Standards and Regulations. Medical equipment must meet specific standards, as they must be manufactured following Good Manufacturing Practices. Consumer products often demonstrate product safety with a UL, CSA, ETL, or CE certification mark. Also, wireless equipment must conform to Federal Communications Commission (FCC) regulations. This is the simplest form of development partnership because you only need to prove that you comply with known standards. It is common to employ third party companies to provide the testing that proves compliance.

Product Fits into an Ecosystem or Environment

If both the standards and technologies involved are fairly stable, this is similar to the government standards case discussed above. Generally though, the ecosystem or environment is not nearly as well defined. Development partnerships would be arranged with companies that help certify that the product works in the ecosystem or environment.

If both the standards and the technology are evolving and growing, much of the work is in interpreting the standard or influencing how the standard evolves. This often involves working on standards committees or hiring consultants who are experts on how the standards have been interpreted by the industry. If there is no single organization that manages compliance, companies will often work together to help prove cross compatibility since this helps everyone. In the hardware industry, groups of companies will have meetings called Plug-fests where different vendors will work together to check on cross compatibility. Subsets of companies will frequently form development partnerships that have a business agenda of defining the market and competitive groups can form up such as the BetaMax versus VHS or Blu-ray DVD versus HD DVD battles. The different partner companies are allies at one level, competitors are a different level and may be development partners only in agreeing on the future standards, or they may be development partners who work together on a technology.

Since this work is highly technical, it generally requires staff from Engineering. However, it is a tricky, political job and often requires senior staff. Even if development proceeds independently at different partners, the direction and features are influenced by the industry.

Product is a Component, Plug-in, Add- on, or Accessory to a Single Company's System

When one company dominates the ecosystem or environment, working in that world means conforming to their standards, making it a component, plug-in, add- on, or accessory to their system.
In this case development is largely shaped by your relationship with that company. This can be a great advantage especially if your company is relatively small and your product is promoted as part of a larger company's

system. However, this is an unequal development partnership, with most of the power residing with the company that controls the system. They can play smaller companies who provide components against each other by hinting at exclusivity while working with all the competition. Engineering will have to devote senior staff, up to and including the VPE, to keep the big company happy.

The more complex the component is, the greater the risk involved in customizing the product for the single company's system. Components that can be adapted easily to different environments are not only less risky, but also can generally produce less value and a lower barrier of entry for competitors. In the hardware industry, these might be OEM components such as the specialized engine parts for cars or they might be add-ons or accessories such as special cases or speakers for iPods. On the other hand, on the software side, these might be special utilities designed to work with the Oracle Database or add-ons to Microsoft Exchange. What is common with these is that your product's success or failure is closely tied to the single company's fate.

Anecdote

I worked for a company that produced RAID cards for computers and the Operating System (OS) vendor dominated the design. They required device drivers six months ahead of their scheduled release date, which turned out to be almost 18 months before their actual release date. This forced us to debug their OS problems when we were only trying to demonstrate compatibility. A major part of the success of that product depended on the success of the new OS and delays in that seriously hurt my company. While the large OS vendor easily absorbed the problems caused by the long delay, my company lost momentum and never fully recovered.

Product Uses Components

Building a product can often be sped up by purchasing either standard or custom components. This is nearly always true in the hardware industry, where products generally use OEM materials or components, from the silicon and chemicals for wafer processing chips, to mechanical parts and packaging. In the software space components are also used to speed product development, ranging from UI products, mathematics and analytic packages, to specialized device drivers. The development partnership here is more one of customer and vendor, and Engineering often has to work with Purchasing or Procurement. In the hardware area, many companies have rules about how vendors can be chosen. Besides the Engineering evaluation of the component, the vendor often has to be qualified as a financially stable enough to rely on. It is also common to require multiple vendors so that no component is single sourced. This is harder to achieve with software, so sometimes the same protection is given by having the software source code held in escrow. Since these decisions can involve a lot of money for the vendors and the discussion can originate in different parts of the company, it is important to be very careful in coordinating these decisions. While it may seem mundane, the purchasing and delivery of hardware components on schedule will often make or break a product.

Contracting for custom components is similar to outsourcing development since you have a unique set of requirements. The main difference is that a custom component will often be a modification of a standard one, while outsourcing development generally means more custom work (See below). Custom components can make sense because it allows the reuse of an established design or design experience that can be tailored to your specific product. Customization of existing components should be easier to specify and test since parts of the component are already defined.

Anecdote

One of my first jobs involved hardware design of a custom battery charger for a medical product. The longest battery life would be obtained by using a component that was only available from a single vendor. The decision was to use this vendor but during the initial production, the Purchasing department was unable to guarantee the delivery of enough components. As the product was being built, the inventory of that part was running so low that we became desperate. It turned out that Radio Shack was one of the customers who took delivery of this part and, for some reason, placed little stock in each store. Thus, we devised a plan where sales representatives across the country would go to Radio Shacks to buy out their inventory of these parts and mail them to the manufacturing line. Fortunately, Purchasing was able to sweet talk the vendor into supplying enough parts so we did not have to implement this plan. But this demonstrates how the success of an entire product can be tied to a $2 part.

Product Uses Development Partners to Outsource Work

This is a relationship where you pay an outside firm to do development work, either for their expertise or because it has a cost advantage. (See the section on outsourcing.)

How Partnerships Work

Some general principles apply to all development partnerships but the exact circumstances will dictate how you work together.

Development Relationships are People Relationships

Whether it is a partnership of equals or a vendor-supplier relationship, establishing personal relationships with the partner is important since it will help smooth out rough patches in the relationship.

Build a Cross-Functional Team for the Partnership

Building the partnership sometimes involves Marketing, Sales, Professional Services, or the Purchasing or Procurement groups. It is important for the different departments within your company to work together to have a coherent strategy and a unified approach to the partnership.

Explicitly Address the Risk of the Partnership

The advantages of partnership always carry risk that should be explicitly understood and tracked as the relationship proceeds. There will always be unknown major events which can disrupt the partnership such as if the partner is suddenly bought by an unfriendly company. However, the predictable risks, like if the partner cannot deliver on time or in sufficient quantity, should be investigated and monitored.

Small Company with Large Partner

From a very small company's perspective, a "dream" is to partner in OEM fashion with an industry-leading heavyweight— one with instant credibility, global reach, quality reputation, and clear success.

From the standpoint of EXECUTING in such a relationship, the small company is faced with the following issues that may not have been top of mind when the deal was signed:

- Do your quality and development practices match what the larger partner needs?
- What is their tolerance for your different practices? What is their level of comfort to risk exposure based on these differences?
- While you might send a dozen patches per year to your hundreds of customers, what does this mean when the larger partner's sales channel can get you 10 or 100 times the number of customers? Is this a supportable quality model?
- Should you choose to comply with the larger partner's quality practices? Can the rest of the company live with the additional cost and time to achieve that quality? What happens to features that had already been placed on the product roadmap but are not pushed out due to these new practices requiring time and resources?

Taking the large OEM partner's viewpoint, you should think carefully about how you will ask the smaller partner to alter their practices.

- Is there evidence to support such drastic requests?
- Is there room for "let us see what happens" or must one be airtight in the quality standard?
- Extrapolate carefully from previous customer-reported defect data and determine if this is likely to continue and be acceptable.

5.6 Licensing

Introduction

Licensing technology from other companies is an excellent way of decreasing time-to-market, spreading risk, and leveraging the capacity of one's sales channel. This can take one of two forms: either by OEM'ing an entire product to sell as part of one's own offerings or by licensing someone else's technology as a component of one's own products. In the second case, you, as the head of Engineering, will be called upon to help negotiate these deals. In this chapter, we will take a look at what is involved.

When to License Third Party IP

Saving the time and money required to develop the same product from scratch is the key advantage in licensing technologies or products from another party. If the given technology is not critical to your core assets, having your own staff that is free to work on more crucial projects and reducing time-to-market are key reasons to opt for buying instead of building in many cases. Here are some of the factors you should consider in leveraging this strategy:

Loss of Control

A potential problem with licensing a technology is your dependence on the supplier's roadmap. If they suddenly change direction and stop producing products you need, you might be stuck. Therefore, it is important to think about second sources. What happens if your main competitor acquires your supplier?

IP

By licensing the property, you are also giving up owning the property yourself. Would the lack of this IP be considered a liability by an acquirer or affect valuation in event of an IPO? Again, a major condition for licensing is that this is not a functionality core to your business.

Another interesting reason for licensing a given technology is if it is something you need but is thoroughly protected by patents. In this case, licensing the technology may be the only way to obtain it, given its patent protection.

Support Model

You need to understand the support implications of the given property. For many products, the licensee is responsible for localization and translation. You also need to be clear on who performs levels 1, 2, and 3 Support.

Setting the Royalty

You need to think hard about your profit margin in setting royalties. If you license too much of a given product from others, you may be left with insufficient profit margin. Again, if you only license non-core components, their license costs will probably be a small part of your product's value proposition. However, as part of the negotiation process, you have to keep it that way. You need to clearly understand your business model to see if the royalty is a burden on the business model. You can also look at mitigation steps such as determining if you can cross-license some of your own IP back to the other party to lower your costs.

Is it Cheaper to do In-House?

To make the final decision, you need to look at a combination of the total costs involved. When doing it yourself, you need to think about time-to-market, opportunity cost for your own staff, and potential patent issues. You also have to consider the margin impact of the license fee and your loss of control and ownership when licensing. Ultimately, the more expensive a task is to do AND the less it is part of your core functionality, the more attractive the licensing option will be.

Contractual Language

There are several considerations when dealing with licensing issues from the licensee or "acquiring side". These include:

- **Rights to sub-license product to partners and distributors**
  If you resell to Independent Software Vendors (ISVs) or OEMs, this may be an important clause.

- **Access to Source Code**
  You may want an escrow agreement giving you the right to the licensor's source code if you are dealing with a startup or a company that is likely to be acquired.

- **Audit process**
  Most licensing contracts require the ability to audit the licensee and verify the number of distributions for accounting purposes. If you are the licensee, you have to pay attention to the audit terms, as they likely require you to maintain up-to-date records of all copies of the licensed product. Failure to meet the audit terms will normally invoke an in-house audit of customer records by the licensor.

- **Branding/trademark terms and conditions**
  Negotiate the rights to rebrand the product if that is important to your market or business strategy and customer base. You must pass along any trademark and copyright information with your product.

- **IP rights**
  As the licensee, these rights are typically non-negotiable. However, there are exceptions such as OS companies.

- **Warranty limitations**
  Most licensing agreements delineate time-based warranties with specific timeframes (i.e. 30 to 60 days from date of delivery to licensee) for notification of critical issues to the licensor. Once notification is made, there are contractual timeframes to respond to the

issues with an adequate response before the licensor can be considered in breach of contract.

- **Liability limits**

   The licensee should ensure that there is an adequate financial liability to a specific amount. In some cases, this pertains to the licensee fees.

- **Indemnification**

   Ensure that the licensor has an adequate indemnification, particularly if the "integrated product" could present a real risk—financially or otherwise— to your prospective customers.

- **Escrow agreement**

   Make sure you get the source if the licensor becomes insolvent or under specific M&A actions.

- **Rights to future enhancements or releases**

   Guarantee that these are mentioned in contract. In many cases, a new major product release may warrant a renegotiation of the royalties.

- **Termination clause**

   Is there an appropriate termination clause in event of product obsolescence or liquidation events such as an acquisition or IPO? Is it possible to obtain the IP outright in such a case?

5.7 Open Source Software

<u>Introduction</u>

If you and your firm have not gone into Open Source Software (OSS) yet, you must have at least wondered out loud if you should. And if you had dipped your toes into using OSS, you may still wonder out loud if you should now take the plunge. If this sounds familiar or if you are considering working for an open source company, then this chapter is just for you. Odds are you are likely already using OSS without knowing it.

In this chapter, we will cover the various considerations that one should take before using an open source project. We will also present the most common models adopted by the companies that publish products in open source format.

We will also discuss the pitfalls of OSS, leading to practical discussion on the key factors and ingredients for OSS success. This will include a variety of OSS topics ranging including the types of licenses, evaluation criteria, ideal organizational structure, finding expertise, fixing problems, contributing back to OSS communities, and more. We will use real life case studies and examples to illustrate some of the discussions.

Some of you may find yourselves in the near future running an Engineering group at a commercial open source company. As of April 2008, three members of the VPE/CTO COP worked in open source companies. Further readings and references are listed at the end of the chapter.

Open Source

What exactly is open source? Commercial computer software is usually distributed in a "black box" form that does not make the source code of the computer software available to the customer. This is known as "closed source" software that is usually distributed as a binary executable. On the other hand, "open source" refers to the practice of providing both the software program AND the corresponding source code for the program in the programming language it is written in. It is usually free for download over the Internet. It also has a legal license attached to it that can limit the user from distributing it without attribution to the original author. Some licenses such as the Gnu Public License (GPL) incorporate terms that are "viral" or "reciprocal" in nature, requiring that any modifications to the software as well as the software it is combined with be contributed back to the public domain.

VCs are Betting on Open Source

Commercial OSS is currently one of the hottest areas in the software industry. There is now a dominant open source firm in every major category of software. Gartner Group calls open source "the biggest disruptor the software industry has ever seen". In the platform middleware software market, Gartner also believes that open source is a viable long-term play, writing: "The open-source option is clearly a long-term phenomenon."

Following Web 2.0 or consumer Internet and SaaS investments, open source has been one of the top three software investment categories by VCs. Since 2000, VC has poured $1.9 billion into commercial open source companies. The past three years have seen $900 million in VC investments in what Larry Augustin[16] calls the third-generation of commercial open source companies. Even Microsoft is shipping some portions of open source software in its newly released Vista OS. There is a general trend of convergence between open and closed source software vendors. Open source is now accepted and mainstream for most IT departments.

Current Landscape and Trends

Several companies and open source projects provide complete stacks including OS, Application Server, Database, and PHP (scripting

---

[16] Larry Augustin, entry on "Open Source Venture Investment Through Q1 of 2007," Larry Augustin's Weblog, entry posted on May 8, 2007, http://lmaugustin.typepad.com/lma/2007/05/open_source_ven.html (accessed on September 18, 2008).

programming language). One of the most common instantiations is the "LAMP" stack that includes Linux, Apache, MySQL, and PHP (or other programming language). Michael Kunze coined the acronym LAMP in an article for the German computing magazine *c't* in 1998. Since then, the number of combinations of open sources and server stack, desktop applications, enterprise middleware and applications has grown significantly. One of these variants is the WAMP stack based on Windows. As with any OSS, you have to be aware of the licensing terms, especially if you intend to include a third party "stack" in your own product for sale.

In the last few years, many companies have successfully monetized the open source market by taking what in most cases was a pure open source project and then providing paid support, indemnification, commercial licenses, feature add-ons, professional services, and training. Recent examples of open source success include the Redhat IPO, JBoss acquisition by Redhat for $400 million, MySQL acquisition by Sun for $1 billion, Zimbra acquisition by Yahoo!, and several others. The ability to create a competitive product by leveraging a community of dedicated contributors is regarded as a major disruptive force in the software industry.

Open source has been around for the past 30 years but it has only gained great commercial viability in recent years. In his book about the history of OSS, *The Cathedral and the Bazaar*, Eric Raymond lays out the roots of why Linux is subversive and why open source is a disruptive force in the software industry. Open source has been disruptive but more importantly, it has also become a big business. Clayton Christensen from the Harvard Business School writes about the disruption potential of open source: "Open source has the feel of a classic industry disruption in the making."

Over ten years ago, no one could imagine running a production Oracle database for key corporate data on an open source operating system such as Red Hat Enterprise Linux. Today, Oracle offers a bundle of both the Linux operating system and its database server and OSS is in production at nearly all of the top Fortune 500 companies. In addition, there is a major open source player in every software category, from operating systems, database and middleware to CRM.

From a market size perspective, the total worldwide software market is estimated to be at $92.7 billion in 2006. The overall OSS market is projected to grow from 13 percent of the $92.7 billion software market in 2006 to 27 percent of the $169.2 billion market in 2011.This represents an expansion from $12.1 billion to $45.7 billion by 2011, which is a tremendous increase in market size. There is clearly a great opportunity for OSS companies to grow in the next few years.

Economic Factors Involved in Open Source in the Enterprise

CIOs of major Fortune 500 companies are more frequently adopting open source projects or products for internal use. Budget constraints and community support are cited as key factors. As the head of Engineering, you are faced with effectively deploying a number of tools or systems to effectively manage, create, test, and document your products on a modest budget. Open source tools have become commonplace within the Engineering department and corporation. Many software companies use Bugzilla as a bug tracker and most use variants of the LAMP stack, but there are thousands of other tools available from the open source community free of use that have broad community of support.

Sourceforge.net, a common web site for open source project management and distribution, lists 174,385 registered projects and 1,828,291 registered users, as of April 10, 2008. These projects fall into 14 different categories including Clustering, Database, Desktop, Development, Enterprise, Financial, Games, Hardware, Multimedia, Networking, Security, Storage, System Administration, and VoIP. Before making any expenditure for software, a savvy engineering leader should peruse the open source projects lists for other options. Some of these projects may be old, have incomplete features, or be of poor quality but a quick evaluation will normally tell you if it is suitable for your needs.

Consider the term "reinventing the wheel". This is especially relevant when considering make or buy decisions. But when it comes to using open source, it could be considered an even more attractive option than either make or buy. Leveraging open source has the capability of jump-starting your software development environment or internal tools functions at zero to low cost. Every software startup has to focus its precious cash flow on developing code that furthers its core product. It cannot afford to waste time and money on non-critical redundant code modules. One caution, however, is that open source projects vary greatly in their maturity, scalability, usability, and readiness for production environments. Before you consider using an open source tool, look at the forums for current issues and if necessary, post a forum question stating your desired application and get feedback. As mentioned above, if you are considering embedding an open source project into your own commercial product, you should review any licensing restrictions.

The ability to extend, patch, and support the code is a huge advantage of open source (as the name points out) over other commercial software. Assuming that you have the skills to support the code, you can actually get the source! Make sure you consider the potential training, sustaining, and community support costs beforehand.

Considerations Before Adopting an Open Source Product

Key Metrics

- **How many active developers?**
  One measure of an open source project's health is the volume of contributions—features or lines of code— being created. The more active or healthy the project is, typically, the more project committers there are and the higher the number of project administrators is. Ohloh tracks open source project health at many levels including developers. As of April 2008, Ohloh lists 94 contributors to Mozilla Firefox, 55 to Subversion, 31 for Apache HTTP Server, and 1399 contributors to Linux Kernel 2.6. Ohloh also tracks the frequency of commits by contributors, the number of lines of code as well as an overall estimate of the project's commercial value based on total number of lines of code, using an average of $55,000 per year at 3,910 lines of code per developer year. Based on this, the Jasper Re-

ports project, for example, is valued at $3.12 million, with 223,000 LOC.

- **Is the Sourceforge.net rating high?**

   Sourceforge.net is one of the most popular open source sites. It maintains its own overall project ranking based on several factors including downloads and project activity. Generally, the higher the Sourceforge.net ranking is, the more reassurance that the project will be viable in the long run.

- **How important is age of community?**

   The age of the community is not the best measure of project health. Like anything else in software, trends come and go. Technologies get replaced and if a project's code does not get refactored as needed, it will die slowly.

Legal Matters

There are over 100 documented open source licenses including GPL, LGPL (Lesser Gnu Public License), MPL (Mozilla Public License), CPL, and many others. Wikipedia alone documents 50 of the more common "open source" software license models.[17] Four of the more common licensing agreements include GPL, LGPL, MPL, and BSD.

- **GPL**

   GPL is viral in nature and requires any source modifications to the product to be provided back to the community and onto your customers. Recently, the new GPL3 version was ratified and did include major changes over GPLv2. GPLv3 offers key improvements like compatibility with other open source licenses including Apache.

---

[17] Please refer to the Wikipedia (http://en.wikipedia.org/wiki/Category:Open_source_licenses) for a more exhaustive review of licensing models.

Moving from GPLv2 to GPLv3 increases the potential for integrating and collaborating with other projects licensed under different terms, which should help to spur further open source innovation and overall adoption. Notable changes in the GPLv3 over GPL2 and the related Affero GPLv3 (AGPLv3) that covers digital rights management (DRM), "tivoization"," patent rights, and requisite availability of source code over a network may negatively impact GPL adoption among some groups of vendors, particularly hardware vendors and others that embed OSS in their products as well as ISVs and SaaS vendors. In some cases, a commercial license may be obtained from the GPL vendor to include their product in your own commercial product for sale and indemnification.

- **LGPL**

    LGPL is a free software license published by the Free Software Foundation. While it was originally written for libraries, it is also applied to other software products. It is considered less "viral" than GPL.

Be careful that your software team is well aware of the licensing restrictions. For instance, you do not want them to unintentionally copy the GPL code into your commercial product. If you are concerned that you may have inherited a product that violates these licensing restrictions, companies like Palamida and BlackDuck provide products and services to validate your source code to determine any open source origins and licensing implications, likely avoiding a lengthy and potentially costly legal action.

Most open source projects are too small to provide adequate indemnification, thus, you need to make sure you weigh the liability risks of leveraging non-indemnified code. Here is an additional list of issues to think about in this context:

- What does the license require of people that make changes?
    - ➢ Do you need to mark the code? Some licenses require clear comments about changes, change dates, and the person who made the changes.
    - ➢ Do you need to contribute the changes back?

- ➢ Is there anything that you cannot change such as modifying attribution, or legal notices?
- Are you planning on contributing back?
  - ➢ Do you want to become a member of the project community?
  - ➢ Do you want to share your changes for the greater good?
- Who owns the IP of the open source project?
  - ➢ Is it a competitor?
  - ➢ Is it a small company that a competitor could purchase or that you could purchase? Would it make a difference if that happened?
- What are your source code distribution obligations?
  - ➢ Open source licenses typically have pretty strict requirements about distributing your code under certain conditions. What conditions does the license impose?
  - ➢ Many licenses allow people who get a copy of your product to request source code for years after you ship the latest version using that software.
  - ➢ Consider distributing the relevant source up front to satisfy your source code distribution requirements. This may remove the legal obligation to provide the source on request later.

Considerations in Opening the Source of a Commercial Product

Some companies take one or more of their commercial products and open source then. Sun is in the process of deploying Open Solaris, an open source version of the commercial Solaris OS. Other open source projects follow circuitous routes. Take Derby for example. Originally a commercial Java Database company known as Cloudbase, Derby was acquired by Informix that in turn was acquired by IBM, who subsequently opened the source via Apache. Rarely are such events truly altruistic. The motivations include:

- Opening a product to start building a community for future upsell of add-ons or symbiotic commercial products
- Getting the community to support and maintain the product
- Getting great public relations karma from giving back to the community. Of course, the other motivations are short-term training, documentation, and consulting dollars from the community.

You also have to consider the following:

- Do you own the right to distribute the source code of your product?
    Many third party components let you distribute compiled versions of libraries but do not allow you to distribute source code.
- Have you analyzed the source code tree that you have to make sure that your code came from where you expected?
    Code analysis tools can be quite handy here. The same kind of due diligence that you perform before incorporating an open source project should be performed before open sourcing one of your own.
- Are you going to empower your competitors? Could a potential competitor use your code against you?
    If so, make sure that you choose the right licensing scheme to mitigate these potential outcomes.

Building and Maintaining a Community

Will open sourcing your project lead to greater interest, more ideas, and more innovation? Who will work on your project? Do you have the staff to maintain the community including the bug trackers, forum responses, and source code management? You have to ask yourself the reasons why the community will work on or support your project. What is in it for them? If it is not compelling, they will quickly abandon the project and move on.

Being Part of the Community

The health or vibrancy of any open source community is only strong if the community gives back to the project. If you receive significant value from an open source project, it is in your best interest to make sure the project thrives and can continue to support your needs. As such, there are several roles "good" community members will perform to benefit the project. These include:

- Check-in your bug fixes or improvements to the project
- File detailed bug reports (preferably with fixes)
- Document the product features
- Evangelize the project by including it in future brochures or press releases. Extol the virtues of the project on other forum web sites.
- Write up successes and post or blog about them actively
- Attend open source community events
- Donate financially to the project and/or help get them funding or press
- Participate in Beta cycles and provide early feedback to the alpha, beta, or release candidate drops
- Give attribution in your About box or another appropriate location to the projects that you are using

What If you Lead a Commercial Open Source Development Team?

How is running an open source team different from running a commercial product development team?

- In a pure open source company, you likely have written the project code yourself to help you achieve some goal, and then decide to offer it up to the community (for the reasons above). But growing a community responsive to requests for assistance and features bug fixes requires one to become attentive to that community. At the same time, it requires that you create a pool of other code contributors from the pool of users.
- In a commercial open source company, it is a lot like wearing two hats. You have to grow the community who are your potential future commercial customers! You have to be active in the project community and provide them with the tools, feedback, and software to

make them successful. At the same time, you may have commercial or Pro versions of your software that require more formal processes, including formalized QA, certifications, and commercial documentation.

How do you measure success?

- If you are in a commercial open source company, the measures of success for your project are not only inclusive of the metrics above for selecting an open source project, but also the financial metrics. These include bookings dollars, number of licenses sold, upgrades, and documentation sales.

Stories

I was an early skeptic of OSS. In fact, it was not until 2002 when I started dipping my toes into the world of open source and to be clear, it was dipping one toe... very gingerly. As a pragmatic, frankly, it was hard for me to imagine why people would code for free when there is so much money to be made. When I noticed that many of the programmers who "volunteered" are mostly doing this to "learn", my skepticism could not help but increased.

My first toe dip into open source was, you guessed it, on non-critical systems specifically JUnit and Cruise Control. We did not just like it so we standardized on it and they were better than practically anything out there, commercial or otherwise. With that experience out of the way, when the engineers proposed the use of Struts as our MVC layer, I was more amenable to it, although still leery because Struts will become the core of our critical web application system. Ultimately, we did green-light Struts since it is a relatively thin layer of code and that the code is clean enough that if we needed to "fix" something, we could do it without much effort. But of course, we also did a lot of testing— functional testing, code profiling, and then performance testing— before we launched it. Over time, we ended up putting in a few enhancements or extensions to the basic Struts and the system worked wonderfully, with or without the extensions.

Other than being free, there are a few more benefits from using OSS. The rest of our technology stacks at the time was commercial software including Oracle, BEA WebLogic, Java, Solaris, IBM MQ Series, and TopLink. Compared to using these other systems, using Struts was like a breeze of fresh air. First, we did not have to negotiate pricing, which alone could normally take weeks. Second, the licensing is free to use anywhere, so there was no need to make sure the use was legal and to keep track of how many CPU licenses were run or, alternatively, having to manage license keys. Third, when we encountered issues like bugs, we did not need to call Technical Support who would take days to get back to us, who then would take a few more days to escalate to the expert support, and who then would take a few more days to escalate to developers.

With OSS, all we needed was to trace down the code, find the issue, fix it, get it reviewed by a second-pair of eyes, test it, and deploy. An alternative is to send it to the Struts community and often someone had a fix for it or the community would put out a fix within days. The overall turnaround for a Struts bug fix was normally within days, as opposed to weeks for commercial software. And when we needed to add enhancements to Struts, all we had to do was to... do it. With commercial software, there would be a feature request process, a waiting period, and your feature request may not even get approved and in the mean time, you would have lost weeks or months waiting.

With these experiences, I became a convert – like a born again. You would think everything else we did would be using OSS. Not so fast! Unfortunately, the establishment, specifically the Operations department, was "not quite comfortable" with OSS. In particular, they asked whom should we blame if something went wrong? Now you see why IBM is making money hand-over-fist supporting OSS and so do a whole host of other vendors like RedHata and Novell; it is all about the blame game and the CYA game. Back to our establishment then, since many OSSs just did not have a credible support structure (someone "prominent" to blame) and our establishment just did not agree to "operate" without it, we still found it hard to push through many OSS projects.

Does the establishment have a point? Yes, it does. How good is a piece of complex system such as OSS when there is no one to stand behind it? This has always been the argument against OSS, like mine was during my early skeptical days. As a matter of fact, many OSSs are written by developers as a process of learning, contributed to the open source society, with little plan to support the system long-term. Which leads to the main point about using OSS: It should NOT be a religious approach and experience, but should be a pragmatic one. Each OSS needs to be evaluated carefully before being adopted.

6. Managing Up and Sideways

How is becoming a VPE different from other kinds of Engineering Management? A lot of it has to do with the nature and style of communication. As an engineer or a mid-level engineering manager, one usually works on solving technical problems while being managed by someone who is interested in a solution to those technical problems. All of this changes the moment you reach the VPE level, or its equivalent in a larger company. All of a sudden, there is no one else who is interested in the technical problems and it is up to you to make sure someone on your team is addressing them. In fact, everyone outside of your organization is interested in business or financial problems and you will realize that your main role is to translate between business discussions and technical discussions. This is one of the hardest things for techies to learn since understanding what the VP of Sales wants is a different problem from understanding what your engineers need. Each of them communicates in a different style and has different concerns.

For you to be successful, you have to relay the concerns of each team member to the other, applying appropriate mediation. Here is a practical example: Suppose one of your responsibilities is managing laboratories full of equipment and you have a team that manages that equipment. The team's concerns will revolve around the kind of equipment being added and the levels of service required. The business viewpoint on this will be if your team is managing the capital spending reasonably and if the energy and facilities costs impact your ability to invest in a new product. This exemplifies the continuing need for senior managers to always up-level their discussions.

Managing always entails setting expectations and avoiding surprise. Communications regarding what other organizations expect— explicit or implicit— from your engineering organization are necessary in delivering satisfactory performance and results. While the first and second level management in Engineering is about performing to the expectations of superiors, at the senior management level, it is about delivering what is needed by peer organizations. While the ultimate objective is to deliver a salable product, each peer organization such as Sales or Finance needs the product to satisfy certain constraints and attributes that are important for mutual objectives. It is paramount to get this clear and to address gaps in feasibility against expectation earlier rather than letting them crop up late in product delivery.

In the following chapters, we will look at the finer points of communication with the rest of the company.

6.1 Politics

Politics defined

Simply defined in the dictionaries as "the practice of responding to conflict with dialogue", the term "politics" has many negative connotations that come from situations where people try to manipulate a situation for personal gain at the expense of others. However, as the definition states, all situations where one responds to conflict with dialogue is a form of politics and generally, the alternatives to dialogue are worse. Thus, engineering leaders must engage in politics to resolve the inevitable conflicts both within Engineering and between Engineering and other departments.

Where does this political conflict come from? There are many interpretations but one of the best is:

> Politics = Humans' self-interests and what they do to push their agendas

At best, self-interest means someone's perspective given their role and responsibilities in the company. At worst, it means someone's personal goals that may not benefit the company. The critical skill of politics is the ability to understand someone else's interests, goals, and motivations. For example, if you know that the VP of Marketing is interested in an increasing Internet traffic number, you will build political power and support by helping them meet their goal. With your understanding that your boss, the CEO, wants to look good to the board members, you can help by praising the CEO in front of the board and by helping them with their presentation. There is a fine line between being supportive and "ass kissing" and everyone has to determine what they are comfortable with. However, the point is that you also have your own self-interest and political skills are an important tool toward achieving those goals.

Politics and Social Skills

Young engineers will often be quite idealistic and will hope that all decisions can be made purely on merit without considering politics. They can feel frustrated and become cynical when they see decisions being made that are not purely "technically correct". Their first inclination is to quit and go to a company where there is no politics, but those who try will find they can never completely escape politics. To advance your career in management, you have to move beyond this viewpoint. Many times, you will find yourself in a good company with good prospects but stymied by the inept. Learning to neither flee from nor simply get in conflict over such a situation and to gracefully outmaneuver one's "obstacles" is a major management skill. Positively applying politics is about how you resolve conflicts without ruffling feathers or at least not feathers that matter.

Now, how far do you go? You should personally draw the line by making sure that what you are helping them to do is in line with the company's goals and is for the common good. For example, helping the VP of Marketing get more traffic certainly helps the company. Helping your boss look good with the board will help him push through various agendas— such as budgets— that will eventually make your company more successful. This will certainly not do any harm, as long as it is truthful.

Listening Carefully: Ineffective Communication vs. Real Political Problems

Sometimes, political problems are caused by communication misunderstandings, rather than real underlying problems. Interpersonal political situations can generally be categorized into one of the three following scenarios.

- **Misaligned objectives**
  People want different things. This is most often worst when one party has a personal objective that is not aligned with the company's objectives. However two individuals can have misaligned objectives and yet both have interests aligned with the company. Honest dif-

ferences in opinion about what is best for the company can often lead to political disagreements.

- **Misset expectations**

  Implied promises, broken promises, and disappointments can all lead to distrust. If this happens once, the parties can usually address it fairly easily. However, if it becomes a pattern of behavior, the relationship breaks down because of the distrust. For a company to function, people have to be able to rely on each other. When this doesn't happen, a wide variety of dysfunctions can occur.

- **Real misunderstandings**

  These pertain to honest mistakes in terminology, idioms, and colloquialisms. This can be common when teams are composed of many members with different first languages. Differences in culture and communication style can also lead to misunderstandings.

If you are in conflict with someone, it is important to listen closely and find out what the other person wants, which is not always what they are saying. Try to respond to their underlying needs to gain their cooperation. One model for diagnosing and dealing with these problems is the notion of crucial conversations. A crucial conversation happens when three things are true. These are:

- There is disagreement.
- There is high emotion.
- There are high stakes.

The absence of any one of the above means there is no crucial situation or necessary conversation. But, if all three are at work, you have to look out! This is when reason sometimes gives way to emotional reactions, quick rash actions, not well-considered options, and an underappreciated analysis of consequences. In such a critical situation, one must be very aware of the conversation as well as the goal it tries to accomplish. Addressing the "issue" or the "content" in a crucial conversation is pointless because the two participants do not trust each other and their relationship is likely at a low point— if not terribly damaged already—when all three of these conditions occur. Thus, in such situations, it is necessary to address the relationship and mutual "safety" first, before returning to the "issue" or "content" that gave rise to the conversation. This is a very superficial treatment but interested individuals can find good references on *Crucial Conversations*.

Politics and Competition

Most people in a company will usually try to cooperate. However, when there are some scarce resources— be it in funding or promotions— about which there is competition among multiple contenders, then there will be politics. People may want to influence who gets a choice assignment, who wins out in reorganization, who gets some extra headcount, who gets a certain promotion, and who does not. This will happen in the nicest companies since it is only human nature. The worst political problems even at good companies tend to occur when there is an incompetent or corrupt colleague who is in your way. You need to be prepared. Many times, the head of Engineering is unskilled to do political battle, since we are often "left-brained" people who believe in innate fairness and who often do not have the articulate and polished verbal communication skills of a Sales VP or Marketing VP. It helps to develop your communication skills to avoid becoming a victim of politics.

Be Patient

As long as the company is good overall, inept people tend to be removed after a while. Often times, an idiot will go away on their own without your intervention. If you can deal with your own frustration, time can be on your side.

Stay Calm

No matter how irritated you may be at what some other person or group is doing, you need to consider the long-term implications of both their actions and your response. Make sure your response reflects your long-term gain, even if that involves biting your tongue in the short run.

Remember that no matter what happens, everybody is going to live in the end. At the end of the day, most work issues are just a game that sometimes you will win and sometimes lose. You have to learn how to identify the concessions you can make and negotiate them upfront if they are not critical for your goals.

Make Sure You Have Your Back Covered

You have to ensure that you have a solid backing from your superiors. Understand and align with their strategy. Build alliances to implement company strategy more effectively. You want to be the good guy, not the bad one and you can do that by building teamwork and by working together.

Read the Landscape Around You

Understanding the motivations of others will help you pick the fights that need fighting and let go the ones that you can compromise. Many times, political battles against you can go for months undetected. After getting surprised a few times by condemnation or criticism that apparently comes out of nowhere, it is important to be well-attuned to the subtle political signs. There is no substitute for asking your boss as often as possible for positive and constructive feedback (written if possible). In the end, it is a huge leverage in your favor if the CEO has your back.

Keep Your Nose Clean

The most effective way to withstand politics is to have your own house in order. If your organization is running well, meeting objectives, communicating well with other organizations, and adapting to business climate, then this is the strongest possible base from which to withstand "politics". This is, however, not a surefire method since others can still undermine by "redefining" the objectives of engineering organizations in such ways as to cast doubt. For example, when the organization was hitting product release milestones with predictability, a CTO still managed to deliver the "engineering isn't spending a high enough percentage of its time coding" bomb into the CEO.

The Importance of "Spies"

One of the challenges of being in a position of power is that individual contributors will often be reluctant to tell you the whole truth especially if others are saying something about you behind your back. A colleague will often be very friendly and cooperative in front of you but is preparing to stab you in the back when you are not looking. Therefore, it is a good idea to cultivate relationships with trustworthy folks on your well-connected staff who hear the gossip and are willing to pass it on. Regularly chatting with these folks can keep you appraised as to what is going on. There is no substitute for good intelligence.

Speak Softly and Carry a Big Stick

Getting involved in emotional conflicts with others is bad. If this happens to you, you have to ensure you always keep the high ground and maintain a professional, helpful, and cooperative demeanor throughout. Even as you plot your opponent's destruction, you never want to give the impression of being anything but a good corporate soldier. Consider this story below:

> I recall only two times in my career getting down to an actual shouting match with one of my peers. He was late with a milestone I was depending on and he would take absolutely no constructive criticism at all. Looking back, there were cultural differences that likely invoked the shouting on the part of the other person and for me it was a humiliating and a non-professional display that is more common in other cultures. You need to practice during your day checking your goals and motivations. An important aspect of diplomacy is to think ahead. Remember that you cannot take a comment back once it is made. One of the best ways to navigate in politics during a confrontation is to be firm but also give your opponent some ways to back off without being humiliated. You should never underestimate the effects of hurting somebody publicly. If you think ahead, chances are you can reach a positive outcome with less damage. One of best lines about diplomacy says it all: "Diplomacy is letting them have your way."

Build Effective Strategies

Armed with patience and good intelligence about your opponent, you should utilize your good standing with Senior Management and

Leading and Managing in Silicon Valley

superior grasp of company strategy to devise programs that gradually isolate your opponent until they are forced out. These techniques work best against colleagues but cautiously can also be applied against immediate superiors provided one has sufficiently good relations with the next higher management level. Another strategy is to simply complain upwards and not down or sideways. This works well in the military but it may have mixed results in a corporate environment.

Politics on One of Your Teams

If you have two team members who are in the midst of a political battle, there are several techniques for managing the conflict. Some of the basic conflict management skills that you can use include:

- Getting each person to document their issue in writing
- Find an unbiased and professional mediator, ideally someone from HR
- Keep working at it since success may take several meetings and interventions

Politics in Other Teams

If a company is healthy and only a few people have issues, you can win. However, it may be hopeless if the entire organization becomes politicized. A key sign that it is time to consider leaving a company is when company politics are pervasive and self-serving. You could be smart and dedicated with your work but there may be subversive biased trend working against you. You may be the victim of some unspoken culture of personal bias. Another sign is when you have confronted the political issues with others diplomatically and have worked to help others meet their goals yet your status still does not improve.

Signs When to Leave When Politics Dominates

Companies, especially in the early years, evolve and change over time. Thus, even if the company you work for was not excessively political when you first stepped in, one day you look around and find yourself in a totally political environment. Here are some warning signs to consider:

- Communication between managers, especially senior managers, is not honest and open.
- Many people in the company believe that decisions are made more on "who you know" than on merit.
- Executives trust their private sources within the department more than the official channels.
- Decision-making and corporate goals become increasingly opaque.
- It becomes increasingly difficult and awkward to explain corporate decisions to your staff.
- Your boss has been hopelessly brainwashed by politics and is no longer listening.

Advanced Reading on Politics

Sun-Tzu's *The Art of War* remains one of the best guides in outwitting opponents, political or otherwise.

Story #1

I was recruited into my current company to do a similar role as I had in my last company. However, once I got here, I discovered that someone else was already doing the job and, thus, I was given only a secondary role. I soon realized though that the other person was truly incompetent and had already made many enemies. He was also very defensive and he often tried to engage me in nasty disputes, copying the entire other executive staff on the e-mails. Having been through this sort of thing before, I kept my cool. I discovered that others were just as annoyed as me with the public e-mail tirades so I simply ignored those. I then built up my connections with our Executive Vice-President (EVP) and clearly laid out what I could do in this role if simply given a chance. I also completely turned around the two teams I had inherited from this person and made sure everyone was aware of the change. Then, lo and behold, after a year or so, the evil person who is already under pressure quit and I volunteered to help the EVP manage the then orphaned teams. Soon, reorganization was announced and I got all but one of the affected teams. Showing good progress with those and keeping up a critical dialogue with others concerning the remaining team, I was also able to get it too reorganized and a significant slice of it added to my team. In the end, I was able to obtain and rebuild practically all of this person's organization, without ever getting in an explicit conflict with anyone. Fifteen years ago, I would never have managed this because I would have been so disgusted by this person's behavior that I would either have walked away or overtly quarreled. But, nowadays, I find quiet negotiation behind the scenes and a multi-year time frame can defeat many such obstacles.

Story #2

I was co-founder of a company in the mid-90s. Six months into the startup, my co-founder stepped down voluntarily so that the board could find a "professional CEO" (he had been replaced at his first startup and was just trying to facilitate this for the same VCs). It took about a year for a replacement to be found, during which time both the CEO (my co-founder) and the board were primarily concerned with the CEO search. So the other VPs and I were effectively running the company. After the new CEO arrived, he spent about a year relatively hands-off, allowing us to do as we had been doing. However, once he decided to actively influence the direction of the company, he brought in an external "marketing" consultant who did not take the time to understand the current business and started recommending we change our company direction and product suite. We had been a personal document management company and he recommended we start another whole product suite around completely unrelated Internet products. This happened at a time where I had injured my knee and was in the hospital for nine days and out of work for approximately three weeks. This was all the opening the consultant needed in order to radically influence the CEO's thinking. The company never recovered. No one was paying for Internet software in the '96 to '97 timeframe!

Story #3

      I was totally shocked to find a peer promoted to Senior VP (thus, becoming my new boss) while I did not even know my current boss was going to create such a position, let alone, promote a peer of mine with less experience. Afterwards, I could recall subtle signs like my peer collecting information and less frequent information from my boss. Thus, reading these signs of interpersonal communication is very important for career development. Likewise in budget battles, when cutbacks are being made, politics can run against you unless you actively promote yourself and your team's effectiveness not only with your boss but with your peers as well.

6.2 Getting and Asking for Help

Introduction

- Is asking for help a sign of weakness?
- Is asking for help a way of team building?
- Is asking for help spreading the credit?

Are you reluctant to ask for directions when lost? The kind of people who enjoy leading can sometimes be strangely reluctant to seek help. A lot depends on the kind of help you are asking for and the way you ask it. For example, if you go to your CEO asking for more funding, you will often be asked "20 questions" to justify the increase. A more palatable way to phrase the request for help would be to say, "Marketing has defined the product requirements in such a way that our current staff cannot meet the target date".

But wisdom is a lot about knowing what you do not know. As a senior leader, you are called upon to be able to form valid opinions on a huge range of topics. While it may be expedient in the short run to pretend to know the things you do not know, it may come back to bite you in various ways. We can think about getting help in these three areas: beyond engineering, within engineering, and in the context of managing your own time.

Of course, if you are reading this book, you have already taken the most important first step!

Issues with Serious Legal or Fiscal Implications

If you find yourself having to make a call on a difficult matter with obvious implications from HR, whether it is in legal or financial standpoint, getting the right expertise, either in-house or from outside, is important. In the long run, showing people you take the prudent and thorough course for the company is better than pretending to know all the answers. If you feel that you may be personally liable for such an issue, it is wise to seek outside legal advice. The company will often seek to take legal action that is in its best interest, potentially at your expense.

In preparation for this, you should maintain strong relationships with your CFO, corporate counsel (internal or external), HR director, or their representatives. While this is easy to ignore because of the distractions of pressing engineering matters, cultivating those relationships will provide you not only the help you need, but also, in many cases, the awareness to realize just when you need help.

Getting Help Across the Organization

A situation sometimes requires you to exercise some leadership alone, particularly if the issue is a matter entirely within the jurisdiction of your own group. But problems often arise in product developments that cross boundaries. For example, the company might make more money if it bundled the product differently but that would require different licenses and the product to be modified in some way to support those differing configurations. Solving such problem requires collaboration across multiple groups from Engineering, Marketing, Finance, Sales, to Support. Building good coalitions within the organization is an important skill for an engineering leader. Since such situations often involve considerable "turf" problems, working in an open and inclusive way and being generous with helping others, builds good organizational karma in the long run even if it is not always in the short run the most politically expedient.

Getting Help from Your Own Organization

While you may feel uncomfortable asking for help from peers or your CEO, there are tangible benefits when asking your own team for help. It is often a sign that you trust them to be open enough about key issues and that you are confident in their ability to help you resolve the issue. However, you need to know your team well enough to make sure this does not backfire on you. You should not try this with a new team until you understand the dynamics. Simply asking for help often results a "brainstorming" process within the team that generates team-building benefits, assuming it is managed correctly.

Managing Your Time and Scope

The hiring process is considered in one light an act of "asking for help". You can view the proper alignment of talent and resources for the best likelihood of achieving objectives as *the management task*. Having the chance to identify a resource or skill that could be leveraged is a management opportunity that affects that likelihood. If that opportunity is not taken, then abiding by the current team may be non-optimal.

This can take multiple forms. As the organization scales, you obviously need additional help from the team to accomplish your mission. But beyond that, it is also useful to recognize when it would be valuable to seek outside consultation, either from consultants or perhaps from your conversations with your customers or vendors to gain insights. Being open to outside help and ideas is an important part of keeping one's thinking current and avoiding the tendency to breath one's own exhaust for too long, particularly after a longer tenure in a position.

Fast growth in an organization creates different dilemmas. You may be very used to undertaking certain tasks as part of your work. But with a growing organization, suddenly, there are new demands on your time and you need to let go of some of those tasks. You may also find entirely new classes of tasks appearing in your organization as it grows. Those will require staffing. Recognizing that you need to ask for resources to delegate key tasks comes with the territory. Asking for enough resources properly is an important part of being able to scale one's own role.

The budget process is also another form of asking for help. Regardless whether you are driven to a top down budget number or not, creating a realistic bottom-up budget as a way of asking for help is always important. It creates a snapshot of resources— going on record—required to be successful and provides a CYA mechanism if a project starts to unravel.

<u>Talking to Peers</u>

At times, you may just want to talk to someone in your own shoes. You may only be the one doing this job in many organizations so there is no one in your office who you can talk to about your problem. Therefore, you need to cultivate connections to professional groups. Getting the opportunity to network and discuss topics of mutual interest is exactly why the authors of this book came together in the VPE/CTO COP. There are plenty of groups of this kind around. The big benefit in joining such groups is that you are able to exchange ideas with people that have similar positions.

6.3 Managing Your CEO

Introduction

This chapter is about getting along with your boss, whether they are a CEO at a small company or a general manager of a business unit at a larger company. We will look at how to work with your boss as well as what happens when you have to participate in the search for a replacement.

Communicating with the CEO

You are expected to act independently, if you are in a senior management role. Since your boss most likely is not that technical, it is easy to leave them out of the loop of many tasks they will not be especially inclined to hear about. This can get you into big trouble! It is crucial to keep your CEO aware of the tasks you are doing as well as the risks your actions cause the company to assume. You should as least conduct these reviews quarterly to avoid surprising your CEO. If something suddenly goes wrong, there will be many questions like "Why wasn't I kept in the loop?"

Part of the value of the VPE is as a member of the strategy team. You want to be engaged with the management team so there is a good shared understanding of how the company's roadmap aligns with your investments, actions, and assumed risks. You should remember that it is the company as a whole— and not the individual— that is making these investments and taking these risks.

Beyond this, if you fail to communicate properly, the management team may not understand and appreciate the value of the investment being made. This can lead to awkward questions as to why your company is spending X millions on this product.

Having a Sponsor

Generally, in any company, you need to have a sponsor who will cover your back when there is trouble. This is often your boss, the one who hired you, simply because you would not have been hired in the first place without that sponsorship. Due to the tendency for companies to reorganize, however, you may find yourself without a sponsor. In this case, you will need to either develop a new one or evaluate your political solution for viability. Most of the authors have had the experience that without someone who believes in you, your position will, sooner or later, no longer be viable. Note that the sponsor does not need to be your boss. One of us identified their VP of Sales as a good choice and worked to develop a relationship with them. In this situation, having someone representing customers greatly strengthened the VPE's hand. On the other hand, if the new CEO abruptly brings in his own team, you know you have lost your backing.

Hiring Your Next CEO

There are three types of situations when you 'hire' your CEO. These are:

- You are seeking a new opportunity and you want a company that has an enlightened CEO.
- You are in a company that is seeking a new CEO.
- You are being merged with or acquired by another company and their CEO will run the new combined entity.

In the first situation, you have more freedom as you can easily decide whether or not to join the company. Unless the CEO performs the role for the first time or is relocating from a distant state or country, there are usually direct or indirect connections you can leverage to get an assessment of the CEO 's track record and working style, before you accept a position (See the background check section below). You can start first with your potential peers who work for the CEO by simply asking them "What are they like to work for?"

In the second instance, you have the opportunity to work with your current team members to evaluate the new CEO candidates, although it is generally from the limited exposure of one to two interviews. Unfortunately, in most of the cases, the VPE has absolutely no visibility into the CEO selection process, let alone, have any choice in the matter. This is not unique to the VPE; most C-level executives are completely surprised when a CEO is suddenly replaced with a new and unknown CEO. Frankly, the board usually has specific and often unstated reasons to replace the CEO and except for rare circumstances, such as keeping founders or key investors in the loop, they don't find it wise to expose the search to the other executives. If you cannot accept the chosen CEO, your options are limited. You could complain to the board (at least those members you have a rapport with), resign, or stick it out hoping the new CEO will either change or will not survive. What you do depends on your belief in the company as well as on your career potential and the compensation system.

Last, in the third situation above, the VPE generally will have no say in the matter. At best you may be a part of the due diligence process and have some visibility into the new CEO's style. If your perceptions of the new management are extremely negative and other peers in your company share your view, escalate this, ideally in unison, to the current board. Many M&A deals have been successfully killed by a lack of "chemistry" or "culture" between the teams. However this is obviously a risky strategy.

Note that in a large organization, the VPE can work for a SVP or EVP rather than the CEO, or equivalently a director can work for a VP; however most of this material still applies in all those cases.

Background Check

Regardless of the situation, you should work your personal network and discover as many things as possible about your potential boss. Fortunately, almost any CEO candidate worth considering will have a searchable history that can be found on the Internet. You can use LinkedIn to talk to others who have worked with the candidate. Get a sense of how they handle problems, stress, difficulties, people, boards, and customers, and discover both their strengths and weaknesses. You can also find in your network some people who went to the same schools the candidate attended and check their alumni updates. Sometimes, this provides insights into proclivities unavailable elsewhere.

Interview Techniques

Assuming you are lucky enough to be part of the interview and selection process, ask very specific questions regarding the difficulties they experienced at other companies. Ask specifically about their relationships with prior engineering leaders and the way they cope with different management styles. See if they respond thoughtfully or give canned responses. Validate your opinions with others who have previously worked for the candidate. It is important to determine if your potential boss will rely on you or if they will have a tendency to micromanage your department

<u>Problems You Can Encounter</u>

Technically Illiterate CEOs

Aside from having the knack for buying and selling, the other main ability required to be a successful businessman is to be nice with people. Many rich and successful executives are masters of these skills yet are technically relatively illiterate. This can be both good and bad. The best executives are those who understand their limitations and intentionally hire a brilliant engineering leader like you to serve as an interface to the technical world for them. In this case, your main challenge is to communicate the business implications of your work. The CEO will be uninterested in your algorithms but they will want to understand tradeoffs between customer functionality, budget, and time-to-market. Success with this kind of CEO depends a lot on your ability to grasp the implications of your choices on the company's business plan and on your skill to state them very succinctly.

Such people also are often focused on relationships since they prefer working with people they know and trust. In this case, spending the time to cultivate your relationship with the CEO and building mutual trust is very important. In some cases, this can take years. This is all about understanding their needs and figuring out how to meet them. Once they understand that you are there for them and have helped through a number of tight spots, they will respect you and will listen to you even when your message is more difficult.

On the other hand, there is also a dangerous kind of technically illiterate CEO who tends to confuse PowerPoint with reality and does not understand their own limitations. These people stand out because they do not understand their own limitations. These CEOs merrily acquire companies with technically incompatible products and then wonder why the companies are hard to integrate or why the other product had to be completely rewritten. They will make demands completely oblivious to any sense of how much effort might be required. The most common scenario where you will encounter this is when your company gets acquired and the new CEO has made their reputation in some entirely different field and brings the same confidence to an area they knows nothing about.

Working with this kind of CEO is likely to be very stressful. If you are very lucky, you might succeed in gradually educating them. This is more likely to become a losing struggle. If you push them too hard, they may simply cozy up to a more sycophantic person who will tell them what they want to hear. Anyone who does not understand their own limitations is very dangerous and is likely to make serious strategic mistakes in other areas too.

The key test of which kind of person you are dealing with is determining up to what extent they are willing to listen to you when you deliver hard messages. How these messages are received will depend on how well you have tuned your message to your CEO's style and on how well you have cultivated your relationship. If you are still not being listened to properly after all your efforts, you then need to decide if this is where you still want to work. If you think the CEO might get replaced (i.e. the company that acquired you might itself get acquired), then simply being patient might be the answer.

Different Agendas

Understanding what the CEO's goals are is also important. Engineers are often idealists who are very committed to making their products as perfect as possible in the long run. If your CEO is building a company for the long run, then this approach will work but they may have entirely different goals. The CEO might be interested primarily in selling the company quickly. In this case, even if it hurts in the long run, they may want to be very tight on development spending to make the financials look better. In extreme cases, they may want to compromise quality to quickly produce impressive-looking product in the hopes of selling it quickly and making it someone else's problem. This approach was common during the dotcom boom and is not unheard of today.

Another example for this is if the company is adopting a "cash cow" strategy of intentionally not spending money on a product to simply maximize short-term returns. If the CEO knows they are a short tem hired gun, this may also influence their thinking. This is particularly the case if the CEO has been brought in by the investor to replace a previous CEO who was not doing so well. Once you get the sense that the new CEO is just in for the short-term, you should be particularly attentive to what their true intentions are.

Being Successful with Upper Management

In general, understanding your CEO's needs and meeting them are the keys to a successful relationship with your CEO. This goes both for what you do as well as how you communicate it. Understanding those needs will help make you successful but in the end, you have to decide if those needs correspond to what you want to do. If your CEO wants your product line to be a "cash cow" and they are squeezing costs, you need to decide if that is what you want from life. If it is not, you need to think hard about your alternative plan. Not having your own interests aligned to your CEO's is not a recipe for success.

6.4 Managing Your C-Level Peers

Introduction

Working with your C-level peers and managing your relationships with them are among the important skills an engineering executive must develop. As you move up from individual contributor to first line manager and then to engineering director, working with people in other departments and building productive relationships become two of your major tasks. As the head of Engineering, your relationship with your C-level peers becomes absolutely critical. All companies have friction between departments. How well a company manages this has a lot to do with how good the relationships between the top-level people in each department are. While it is common for individual contributors and lower level managers to vent their frustrations about other departments, the engineering head must draw a fine line between showing empathy with their department and not contributing to the discord between the groups.

If the engineering leader does not have a strong working relationship with the VP of Marketing or any of the other business groups' VPs, it is harder for the respective staff to get along. In the worst case, when the department heads cannot blend well, the environment then becomes extremely political. For instance, if the VP of Business Development does not get along with or is unwilling to talk to the head of Engineering, the tendency will be to try to gather information using another way. Back channels for communication flourish and an Engineering manager may find that some of their own staff is conveying information to other departments to gain status or curry favor. As unpleasant as it can be at times, the VP or C-level executives must find a way to work together and communicate.

Where Are They Coming From?

Starting in the interview process, you need to get to know these folks and see and understand where they are coming from. You want to know everything about their background, motivations, and habits:

- Learning how each peer wants to communicate and collaborate
  - Their pets
    - Pet projects
    - Pet peeves
    - Pet employees
  - Are they in for the long haul?
  - Are they in for a specific check box on the resume?
  - Are they in for a specific milestone?

- Where are the current alliances?

The more you can understand how the world looks through their eyes, the easier your adjustment will be in terms of your communication style and approaches to working with them. This will help you grasp who to work with and who to work around. Knowing what they likely want from you will help you in reaching accommodation with them. If you can meet their needs, then they are more likely to meet yours. It will also save you from potential political dangers as well as from being used as a pawn for someone else's political struggle.

Setting the Ground Rules

When you start with a new company or when your new key C-level peers start, establishing the ground rules for interacting upfront is highly recommended. It is also important to understand the expectations, goals, and management styles of not only the CEO, but also all of your peers. Many of them may not— or pretend not to— have the faintest idea how engineering product development cycles are managed. As a result, they may have completely unrealistic expectations from you and your team.

The following are the things you need to make clear to the entire executive staff when you start:

- How engineering commitments are made (the process)? This includes both timing and budget commitments.
- Who among your team members is authorized to make a commitment on behalf of you and/or the Engineering team and for which product/s?
- What is the confidence level in these commitments? (i.e. 80 percent or 90 percent confidence)
- What are the assumptions and risks associated with the commitment?
- What is the cost of changing an existing commitment and inserting a higher priority task?
- What is the difference between an estimate and a commitment? It comes down to the degrees of planning. It takes more planning and effort to create a 90 percent confidence schedule versus a 50 percent confidence schedule.

In a perfect world, you also have a similar set of "agreed" ground rules from the other peers you depend on (i.e. Marketing for product requirements, Support for customer issue information, and Business Development for partner and OEM commitments). Nobody likes surprises and these ground rules will minimize surprises when discussing deliverables both to and from your team.

6.5 Managing Your CTO

Working with the CTO

The role of the CTO at a hi-tech startup can be considered in many ways as the company's most critical role early on. It is the CTO who typically takes an idea and turns it into a prototype that is "sold" to the investors and/or marketed to prospects. The CTO transforms a company vision into reality. However, they often get an unwarranted reputation for being prima donnas and difficult to work with. Nevertheless, you should note that there is plenty of "attitudes" among other executives as well.

While the title of this section states "Managing Your CTO", the reality in many companies is that the CTO may report directly to the CEO or president, so a better title for this chapter may be "Working with the CTO". When it comes to working with your CTO, it is important to look at a typical CTO job description and how it interfaces with the VPE role. Below is a sample set of CTO responsibilities, taken from Sevin Rosen's VC Web site.[18] Naturally, all of these topics are also things that the VPE might wind up doing themselves!

- **Lead the execution of technology strategy for technology platforms, partnerships, and external relationships**
  The VPE should coordinate with the CTO the creation of an architectural specification— primarily authored by the CTO and other senior engineers— that discusses technologies, critical components, interfaces, platforms, and directly addresses how the "product" will meet the current and future "product vision" of the company. The

---

[18] Sevin Rosen Funds, "Chief Technology Officer Job Description," http://67.208.32.43/openee/upload/CTO%20job %20descriptiona.pdf.

VPE may facilitate and support the CTO's running of a regularly scheduled architecture review board to ensure timely resolution to key architectural or design issues. The VPE must ensure that the Architecture Committee has an adequate representation from Engineering and that time is allocated to support it. While the CTO will typically evaluate a partnership from a technical perspective, it is the VPE who must look at the big picture, including staffing implications, product integration, and timing.

- **Build and manage a top-flight technology team and oversee Research and Development, as well as Project Management**

    The CTO should be actively involved in all senior engineering hires. The CTO's affirmative vote is considered mandatory at many companies before hiring key engineering talent. The VPE may work directly with the CTO to perform targeted searches for such engineers.

- **Provide visible leadership for the company within the technology community**

    The VPE must place the CTO in the position of last arbiter of technical decisions or feuds. At the same time, the VPE should ground the CTO in reality and ensure that technology, process, or tools decisions are pragmatic and realistic. If the CTO reports to the VPE, the VPE must ensure there is adequate time allocated to external visibility (i.e. papers and conferences).

- **Anticipate and react to major technology changes to ensure the maintenance of company leadership in the competitive landscape**

    As the CTO figures out the next direction to go to, it is the VPE's job to figure out the issues and costs involved in implementing this task.

- **Establish technical standards and ensure adherence**

    Having the company directly involved in the creation of standards can have huge business benefits by positioning the company's products as reference implementations of the standard. Working on standards normally involves both collaborating with the CTO on a policy level and providing engineering resources to do experimentations and ensure compliance in the products.

*   **Discuss technology directions with customers**

    In many companies, an important role of the CTO is to explain the company's technology to customers. Companies often understand that products evolve over time and that when they buy into today's product, they want to make sure that after five years, the product should have grown with their company and is still meeting its needs. These conversations with customers can be a valuable source of feedback and the VPE should listen closely to the results.

Why Companies have a Separate CTO and VPE

Companies vary in how they handle these two roles. Some companies have only one of the two roles staffed, others have a single person with both titles, and still others have a separate person in each role. While there may be historical or idiosyncratic reasons for this, there are some generalizations that can be made.

Companies that view new technology as a strategic part of their business often have a CTO since the C-level title will attract senior executives. This is especially true if the company has other C-level titles, such as CFO, CIO or Chief Marketing Officer (CMO). If a company has multiple C-level executives but does not appoint one for technology, then this is an indication that they do not view research and technology as central to their business. Some companies do not have any C-level titles except for the CEO and perhaps a CFO. In these cases, the lack of the CTO title might not imply technology is less of a priority. On the other hand, the existence of the CTO title is sometimes purely historical or based on the desire to hire a specific candidate.

The lack of a CTO does not mean technology is not important to a company. But as we have mentioned above, a CTO's job is more strategic and involves more research and, generally, the use of cutting edge technologies. Technology can be important but if constant evaluation of new and cutting edge technologies is not critical, then the work is more of a combination of management and technology and this is usually the VPE's role.

While a CTO may or may not manage a staff, the VPE always manages the Technical team, organizes the work, and drives product schedules. In companies where both roles exist, the CTO will usually do the strategic work and future product roadmaps, while the VPE will usually manage the team and the interactions with Business. While there are some times when the VPE reports to the CTO, it is more common for both to report to the CEO. However, the VPE is expected to take technical direction from the CTO.

The most common point of friction between the CTO and the VPE is that the CTO would like to control the nature of the technology within the company while the VPE has schedule and product responsibilities. The classic problem sets in when the CTO would like to change to a new cutting edge approach but the VPE, on the other hand, would resist because of limitations in resources or risk to revenue or schedule. This natural dynamic can be healthy, if both sides understand each other's roles and if they work well together.

One common scenario in startups is that the founding technical leader is regarded both CTO and VPE and as the company expands, they split the role. Generally, the founder will retain the CTO title and the company will hire a new VPE. In this situation, the incoming VPE has the additional challenge of dealing with the fact that the CTO is a founder and previously ran the group. The key is for the CTO to realize that they are changing roles and for them to embrace this is by letting go of the responsibility that the new VPE will perform. Part of the new VPE's job might be to work with the CTO to help define this.

Initial Engagement with the CTO

In companies where there is a strong dependency on patents and formal R&D, the roles of the CTO and VPE are clear and reasonably well defined. However, as in many other companies, the CTO and VPE roles are often mixed. A classical scenario is a top engineer who launched the first product and as the company grew became more and more isolated and felt displaced. Managing a situation like that is quite a challenge because it involves sitting on the table and negotiating with the CTO about who is going to be in charge of each of the many facets of Engineering.

This is the type of negotiation that should be planned well in advance and ideally should be a collective effort among the CEO, CTO, and VPE. A key factor in managing the relationship with the CTO is clearly defining where you, the VPE, can help and where you expect the help of the CTO. This process sets the stage for collaboration instead of competition.

Here are some key questions to think about as part of this process:

- Was the CTO or ex-VPE part of the founding team?
- Replacing the CTO or VPE is a very different scenario than augmenting the team due to a perceived need on the incumbent team— very different dynamics
- If replacing, is the former CTO still present or now gone?
    - ➤ Either can be good or bad
    - ➤ Gone implies some expertise departed the company
    - ➤ Gone implies that you have a fresh opportunity to create the organization you imagine without having to answer to an incumbent executive
    - ➤ Present means you have a resource that can provide you context and be supportive
    - ➤ Present can also present a problem, in that the former may feel deposed and therefore, feel threatened by you

Anecdotes

Story #1

One of us was recruited to replace a founder or CTO. This fellow worker felt quite threatened and due to the reduction in responsibilities, he had ample time to lobby others to oppose the changes proposed by the new person (me). The problem was not with the CTO: the CEO never clarified the reporting relationship among the VPE, CTO, and CEO. He promised that the CTO would work for the VPE (me) when the VPE arrived but after the VPE arrived, he "left it for us to figure out", which was, in retrospect, an indicator that I should have exited the building right then and there. The CEO lost his job because he could not manage the CTO and therefore, when the company was sold, he was no longer the CEO. Someone else was brought in to fill that position, though the new individual added no value to the acquisition process. This diluted the founding CEO's value at least 50 percent.

Story #2

Since the VPE and CTO have overlapping responsibilities, it is very important to have a good working relationship. Who has what responsibilities and what should happen if there is a difference should be clarified. It is also important that the CTO maintains the ability to pilot projects, help with designs, and specify and tune the architecture. At one company, the VPE did not want the CTO to be able to pilot projects or have his team create the designs for new components. He did not want this because the engineers felt like they should be doing all of it. I believe that managing that expectation is the VPE's job. It is fine for the CTO to work with the engineers on designs. It is alright for the CTO to have a capable team that creates pilot projects. To help ensure that hurt feelings are not too much of an issue, I feel that rotating engineers into the Design team is a good way to cross train and let people know that they will have a turn as well. I also expected that the CTO's team should do the entire design or all designs. I think the high level pieces and major thrusts should be under the pervue of the CTO. It is also a great practice to make sure that there is open communication between the VPE and CTO and between Engineering and CTO. It is fine for engineers to ask questions about designs and participate in them as well as to help come up with refinements to the product line and refactorings. They need to feel free to participate. Otherwise, they will feel left out. If some people feel hurt and slighted or if some want to participate in the design and review processes more, make sure the CTO knows and understands this. The CTO also has to understand that person's skills and availability (or lack thereof). This will help both the VPE and CTO to manage the expectations of the engineer and help them further their career.

Story #3

Some CTOs who fail to perform technical oversight can cause problems for their respective companies. When working on an Enterprise Management Console, the design was not created in a way that would scale. The CTO did not have enough visibility or involvement to anticipate the problem that was coming. The architect kept most of the engineers on isolated projects. The first sign that there was a scalability problem was when we attempted to test the system on 35,000 servers. The system was implemented leveraging acquired third party networking technologies without fully understanding the implementation of those technologies and the consequences of that implementation. When the system was turned on for 35,000 servers, the resulting network overload took out the server and impacted network performance. Once we understood the problem, we had to re-architect the network communications, change the UI, and debug from scratch. This showstopper bug could have been avoided by having better oversight and questions asked early on in the project.

6.6 Board Relationships and Communications

Introduction

A board is "a group of individuals that is elected as, or elected to act as, representatives of the stockholders to establish corporate management related policies and to make decisions on major company issues. Such issues include the hiring/firing of executives, dividend policies, options policies and executive compensation. Every public company must have a Board of Directors."[19]

Board members are generally company founders, company executives, and major investors. Often referred to as "the board", they are supposed to represent the shareholders and thus, provide oversight to the executive team. While public companies are often criticized for having "rubber stamp" boards, there is at least a set of formal processes requiring board involvement. At startups, the board might be a polite fiction. Since board members represent shareholders, the board of directors at startups depends mostly on what sort of investment there is. Major professional investors like VC firms or private equity firms will generally want a board seat, however, Angel investors or small private investors are often not represented.

Understanding the nature of the board is important to a VPE because its strength completely changes company politics. A strong board will limit the freedom of the CEO and executive team and can even force the hiring of their own "pet executives". However, they can also balance the actions of the CEO and provide perspective to the management team. A

---

[19] Answers.com, "Board of Directors," http://www.answers.com/topic/board-of-directors.

good board should provide guidance and be a sounding board to the executive team. Working for a company that does not have a good board or whose board is uninvolved is a very risky job for a VPE. This is especially true with a startup where lack of a good board can mean a CEO running a dictatorship.

Another key issue for the VPE is the kind of exposure they get with the board. An involved board should want to hear from the executive team and not just rely on the CEO. The board oversight role is severely hampered if a few executives are filtering all their information. It is worth asking this when interviewing for VPE positions because it provides insight into the company's workings.

The VPE-Board Relationship

Defining Goals

In managing board relationship as a VPE, it is important to first determine your goals. Both you and your CEO will usually have at least one same goal: to manage board expectation and avoid surprises. However, you probably have secondary goals that a CEO or founder does not have. Your secondary goals may include gaining positive visibility or networking with a well-connected board member.

Once you establish your goals, your next step is to work it out with your CEO such that both of you agree on what types of relationship you can establish with the board members. Note that the CEO needs to manage board members very carefully so they may be somewhat hesitant to let you have a free reign. For example, if you give a different account from the CEO on certain sensitive problems in the company, trust would have been breached. This could lead to many different issues, potentially including termination of you or the CEO, which could in turn mean the demise of the company and possibly, your career.

Setting and Managing Expectations

It is important to standardize and agree on the process for setting release dates and content. Is the company "roadmap "feature"-driven or "date"-driven? Many companies have a train model that requires regular timely releases.

When dates are communicated to the board, what is the level of confidence? Should a percentage of confidence be applied to denote risk? Some of this depends on the CEO and on the company culture regarding "risk-taking". If the company culture including the board encourages healthy risk-taking, it is assumed that occasionally some projects and releases will fail to meet expectations. If not, dates and features have to be managed carefully. Gathering this "sense" from each of the board members during your interview process is always a great idea. If the board is not aligned on this strategy, it is better to play it safer and set high confidence goals and dates.

<u>What Boards Want to Hear from a VPE at Board Meetings</u>

The typical VPE presentation to the board includes the following topics:

- Budget and hiring status
- Key organization changes (if any)
- Metrics update (charts showing bug trends (internal and customer), budget adherence, staffing, and turnover)
- Process improvement initiatives
- Major objectives and milestones (i.e. releases, projects)
- Status (schedule). . . major milestones only (no Microsoft Project Schedules!). It is best to include a comparison from the previous board meeting (if there is a change) to the original schedule.
- Risks and issues - What are you going to do to mitigate the risks and issues?

➤ One of the worst mistakes to make at a board meeting is to rattle off a list of issues and risks without proposing some suggested solutions or a plan to attack them.

➤ Another HUGE mistake is to blindside a peer in the board meeting and blame him/her for issues or impediments with your progress. This is the last resort if you have articulately advised the peer about the issue with advanced notice and in failing to respond in a timely manner or if you advised them AND the CEO that you will be bring up the issue at the board meeting.

Problems

Board Does Not Ever Meet with the VPE

This should not happen at a technology-driven company, even for an early stage startup. Presenting to the board is a good way for them to exercise their oversight and it provides the VPE with insight into the CEO's perspective. However, early stage startups that are not a technology play may have board meetings that do not include the VPE. This should be considered a warning sign regarding how much the board and the company as a whole values both technology and the VPE. It is possible that this is due to ignorance if the CEO and board are inexperienced and thus, it is worthwhile to discover their views on this. If the board does not ever listen to the VPE's presentations, then they are not likely to be of any help. One indicator of the board's perspective is whether the board is involved in the hiring decision or not. A critical executive hire should involve the board and it is not unusual for them to be part of the interview process. Board apathy over executive hires is a key indicator of a weak or uninvolved board.

Board Does Not Need an Update from the VPE This Month or Quarter

It is rare when a VPE's or other CEO's direct report can skip a board meeting, unless it was directly related to a specific large sales opportunity. Every attempt should be made to attend every meeting as this is for you own sake also. There is a lot that can be inferred from comments and questions made by board members during the meeting even if you are not presenting. Later stage startups like Round D and Mezzanine may focus more on a strict financials-based board presentation from the CFO or VP of Finance and cover Engineering and Development status on a rotating basis. In any event, the VPE should still attend every meeting and should not be excluded.

What to Present When the CEO Does Not Want You to Present the "Bad News"

If the CEO is hesitant to discuss bad news in a board meeting, there are ways to turn an issue into an opportunity. For instance, you are two months late with a major release and are drilling down on the causes. One major factor was related to engineering time required to win major customer deals by providing incremental and unplanned product features. In this case, you can offset negative news with positive ones but if you cannot do that, you have to make it clear that the bad news was a one-time thing and that the lessons were learned and the mistakes will not be made again. Ideally, you can point to process changes that have been made or identified to prevent the problem from recurring.

When it is Appropriate to Go "Skip Echelon" Directly to the Board vs. to Take an Issue to the CEO

This is a last resort scenario. You should only do this knowing that you are taking a huge personal risk with your own career at the company. The only legitimate reason for taking such action is an issue that presents a significant legal or financial liability to the company, which has not been addressed satisfactorily by the relevant parties or the CEO. These could include:

- Possible case of harassment
- Illegal accounting practices (i.e. SOX violations and revenue recognition)
- Intentional misstatement of serious company financials or metrics
- Misappropriation of company funds

If you continually find your proposed board slides filtered by the CEO before the board meeting, you have to be wary that key information may not be getting to the board. For example, if serious risks, issues, or constraints are not relayed to the board, there will be little or no tolerance for your project's failure later. It may be time to demand from your CEO an unfiltered presentation or, as last resort, go straight to the board.

When it is Appropriate and Necessary To Do This

In *A Simple Guide to The Basic Responsibilities of VC-Backed Company Directors* written by the Working Group on Director Accountability and Board Effectiveness, certain board responsibilities were mentioned. These include:

- Overseeing and promoting fiscal, legal, and ethical governance standards
- Identifying barriers to company progress and proactively dealing with these barriers

Failure to act in good faith can have serious adverse consequences to a director such as being exposed to personal liability for breaches of the duty of care or losing coverage under indemnification provisions or insurance policies. Likewise, an employee may face personal liability for inadequately exposing serious company liabilities at the appropriate levels. Another tenant of boardroom conduct is to avoid surprises. This would indicate that the best way to communicate this category of information is by writing directly to all board members in advance of a board meeting.

What to Do when Asked a Non-Engineering Question in a Board Meeting

If a situation like this happened, it is safest to defer the question to the appropriate functional VP. It is in bad form to presume authority for another department by responding to such questions. Place yourself in their shoes. For example, how would you feel if the VP of Sales responds to questions on engineering topics like staffing or budget? The possible outcomes are ripe for disaster.

What to Do when Asked an Engineering Question in a Board Meeting and Do Not Know the Answer

There is a strong temptation here to answer something, even if it is just a guess. Avoid this temptation. Answers to board member questions should never begin with, "I think it is something like. . ." If you do not know the answer, then the best thing you can do is to say you do not know but will find out and communicate the answer separately.

7. Other Responsibilities

Another aspect of the engineering leader's job is to interface with the various groups outside of Engineering. In the preceding chapters, we have already discussed Engineering's connections to Senior Management, Human Resources, and Support. In this section, we will look at the rest of the organization: Finance, Sales, and IT. We will also tackle certain legal matters, especially the protection of IP.

7.1 Working together with Sales

Introduction

Collaborating on sales calls is the most common scenario for the development leader to be working with Sales. In this chapter, we will look at the dynamics of these engagements. As we go through this, you should always remember the following:

- We each represent our company in every event, at all hours, and at any location.
- Listening is sales; bringing a customer's insight back to the company is a part of the selling process.
- Saying NO can be sales as part of maintaining credibility and not just saying YES to anything a customer asks for
- Know when to talk and when to shut up
- All interaction has a selling component since it is human nature to communicate and convey opinion and understanding!

Let us look at all of these in detail.

The Sales and Application Engineering

The Sales and the Engineering departments can have many different kinds of relationships with each other. This is especially true for highly technical products, which require Sales or Application engineers. In some cases, the Technical staff supporting sales reports directly to Sales and in other situations, they report to Engineering. Sales engineers will generally accompany the Sales staff on customer calls and be the technical contact for customer questions. Application engineers usually go a step further and help customers integrate or customize the product, as a certain amount of work will be done for free as part of the normal sales cycle. Companies often sell application work that goes beyond sales support. These Application teams might also be organized as Professional Services teams that can bring in significant revenue. In OSS companies, this might even be the main source of revenue When a brand new technology product is developed or for smaller companies, there are often no appropriate Sales or Application engineers. In these cases, the staff from Engineering may be loaned out on an ad hoc basis. When a client is important enough, the Engineering staff may work with the customer even if there is a dedicated Sales engineering team.

The Sales or Application and Support engineers are the primary customers for internal technical training and support. They are usually the primary technical resource for the customers, the Sales and the Marketing teams. These teams can be the best resource for getting customer feedback, finding good beta customers, and detecting customer problems early on. In larger companies, there are usually formal training sessions— sometimes, even internal technical conferences— where the locally based Support, Sales, or Application engineers get together for technical presentations on the new products and technology. Engineering will generally prepare the technical materials and give these presentations and it can be a good opportunity for the Development, Support, and Application teams to mix.

When the company's product is integrated into a larger system or is a platform for development, these companies then may have their own developer's conference. The Support, Sales, or Application Engineering staff usually leads these developer conferences but the Engineering Development staff will usually be involved, especially when there are major new products.

Professional Services and Engineering

Professional Services is related to Sales and Application Engineering, only more focused on post-sales activities. There is often good overlap in the skills of the Engineering and Services teams so it is possible to share resources, which is generally good for the business as a whole. However, this may not work well for you unless you have good working relationship or understanding with the VP of Professional Services.

The basic cause of friction between Engineering and Services are the different performance models. Professional Services has a very concrete measure: hours billed. Performance means maximizing billed hours. By comparison, Engineering has fuzzier measures such as product delivery and product quality. Performance means maximizing these fuzzier measures. This creates a basic inequality between you providing a resource to Services, where measuring the exact negative impact on your organization's perform- ance is difficult, and Services providing you a resource, where Services can make very accurate claims on the cost of the loaned resource. The outcome you want is for both organizations to show they are maximally utilized. This can happen if you have established a good working relationship with your peers in Professional Services.

Sales and Engineering Working Together

Conflicts in the working styles between Sales and Engineering are some of the classic stereotypes in the corporate world. People on both sides have humorous anecdotes about the antics of each group. The conflict is rooted in the difference in the types of personalities that tend to go into each area as well as the goals and problems each department face. People who work in Sales tend to be more extroverted and people- oriented. Their goal is to sell the product while their problem is that their customers are busy and usually, only a small fraction of the customers they talk to will actually buy. Sales people are judged by the amount they sell and, in many cases, are compensated by commission so they are highly motivated to improve their numbers. Sales teams therefore tend to opt for simple clear messages to try to persuade the customer and keep the sales process moving forward. Normally, their concern about working with engineers is that they will want to be so accurate that they dilute the message. For example, Sales would like to say something like, "Fastest in its Class" and they would be worried that the engineers will weaken the message with complex qualifications and details such as "Fastest in its Class when comparing fully loaded systems and using standard hardware and not including special customizations".

Engineers, on the other hand, tend to have less extroverted person- alities and are judged on the quality of their work and their attention to detail. Engineers tend not to make inaccurate statements that lead to more complicated nuanced statements, rather than the bold messages that aid Sales. Engineers on sales calls will cringe when the Sales staff makes blanket statements and their great fear is to be held accountable by the client for an incorrect statement made by Sales. Engineers are also frequently worried that they will have to end up building a product to satisfy bold statements made by Sales.

Story #1

Early in my career, I was on a sales call where the Sales team described the product as "real time". Since it took over five minutes to generate an image, Engineering questioned them after the sales call and the Sales person said it was real time on a different scale: it was "geological real time".

Story #2

There are also times where it is helpful to be an engineer in sales discussions. Frequently, the technical member of the team is asked to validate if the performance will be acceptable. I have been on calls where that was a huge concern for the prospect. After a while, I started asking for concrete information to compare it against and found out that the competing solution was a large room full of filing cabinets. It is nice to reassure customers that your solution will meet their needs. That is something that only a technical person can do when there are technical concerns regarding scalability, performance, security, stability, and the like.

As a development manager, there may be times when you are expected to work together with Sales serving important customers. Learning how to be comfortable in a sales situation and how to instill confidence in the Business teams that you can work with them are crucial for an engineering leader. One way to think of it is that you are working as part of Sales and the Sales person, usually someone senior, is taking the lead. Unless they say something that is completely wrong and harmful, your role is to support what they say. It helps to have some pre-meetings with Sales so you know what to expect. It is also beneficial for them not to say something that will come back and harm them. Most of the time, this preparation will smooth out any problems.

Most of us with an engineering background focus on the "how things work" aspect rather than on the problem that any specific feature is going to help the customer. During the sales process, the goal is to present a compelling story about the product. As a technical manager, you have to understand the Sales person's rationale behind it and help him/her to present it. In most cases, the technical folks' role is to make the customer feel confident that the group or company has expertise to solve that particular type of problem. Generally, the technical manager should focus on giving just enough information so that the customer becomes comfortable with the solution. The manager should avoid giving too much information because it could limit the Sales person. It is common for the most important items to the customers during the initial contact to change after some time and to be substantially different during the final phases of negotiation. It is also important to work with the Sales person ahead of time and figure out how technical the various parties are and how deep the conversation should get technically. In early conversations, questions about issues like performance, scalability, and integrations should be answered at a high level with an offer to dive deeper in further discussions. With our tendency to build things and solve problems, CTOs and VPEs frequently want to dive deep into technical details during any customer discussion. Find out ahead of time if this is the time, place, or right audience for this discussion.

The nightmare scenario is when a high level Sales person will knowingly make false or misleading statements to try to get the sale and your presence as the titular head of Engineering is at least a tacit backing of that statement. In those cases, what you need to do is to consider two major things. First, you have to determine if the misleading statement will cause any danger or harm or if it is just a meaningless hyperbole that will not influence the final decision anyway. Second, you need to consider your own personality and whether you are comfortable in a role that can expose you to this behavior or not.

Story #1

In the early '90s, I was running a very successful program with competitive wins spanning more than six years of bids against the likes of Lockheed, Martin Marietta, SAIC, SRA, Harris, PRC,

Westinghouse, GE, GTE, and Ford/Loral. In one particular Request for Proposal (RFP), the competition came in with a bid approximately 50 percent of what we bid and what we believed we could build the system for. I refused to lower our bid because I knew we could not deliver for less. Six months after the project kicked off with the competition, the customer canceled their project and signed with my original bid because the competitor could not deliver and the customer had enough evidence by then.

Story #2

In the mid 2000s, I was on an early sales call with a prospective customer. During the conversation, there was a question asked about integration. I started digging deep into integrations, options, possibilities, what they needed, and how it would be coded. Unfortunately, this was not the right time for this discussion and these were not the right people. During meetings with individuals who lack enough technical depth or business use case depth, it is more important to answer at a higher level and not getting pulled into the weeds. Getting pulled into the weeds derails the pace of the meeting and may prevent critical discussions from taking place. While we did win the deal, it is important to understand when it is time to say, "Yes, integrations are really easy with our product and are quick to implement" and when it is time to discuss in great detail what will be integrated, how it will be integrated, the exact timing... Keep asking yourself, what does this audience need to hear? Do they need a high level overview, general confidence and experience, or detailed instructions and how-to's?

Story #3

Shortly after my arrival at QQQQ, I was asked by the Sales VP to provide one of my engineers in support of a conference call because that engineer had experience with SAP integration. When I approached the engineer about this, he said he does not have any such experience but had only looked into it briefly in a previous exploratory exercise. Since no provable credible experience would be gained by making the engineer available, I thought to keep him on his current task and take the call myself, because in Siebel deployments, I had been aware of how other Siebel-SAP integrations had been attempted and what the various possible technical approaches could be.

When my first utterance was, "Well, we have not actually done this, but here is how it could be done. . ." I was immediately stifled by my Sales VP, and he and his staff answered "yes" to all the customer's questions. At debrief, he calmed down a little bit but he was still strong in his position that "whenever the customer asks, the answer is YES". I was clear that I was not going to misrepresent either the company or myself. The Sales VP said there is always an opportunity to correct the response later but one should always answer affirmatively at first. I basically have a serious problem with Sales people who sell this way. In a separate data point, after a very nice customer go-live congratulatory e-mail, the customer highlighted four bullet points. Three were very positive, but one expressed documented disappointment that despite our RFP response that we employed no Java applets in our UI, we did in fact employ Java applets in our UI. There was no room for misunderstanding on this point; it was clear case of misrepresentation. On both cases, I told the CEO that I would no longer support sales tactics following such practices.

7.2 Budgeting Practices

Budget

A budget is basically a plan for expected spending. A well-documented budget typically details expected expenditures by category for a one-year planning horizon by month. It is a process that directly follows a rigorous company vision and strategic planning cycle to ensure that spending is aligned with the company directives and go-to-market strategy.

Budgets are useful in two major ways. For upfront planning, a budget allows you to understand how much your proposals will cost and to determine if you can afford all the things you want to do. As the year progresses, you will check your actual behavior against the budget to validate progress. A budget also provides a check-and-balance if the execution matches the original plan or, in the event of a significant deviation from the plan, what the fiscal implications of those deviations are. It tells you if you are hiring fast enough, too fast, or are behind in your hiring. It lets you know if spending in various categories is already out of control and is impinging on your ability to invest in other things. It also tells you how much headroom you have to take on new projects. Therefore, budgeting is a dynamic process involving planning, monitoring, and iteration.

We will start by discussing the simpler budget exercises found in smaller companies and then move on to the portfolio management practices found in larger organizations.

Components of a Budget

Budget Calendar

Budgeting is normally done on an annual basis. You have a planning period, typically a fiscal year divided into quarters. The fiscal year might be the same as the calendar year or have some other start date set by

your company. You usually prepare a budget at the beginning of the year
and then you update it quarterly.

Spending Categories

The following are some of the categories likely to account for most
of your budget:

- **Salary**
  Salaries are usually the largest single expense for a hi-tech company. These costs will be fully loaded including taxes and benefits,
  which usually run less than 40 percent over the raw salary. It also
  includes projected salary increases. This category can fluctuate tremendously depending on your usage of offshore labor. It is important to budget using the fully loaded cost of the employee to keep the
  cost to the organization as realistic as possible.

- **Outside services**
  Contractors and outsourced work will show up in the outside
  services line of your budget. If there are multiple significant outside
  services planned, multiple line items would be appropriate.

- **Depreciation and leases**
  Your capital equipment gets charged to you in 1/36 increments
  assuming a standard three-year depreciation or lease cycle. Thus,
  your new capital purchases and leases hit the current period only
  marginally and most of your costs in this item are for the equipment
  you purchased in the past. Generally, leases are preferable to purchasing capital goods because they allow you to immediately expense the item. However, leases may require a lot of paperwork,
  financial due diligence, and force you to return the item after three
  years or buy it outright at that point, which can be problematic if the
  economic life span of the item is more than three years. Make sure
  that you negotiate a good buyout option in all of your lease agreements. The cost of the item at the end of a lease is critical. Many
  times, you may not be able to locate a particular network switch
  three years later and you will have to pay a premium for an old item
  that you may no longer use.

- **Expensed equipment**

   Expensed equipment includes anything that cannot be capitalized. This includes small purchases, leased equipment, and equipment having a short life span. Hardware prototypes are excellent examples of costly goods that need to be expensed rather than capitalized. Sometimes, collecting small purchases together into larger purchases will change them from an expense to a capital equipment purchase. Buying a peripheral with a cheap computer may help it transition to the more advantageous capital expense category.

- **Allocations**

   In most large companies, you will be charged an allocation for shared services provided by other groups, typically facilities or IT. These allocations need to be watched carefully because, for example, if you hire a number of people and need a new building, the sudden increase in facilities allocations can crimp your budget when that building comes on line.

- **Cost of goods**

   While directly unrelated to expense items, an engineering leader has a key role in projecting any licensing or cost of goods components from a third party or bundled software. As an example, we include more than five third party products bundled with our product suite. Finance must account for the COGS related to these third party expenses. If you are paying for licenses of external software or services that are used in your product, keep in mind that future or expanded versions of that product or service may require payment increases.

- **Travel, communication, and other categories**

   There will be some smaller categories to cover things like travel and communication expenses. Amusingly, since most of the big expenses in an engineering organization are fixed, the few variable areas like travel will prove endless bones of contention far beyond their capacity to influence the overall spend. It is important to note that the travel arrangements for your troops send a clear message to them of your valuation of their worth. If you have a town car waiting for them at $45 they will feel more appreciated than taking a taxi at $25. The net difference in the travel expense is very little, but the difference in the message that the engineer receives is huge.

The Budget Process

Good budgeting is properly considering the prioritization of spending categories. Does it make sense to spend more than $100,000 for a software test automation tool? That could hire several people overseas. What is the right tradeoff? Besides dollars, what does it do for you from the perspective of quality, timing, agility, and ability to quickly diagnose problems?

Good budgeting is also properly considering the prioritization of risk. Budgeting needs more "management reserve" in areas of risk and uncertainty. You should not lock yourself to a tight dollar quote on items you have not previously had experience with. There is nothing more fun than getting that $2 million computer delivered only to realize the power needs to be completely rewired and you need a structural engineer to make sure it will not fall through the floor.

Building a Budget Spreadsheet

An engineering leader will prepare and present a budget in several situations that include:

- Planning phases of a budget before approval
- Review of last year's budget and comparison with new budget
- What-if scenarios during funding negotiations

A good approach used to build a budget spreadsheet is to divide the spreadsheet into two tabs: assumptions/formulas tab and the budget tab.

The assumptions tab will hold the items used in the calculations and their respective values, for example: cost/1U rack space, rent $/sq foot, and depreciation of equipment in years. It will also hold items with basic formulas like discount formulas based on usage. For instance, if you rent two racks, you would get a 10 percent discount. There will be situations where the quantity of an item depends on the quantity of another. For example, the number of employees multiplied by the office space. Documenting your assumptions is a way to document your model. The second tab will hold the main area of the budget spreadsheet and will use the other tabs as inputs for the local items. This simplifies the maintenance and facilitates reuse. It also allows the budget area to be formatted for presentation instead of data entry. Each line will contain an item and for each item, there will be 24 columns corresponding to "quantity" and "dollar amount" for each month.

Once the basic infrastructure is in place, it is simple to tweak the numbers in order to match the requirements and availability of funds. There will also be situations wherein based on the monthly expenses, one could calculate the present value of funds needed, considering a rate of return of some type of investment. Organizing the information using tabs allows the manager to create several different views based on the audience and assures consistency of the numbers presented. Another important point is that by describing the assumptions and metrics used, the manager can report on improvements on productivity and use of new technology, and the like.

It is also important to note the source of the numbers that are used in the assumption. Did the cost per rack numbers come from one particular agreement that is already in place, a quote, or industry average? Noting where and how you acquired the numbers will save you a lot of time later. If some of the numbers came from the IT team in an email message with a particular subject and date, you can note those in the tab and make it easier to find later on. There is almost nothing more frustrating than reverse engineering numbers only to find out that you just found the numbers you started with.

Setting Targets

The first step in most budget exercises is setting a target. Generally, in most companies, Engineering's cost is set to be some part of revenues. Early on in the planning process, the executive team will create a revenue plan for the coming year, forecasting 29 percent growth, for example. Then if Engineering is fixed to 14 percent of revenues, a little multiplication will yield the target budget for the next year.

If you are a Round A company, spending 40 to 50 percent of total company spend on R&D is common. As the product matures and the company reaches Round D or later, R&D expenditure will normally drop to 15 to 20 percent. This, of course, depends on both the industry and product but if your R&D expenditure is out of line with these guidelines, then it behooves you to negotiate a higher percent of R&D ratio with the CEO or board. If your company is under investing in R&D they will be paying for it over the next few years or until the end of the company. Moreover, if your company happens to be over investing in R&D be prepared to justify why the current investment levels are needed or be prepared to have them lowered to industry expectations.

Building the Budget

Budgets are best built bottoms up, looking at both ongoing projects and at the proposed incremental projects for the coming year. The existing spending is typically known very accurately from reports from Finance department and one has to apply some heuristics for the upcoming spending. Naturally, the sum of the new and old spending will exceed the given target. That is when it is time to think harder about the roadmap to figure out what you can afford! At the same time, you should definitely avoid padding budgets. All projects grow to fill the available resources. Thus, it is best to be very realistic in your planning and have a mechanism for adjusting the budget as conditions change.

How One Quarter Affects the Next Quarter

Finances are normally tracked on fiscal quarters. One of the challenges is that when you hire many people late in one quarter, they will only have minor impact during that quarter. However, their full impact on the budget shows up at the beginning of the following quarter. Likewise, mappings between headcount and budget are never completely linear even within one budget period because the timing of when during the budget period you hire and the rate at which you are able to hire will make a big difference.

Effect of Seasonality on Budgets

A business growing quickly may not grow equally fast at all times of the year. This can result in one quarter showing far more growth than the next. This can pose a challenge to Engineering budgets because if the budget is at all tied to revenues, it may be subject to somewhat unpredictable fluctuations. To control these, you may want to divide your budget into a fixed component that is sure to be funded and an optional component that you fund if the resources allow it. It is also important to have discussions with the management team to make sure that you are able to hire effectively and retain key employees. It is alright to have cycles, but if you hire to the average case, you should be able to keep your employees through the down quarters.

Allowances for Salary Changes

In planning the budget for the next fiscal year, you need to provide a reserve to cover the cost of salary increases and bonuses. Considering this is especially important if you have offshore operations where the existing employees may routinely get quite large pay increases for retention purposes. Furthermore, you also need to consider the salaries of new hires that, in a market with increasing salaries, may cost more than some of your current hires. In that case, you also need to remember which part of the pay range for a given grade you are likely to place new hires to and build that into your budget assumptions. While you can often bring people in the lower part of the range, you may have to pay at a premium price if you are competing with other companies for the top talent. That can make a significant difference in your budget, depending on the number of people hired. This is a good time to think of star performers hired below their appropriate pay scale. Many hot young engineers will come in on smaller salaries to prove themselves and then expect, and earn, far higher than average raises.

Currency Fluctuations

If your operations are international, you also have to factor in currency fluctuations. In many companies, international operations use separate accounts from the domestic ones and you have to think how to combine these separate accounts into a single budget. Your colleagues from Finance will usually guide you on what formula you will use to do this combination.

Monitoring the Budget

You should review your spending monthly as provided by Finance against your budget. In addition, there should be a quarterly review of the company's overall roadmap plan and that review should be connected to a review of the budget to ensure that they remain aligned.

Do not be Under or Over the Budget

Most VPs are measured and paid bonuses based on the actual spending under budget. However, too much under spending can have equally negative implications including not meeting the company priorities or roadmap wherein ideally, your actuals are at or "just" under the budget goals. However, there are occasional exceptions. For example, you are in the middle of a quarter and you have three open requisitions to fill. However, the sales curve is WAY behind the bookings curve or target. It would be wise to consult the CEO before proceeding with hiring, even though they are budgeted expenses.

Good and Bad Times

Creating a budget and staying on track when revenues are growing quickly is easy. While at TTTT, my budget was growing by about 300 to 400 percent per year for nearly four years. The challenge in that case is to hire solid employees quickly enough to meet objectives.

Cutting the budget in bad times is a harder story. Performing layoffs to meet a budget objective is the last resort. Some companies view layoff as an opportunity to cut weaker and non-critical employees. However, weak employees should be worked out in good times and bad. At some point, successive budget cuts without considering product focus becomes a vicious cycle: trim budget, sales drops, trim budget. If cash flow is the issue, additional funding may be necessary, assuming the business fundamentals are strong. This is where being an engineering leader takes some guts.

Knowing when to stand your ground and risk your job to preserve some crucial mass or morale in Engineering is a difficult line to draw.

Portfolio Management

As a company grows, the suite of products being built tends to become so large that it is very hard to tell how much is being invested where and what the actual ROI is. Budgets are usually built by department. As departments get bigger, it becomes very hard to track the components of the departmental budget. There is no easy way to separate projects from one another. Furthermore, pet projects become impossible to kill, staying alive year after year hidden inside of large budgets.

The way out of this is to institute portfolio management. A portfolio management system tracks the total set of deliverables from an organization and the spending allocated to them, both from a historical and planning standpoint. Such systems allow one to understand precisely how resources ramp onto and off projects, how much money is being spent at a given time on a project, as well as what the overall expenditure on a project is. Portfolio management systems are normally enterprise software packages that can be bought off the shelf from many vendors such as IBM or HP. These systems usually have two components: a data entry part and a reporting part. The data entry part requires setting up different projects and have managers add and update resource loading data regularly. Often, the system can also be used to do what- if analysis on the resulting data. The reporting aspect, on the other hand, provides a dashboard to summarize and analyze spending from various viewpoints.

Implementing a portfolio management system requires some cultural change since it forces everyone to do the clerical work to record exactly who is working on what and when. This involves tracking people, skill sets, and projects. It also provides different powerful analytic capabilities for the organization. Managers who are trying to assess if they can commit to a new plan can use the system to do resource analysis to understand if they have enough of each kind of skill set available at a given time to support the proposed plan. At a higher level, one can also understand if spending on each product is consistent with the return on those projects and drive appropriate investment decisions. Portfolio management comes into its own once a company has many mature products and is trying to balance incremental investments in them. The whole process is probably too heavy for organizations trying to do very rapid development in a high change environment. Unfortunately, few large organizations that would need portfolio management have the desire or ability to act that quickly.

7.3 Intellectual Property

Legal Matters

The company's corporate counsel and the entire legal department, for large companies, have diverse responsibilities. These are:

- Representing the company in litigation
- Ensuring compliance with applicable laws
- Reviewing all contractual agreements and legal or regulatory documents, both large and small, to mitigate risk and preserve the company's advantage
- Filing forms, paperwork, and documents to further and protect the companies interests (including patents, copyright, trademark, service mark, and incorporation documents)

This broad charter means that the lawyers will be involved, at least in the background, in many areas of the organization. Many of your interactions with the legal staff will practically be over terms of contracts for procurement or M/A, HR policies and decisions, or financial documents and policies. We have covered these topics elsewhere in the book under the relevant chapters.

In this chapter, we will focus on one very important topic. Generally, a hi-tech company's competitive advantage and, indeed, a good deal of its book value ("Good Will") depend on the IP the company creates. This IP by its nature is both proprietary and confidential. Protecting this property is critical for a number of reasons:

- Keeping trade secrets from competitors
- Keeping ahead of competitive companies
- Creating a revenue opportunity for licensing IP to others
- Providing a legal defense against patent infringement lawsuits

Generally, there are two main areas for managing IP: legal (i.e. patents, trade secrets, and copyrights) and security-related. Being closely linked, these two areas govern the right to access information and the ability to access information, respectively. Typically, you cannot defend challenges to your legal protection without showing a good faith effort at physical protection. On the other hand, your physical protection will never be foolproof enough to obviate the need for legal protection.

Legal Protection

There is a wide range of legal tools available for protecting IP including patents, trade secrets, trademarks, and copyrights. The exact details of these differ from country to country. Since the authors are engineering leaders and not lawyers, we will not go into great detail as how to all these things work. However, we will outline some of the key management issues.

Copyrights are generally assumed by many people. You actually have to file for a copyright on a given work. To do this a portion of the work must be submitted with the filing. You can either perform a representative sampling of the work or present a set of the first and last pages. One interesting thing is that you can actually delete up to 10% from the document you submit. This is intended to protect trade secrets contained in submitted materiel. If you have a model where an Open Source product and a commercial product are built from the same code base, you can potentially file one copyright for both and redact the professional code. One easy way to do this is a to use a browser and markup to make the font for text that should be redacted black text on a black background. You then print out the document and send it in. With a robust build system, this kind of document should be easy to create automatically. If you file for the copyright within 3 months or before infringement, then you can get attorney's fees and statutory damages. Please see http://www.copyright.gov/ or consult your attorney for more information.

Patents are generally the most important of the legal tools. Once granted, a patent in a given country allows its owner to control access to the topic of the patent for some period of time in that country. The classic advantage of a patent is that it allows the holder of the patent to recoup the expenses of developing a product by delaying the entry of competitors into the market and/or by licensing the patent to others for royalties. This mechanism has evolved over hundreds of years and still works fine in its original intended form.

The challenge is that modern technology has exceeded the bounds of what can be effectively described in a classical patent. This has two bad consequences. First, patent examiners cannot tell what a valid patent application is and are easily fooled into granting patents that are either obvious or non-original. Second is the litigation, either to prove that someone has infringed your patents or to defend yourself against infringement accusations, which is costly and risky to argue because it is difficult to get the judge and jury to understand what your point is. Accordingly, any situation that requires a patent to be litigated is a bad thing and must be avoided.

You need to remember that many companies use patents as an offensive weapon. There are two ways of doing this. First, criminals intentionally obtain patents on obvious ideas by fooling the examiners and then sue anyone who implements this idea. Second, companies with legitimate patents will accuse other companies, especially smaller ones, of infringing their patents simply to spook them into various kinds of concessions to avoid the threat of expensive litigation. There is only one effective defense against these problems: you need to have as many patents as you can possibly create. Then, when someone sues you, you can retaliate by counter-suing with one of your own patents. The threat of mutually assured destruction will often protect you against these actions. You need to have many patents because you may be attacked with multiple patents yourself and you need to find patents to which the other party is likely to be vulnerable.

The moral of the story is that your corporate counsel will be after you as an engineering leader to help them create the largest possible patent portfolio. The primary way to accomplish this is by creating a program that will encourage employees to identify as many patentable inventions as possible. This is best done with a highly public recognition program where employees receive financial awards, both for filing invention disclosures and for actually obtaining a patent, as well as abundant celebration within the company for doing so. For example, here are the rewards one of our companies provides:

Type of Award	Number of Inventors		
	1	2(Shared)	≥ 3 (Shared)
Invention Report Award	$500	$1000	$1500
Filing Award	$2000	$4000	$6000
Issuance Award	$2500	$5000	$7500
Multiple Patent Award	100 shares		

At that same company, the people getting patents are celebrated at company beer bashes and on posters in the hallways.

This serves a couple of purposes. First, by motivating people to participate in the patent process, you are helping create the arsenal of patents the company needs. Second, it encourages and rewards innovation and thus helps create even more IP. Aside from creating new patents, M/A activity is also a good source of additional patents.

Unfortunately, if litigation arises, you and your staff are in for a very time-consuming exercise. This explains why it is very important for you and your staff to carefully follow the guidance of your counsel on best practices around patents and patentable technology. In "Reality Check", Guy Kawasaki says, "It's highly unlikely that patents will make your startup company defensible, because you won't have the time or the money to do battle with a Microsoft-size competitor."

Patents should be filed as soon as the idea is created. In the US, the patent is supposed to be awarded to the entity that first invents an idea. If someone else files a patent for something that you created earlier, you can invalidate their work and/or still file for a patent yourself. In most of the rest of the world, the patent is granted to the first entity to file a specific idea. This is a very different process. Generally, if knowledge of a patentable idea gets outside the company and/or is disclosed, your odds of getting a successful patent filed go down. In order to protect yourself, provisional patents are very easy to file and do not need as many details as a full utility application. A provisional patent is like putting a stake in the ground saying you are going to protect an idea. You then have roughly a year to fill in the details and file to convert the patent to a utility patent and roughly 14 months (varies by country) to file in foreign countries.

In addition to the time of your employees, patents will typically take thousands of dollars in legal fees to file through the utility process. A sample cost would be around $5,000 if you do a lot of the work yourselves. To convert a provisional patent to a utility patent costs roughly $500 plus any legal fees. Filing a PCT (reserving the right to file in foreign countries later for 30-31 months) costs roughly $5,000. Filing in each country costs somewhere between $5,000 and $15,000. Foreign filing includes costs for in country lawyers, legal translation, and filing fees.

There are also legal requirements to maintain protection. For trademarks, you must go after any infringement of your trademark. If you do not, you loose the right to do so for similar infringements. For example, you cannot see someone using my company's name inappropriately in their advertising and decide to let it pass. Once that is done, everybody gets a pass. Patents, on the other hand, are far better at protecting the company and offer far more flexibility. Until the patent is issued, there is no liability and no protection. After a patent is issued, you can choose against whom and where you enforce the patent. There is no requirement to go after any specific case even to maintain the right to go after an identical use somewhere else.

Security

IP is not merely patentable. It is also a trade secret; that is, your proprietary source of competitive advantage and that property needs to be kept secret in order to protect this advantage. This means controlling access to your IP so that only authorized parties have access to it. Notice that both patents and trade secrets are, to some extent, mutually exclusive because the material in the patent is published (after a delay) and hence not a trade secret anymore once the patent is granted! To understand security around IP, we need to look at the following areas:

- Kinds of information
- Kinds of audiences for that information
- Techniques for protecting that information

Kinds of Information

A company usually has many kinds of information relating to its IP, which have different security requirements:

- **Public information**
  This is anything that is generally viewable, ranging from published specifications to patent texts after being awarded or published by the United States Patent and Trademark Office (USPTO).

- **Confidential information**
  These are the trade secrets that we want to control purely for competitive reasons. Strategy documents, internal memos, policy documents, audit results, procedures, and source code all fit within the confidential information category.

- **Secret information**
  This is the information we need to control for legal reasons such as financial statements, credit card information, medical information, personally identifiable information, customer's data, customer's IP, vulnerabilities in product or company security, or HR data wherein its disclosure to the wrong people would have legal or regulatory implications.

Part of properly managing IP involves clearly distinguishing these cases and having appropriate policies in place that are enforced consistently.

Kinds of Audiences

One of the challenges in the modern world is that there are so many constituents involved like:

- Employees
- Contractors
- Partners
- Outsourcers
- Vendors
- Customers
- Journalists
- Analysts
- Politicians
- Elvis

We may also want to differentiate these subcategories. This problem is complicated since simple rules for distinguishing among different groups are often blurred. A company can be a partner in one line of business and a competitor in another. A contractor might be in-house and almost like an employee or working elsewhere for a firm that also does business with one's competitors. Contractors also have a habit of working for multiple companies. Typically, when a company is small, these problems are minimal because there are a small number of collocated employees who are mutually well known and it is easy to define the universe. However, this becomes a complex problem for a larger distributed company.

Protecting the Information

As a company matures, the quantity of important IP to protect steadily increases. This will become an increasing concern for the CEO and the board. This will lead to pressure to implement various security measures. The challenge is that in any organization one of the main drivers of productivity is the free and open exchange of information. Your challenge as an engineering leader is to balance the need to mitigate the security concerns with the need to preserve the open flow of information. In many cases you may find it useful in concert with your IT counterparts to engage with a security consulting firm to do a security audit, both to precisely quantify the risks as well as to define practical counter measures. Without any claims to exhaustiveness, we'll outline some of common areas of concern below.

The first point is that your secrets remain secret only as long as you work at this and you only have legal remedies to the extent that you can show you are taking good faith efforts to protect the information.

There are two kinds of bad situations that can happen and you have to prepare for both cases. These are when:

- You expose too much information by policy (or lack thereof), thus, allowing the information to get disseminated.
- Someone intentionally bypasses your protection and outright steals the information.

The first level of protection is to have adequate policies in place. This means having clear rules as to what kinds of information are available to each class of individuals and how they need to handle it. The resulting policy will be a matrix describing rules for accessing, updating, storing, and transmitting each class of information, depending on the kind of individual. For example, employees might have full access to confidential information but a vendor only upon signing a non-disclosure agreement (NDA). You may choose to make certain classes of confidential information available only to certain classes of employees.

The second level of protection is to guard against malicious theft of information. There are multiple areas of risk here. First, a competitor might simply sneak into your office and make off with some data. Second is a disgruntled employee who might take a handful of information with them to a competitor. Third, your own people might inadvertently disclose information that they should not. Fourth, hackers might break into your network and steal the information. In a small company where you know everyone and trust them, these issues may not seem so real. But in a large company, they can become completely intractable. The challenges arise from the complex relationships with vendors and outsourcers in far-away countries with weaker legal protection. It often becomes very difficult to tell how trustworthy given parties are. It is also important to keep in mind that employees commit a large percentage of intrusions.

There are a couple of defensive steps to take in this regard. First, you need to make sure your whole staff is fully trained on your information security policy. It may seem obvious but engineers are by nature too gullible and often need to be reminded of the importance of being careful with confidential documents. Second, you must implement physical security in your facilities like locking doors or requiring badges. If you do not trust your staff particularly in remote locations, you implement measures like banning of laptops or disabling removable HDDs and writable external media. Third, you have to make sure all contracts with third parties clearly spell out IP protection and make sure that the third party takes full legal responsibility for protecting information you disclose to them. Also, be careful to only disclose to your less trusted parties what they need to know.

Another major area is network security. In a small company perimeter security may be enough, keeping outsiders out, and having the interior of the network wide open. In a large distributed organization this approach fails because with all the contractors, partners, and the like who have access to the network, the line between inside and outside becomes hopelessly blurred. In this case you need to focus more on protecting individual applications on a need-to-know basis. That also makes security more modular, by allowing you to address the network a system at a time.

At times you may find it impractical to fully protect a system solely by access control. In that case, especially in countries with decent legal protection, a good alternative to physical control is logging. Allow people freedom but log what they do. You can then study those logs including the logs of access to buildings and rooms, network logins, and especially source control access. There are good tools for analyzing and detecting suspicious trends in such logs. You must also keep the logs for a long time. This turns out to be a very effective way of detecting illicit behavior and having the logs makes for cut and dried cases the district attorney will be happy to take on. For example, at one company, a junior employee left and surfaced as a senior leader of another company offering a product almost identical to the original company's product. Examination of logs showed that in two weeks before leaving the company, he generated 1,000 percent of his usual traffic on the source control system. This was sufficient evidence to obtain a search warrant on his home, where the stolen source code was found. He was subsequently sent to jail for this.

Conclusion

Security matters can seem dreary next to the excitement of product development. However, if taken seriously, these can protect the company from potentially ruinous financial exposures. It is important to collaborate with both your legal counsel and your IT department to come up with good solutions. Remember though that they will always err on the side of caution and it is your job as a leader of your group to make sure you also protect your group's freedom and its ability to innovate without undue interference. Balancing these demands is part of the challenge of being an engineering leader.

7.4 Information Technology

Introduction

The Information Technology (IT) department is responsible for all of the non-development specific computing services in a company. In startups, it is common for the VPE to be responsible for IT. On the other hand, in large companies, the VPE needs to understand how to interface with IT. In this chapter, we will look at what the VPE needs to know about IT. We will start by giving an overview of what IT does and then look at how this matters to the VPE, depending on the scale of the organization.

Requirements for IT

The following are the three main drivers for any IT organization:

- **Operational**
  The modern company is utterly dependent on its computers to function. Thus, failure of IT infrastructure can have catastrophic implications. For example, most public companies transact a large chunk of their business during the last week of every quarter. If the financial systems fail during that time, the company may not be able to realize enough revenue to make its numbers. Accordingly, IT systems have to be up 24/7 no matter what. Guaranteeing this uptime makes IT departments inherently change and risk averse.

- **Legal**
  The modern company has to comply with numerous laws respecting security, privacy, and financial reporting requirements. This ranges from Sarbanes-Oxley to ISO 25001 to export restrictions. Compliance with these laws falls squarely in the realm of IT. This adds a great deal of complexity to IT planning processes.

- **Financial**
  In most companies, IT reports to the CFO and is viewed as a cost center. Thus, there is always a huge push to control costs.

The combination of complex legal requirements, high demands for reliability, cost pressure, and the ongoing demands for additional application functionality make managing an IT department a stressful affair, requiring a great deal of thought to achieve a good outcome.

What an IT Department Does

Generally, an IT department has to manage a physical infrastructure and a set of applications running on that infrastructure using a set of well-defined processes. We will discuss these later. In addition to what we discuss here, companies following the SaaS model have further requirements.

Infrastructure

IT is normally responsible for the company's entire physical infrastructure, sometimes excluding certain engineering specific requirements.

- **Data center**
  The IT department needs to manage the company's datacenters, ensuring adequate capacity, reasonable power costs, sufficient bandwidth, and decent geographic coverage. These can be either internal or outsourced.

- **Networking**
  IT is responsible for the company's networking. This includes external Internet access and links between company facilities. Key issues here are having adequate bandwidth, reliability, appropriate security, and moderate costs. For external links, this is a matter of negotiating reasonable rates for enough but not excessive bandwidth, with particular care needed for intercontinental connections.

- **Servers**
  IT needs to procure and operate the required hardware in the datacenters including servers, routers, switches, and the like. Key is-

sues here are achieving enough standardization to hold down costs and keeping reliability and service costs under control.

- **Storage**

    Modern companies require huge storage capacity, especially with legal requirements to preserve large number of company information essentially in perpetuity. Storage needs to be managed well, providing enough capacity and performance for demanding applications as well as considering backup and disaster recovery needs. Doing this cost-effectively requires differentiating between primary storage (where performance is paramount) and secondary storage (used for archive where cost is paramount). De-duplication is vital to reduce the cost of the secondary storage. Appropriate mirroring is required for redundancy and geographical performance reasons. Also, manageability is important to control the cost of administering large quantities of storage.

- **Desktops**

    Generally, IT provides and manages the desktops in a company. The key challenges are having a reliable and easy to support product, keeping up with evolution in the technology, and making sure the devices stay updated especially with respect to anti-virus software. A headache in many companies are arguments about how much leeway users are given over installing their own applications or making operating system modifications. More extremely, there are debates about the different kinds of computers such as the use of Mac's in a mostly PC world.

- **Printers**

    Printers are a special class of devices also falling under IT. Printers need to be provided and serviced. Nowadays, printers like copy machines are outsourced in many cases since it is a distinctly non-core competency in IT.

- **Mobile devices**

    The proliferation of laptops, Treos, Blackberries, and iPhones has created a whole new infrastructure universe for IT departments. Mechanisms for syncing these devices as well as for updating them have to be provided. For example, Treos require one's Exchange servers to be running the Good Mail server to sync the mail to them. At the same time, there are huge security issues because of the mobile nature of the devices as well as the inability to guarantee that they have been updated or backed up.

- **Telecommunications**

  Telephones used to be a separate entity, usually managed by facilities. However, with the advent of IP telephony, phones have often simply become another aspect of the network.

Applications

The modern organization requires myriad applications to function. Here are just some of the more common ones. Generally, the IT department in these areas is constantly pressured to provide new applications and functionality, while still holding to reliability and cost constraints.

- **Communication**
  - ➢ **E-mail**

    Most companies stop functioning without e-mail. In 99 percent of the corporate world, this means Microsoft Exchange servers. The alternative for many smaller companies is using outsourced web-based mail or open source solutions.
  - ➢ **Web sites**

    Most companies these days have one or more web properties and services. These are frequently maintained by IT.

- **Business applications**
  - ➢ **Accounting system (Finance)**

    The finance system is the most critical application. It must work as no bugs are allowed.
  - ➢ **Order fulfillment system (Manufacturing/Finance)**

    The order fulfillment application is generally the second most critical application. It basically tracks customers, orderable products, customer orders, and their fulfillment. The combination of the financial and order fulfillment system is commonly required to recognize revenue.

> **Sales tracking (Sales)**

In a company with a direct sales model, the sales tracking application is needed to allow management insight into the sales funnel, which is important for successfully predicting financial performance in the coming period.

> **Call center software (Support)**

The Call Center application is the lifeblood of the Support team tracking customers, their issues, and the resolution of those issues. This application is often directly accessible by customers as well.

> **Employee tracking (HR)**

The HR department needs an application to track all employees and their attributes, ranging from time off to salaries to the organizational chart. This application is usually a major tool for the employees too.

> **Business intelligence (Executive)**

Feeding of the other applications, the business intelligence system is critical for executives to get insight into key metrics in their organization. Without an effective business intelligence system, it would be very hard to build accurate forecasts of sales and finance.

> **Information management**

As the organization gets larger free-form data, as opposed to the structure data in databases, such as the financial or order data, it starts to become a large problem because locating the current data amid all the obsolete ones becomes physically hard to do. Also, security issues loom. At this point, it becomes important to provide information management solutions such as content management systems and Wikis to organize and track this kind of information.

Processes

Because of the high and contradictory demands on an IT organization, IT requires a stricter process model than a typical engineering organization. Processes in IT usually revolve around four main areas: service, security, data protection and recovery, and capital planning. The ITIL framework governs all of these.

- **ITIL**

  ITIL is an application of the CMMI framework to IT. It has been demonstrated that following ITIL is a best practice for mastering the myriad challenges facing an IT organization. For most teams adopting ITIL, the most interesting conceptual innovation is the careful distinction between incident and problem management. Incidents are the particular issues that require attention while problems are the underlying causes. The idea is that incident management is about managing stakeholder communication, whereas problem management is about fixing the problem. Separating these two often avoids much duplication and allows for more scalable problem resolution.

- **Service**

  The main interface to IT for most users is through the help desk. IT needs to support the infrastructure, provide training, and help with questions, problem resolution, and project management. Doing this accurately and cost-effectively requires thoroughly worked out support procedures and documentation including run books, knowledge bases, and a rigorously followed process infrastructure. Well-defined service level agreements for different classes of users are the most important. It also helps to hire people named Mordac.

- **Security**

  This has become a huge and complex space, which we can barely do justice to here.

  ➤ **Security policies**

  The company needs clearly stated and comprehensive security policies, usually governed by standards like ISO 25001.

  ➤ **Security audits**

  Policies and their application need to be regularly audited both for liability and risk management reasons.

  ➤ **Identity management**

Given the range of deployed applications, an effective single-signon system is required to enforce fairly robust passwords.

➢ **Perimeter control** – Hackers need to be kept out!

➢ **Virtual private network (VPN)** – Employees and partners need to be let in.

➢ **Anti-virus**

Viruses are far more catastrophic in corporate environments than at home because of the sheer quantity of systems that can be impacted. Laptop users who bring infections in-house are the bane of all IT departments.

➢ **Monitoring** – Networks and machines need to be audited for risks.

➢ **Document classification and retention**

Sensitive data needs to be identified as such and retained appropriately.

➢ **Access control**

Access to sensitive data needs to be protected for privacy reasons (i.e. HR and customer data) as well as for legal reasons (financial data).

• **Data protection**

Backups must be available of key data and restores need to work on demand! The backup and restore procedure must be regularly tested. If it is not tested, it does not work.

• **Disaster recovery and business continuity**

The 9/11 incident underscored the importance of making sure that the company can continue to function even in a catastrophic destruction of equipment as well as key employees being incapacitated. The disaster recovery procedure must also be regularly tested. If it is not tested, it does not work.

• **Capital planning**

To control costs, there should be ongoing assessments as to which functions should be done in-house versus outsourced, which equipment should be purchased and which leased; as well accurate plans should be made to forecast demand.

IT and Engineering

As you can see from the list above, IT has a daunting list of challenges. Furthermore, IT is very different from Engineering, even though they both deal with computers. Engineering is focused on high-speed development, high levels of changes, and a higher tolerance for risk. Since Engineering investments ultimately create revenue, cost is usually not a primary driver. Engineering organizations can also tolerate fluctuations in reliability better than the accounting department, for example. On the other hand, IT requires maximum reliability, tries to control change, and becomes very risk averse and concerned about cost. This creates a fundamental tension that the VPE should always respect and has to be aware of.

IT in a Small Organization

In a small company, it is common for the VPE to run IT. Given the complexity of the issues outlined, running IT can be a huge distraction for the VPE. The best advice that can be given for a small company is to outsource as much as possible. Using managed hosting services and SaaS applications can cut entire classes of overhead. Furthermore, since a small company has little information to steal, security is not that much of a concern. The problem starts when growth happens. Once the company grows large enough to have significant custom IP, security suddenly becomes an issue. There will be needs to tie together the applications. The hosted applications will not have enough extensibility. Now the real fun begins! You have to create your own infrastructure and manage it. Topics include:

- IT team size that is appropriate and needed
- Help desk support
- What restrictions are placed on end user desktops and laptops
- Central corporate file systems and storage
- E-mail
- Backup strategy – What gets backup when? Offsite storage?
- Reporting systems – Datamart/Data warehousing, Data collection
- Financial systems
- Security and access control
- VPN setup and remote access

- Ensuring IT co-exists peacefully with development and quality assurance
- Internal SLA and escalation policies

IT in a Large Organization

Once past the startup phase, IT quickly splits off from Engineering, acquires a CIO, and usually reports up to the CFO. At this point, the interesting questions for the VPE revolve around how Engineering best interacts with IT. The good news is that almost all the topics mentioned above are not your problem anymore. However, you will still wind up interacting with IT many times.

Setting up a Separate Engineering IT Organization

Once IT is on its own, Engineering should set up its own team to manage its computing resources, which can then be appropriately separated, both technically and organizationally from the corporate environments. This is the easiest way to provide Engineering with the services it needs promptly, without causing undo conflict with IT because IT will never be responsive enough.

Communications with IT

It makes sense to have a regular dialogue with IT. Since IT is usually overloaded with requests and is under-funded, most IT departments tend to listen to the squeaking wheel. With Finance and other back-office functions being the legitimate main driver with IT, they will often ignore Engineering needs. Constant dialogue can help work against this. Setting up standing committees to look at security and financial issues is also useful. Generally, it is best to let IT own the security issues and simply work with IT to understand how to apply their policies to Engineering while minimizing productivity implications of their policies. On financial matters, collaboration pays off a lot, as using standardized procurement processes such as negotiating volume purchasing agreements on standard parts can significantly cut costs.

End Matter

In the last pages, we have covered a lot of ground and the more we wrote, the more we appreciated how many different skills and areas of knowledge an engineering leader has to deal with every day. But for those who have the proper balance of craziness, intellect, people skills, and technical know-how, we think presenting a new challenge every day is a wonderful job. We mightily hope you have enjoyed reading our book and learned something in the process. If you still want to learn more, join us on the web at http://leadingmanagingsiliconvalley.com.

About The Authors

Marilson Campos

Marilson Campos has been leading the development of engineering products for the last 20 years. He currently oversees all engineering functions of the GlobalEnglish learning services and is responsible for the delivery of the company's product roadmap. Prior to joining GlobalEnglish, Marilson served as CTO/VPE for Fortune 100 as well as startup companies, including JP Morgan, ActiveTools, and TechSys, among others. He has spent his career developing organizations that create highly scalable systems utilizing agile processes. He successfully built several large-scale software products, including Cade.com.br, the largest search engine in Latin America, which is now part of Yahoo! His portfolio also includes a number of enterprise web portals and a wide range of e-commerce projects. He enjoys traveling with his wife and his two kids.

Leo Dagum

As VP of Information Architecture Engineering at Business.com, Leo Dagum is responsible for all development and related engineering functions in web information retrieval, business intelligence and yield management. Prior to Business.com, Leo was VPE at Rapt Inc., a global provider of profit optimization software with Fortune 500 customers across multiple industry verticals. At Rapt, he successfully drove major new product initiatives and introduced new optimization and analytics technologies into Rapt's flagship product while also transforming engineering development from a traditional Waterfall model to an Agile methodology.

Prior to Rapt, Leo held management and research positions at Silicon Graphics and NASA Ames Research Center. He received his Ph.D. in Aeronautics and Astronautics from Stanford University and B.S. in Engineering Physics from Queen's University, Kingston. Leo enjoys surfing, backpacking, and traveling with his wife and three wonderful daughters.

Sam Hahn

Sam Hahn is VPE at eGain. Before joining eGain, Sam was VPE at Purisma, where he was responsible for all product development activities. Other positions he held include Director of Product Marketing - Architecture and Infrastructure at Siebel Systems, VPE at Sales.com, and co-founder and CTO at DocuMagix. Sam is active in various professional groups in Silicon Valley and is a partner at Sand Hill Angels, a private equity firm. He has a B.S. in Mathematics from Stanford University.

Thomas Hempel

Thomas Hempel has 22 years experience in Management. Currently, Thomas is senior director of Engineering at NetApp, Inc., where he is in charge of Support Automation Products, Infrastructure, Processes, and Information Engineering. He is in charge of all capital planning and engineering labs. His achievements at NetApp include building and making productive six different global but unified organizations, working with the Service organization to create profitable products like Autosupport Premium, and helping create the company's industry leading DITA-compliant information architecture. He has also led the lab organizations in creating world-class energy efficient data centers and is currently leading the virtualization and consolidation across the Engineering organization.

Previously, Thomas worked as VPE at E.piphany where he led the switch to Agile development as well as making the Octane products actually work. He has long been interested in the connection between tools, processes, and productivity, as well as how to make offshore development work. A Stanford graduate, he likes investing, trains, Phil Lesh, and wandering around Shanghai.

Ed Komo

Ed Komo oversees all development and engineering functions of the Jigsaw site and platform. This includes the business intelligence, data warehouse, accounting, and back office reconciliation systems. Ed joined Jigsaw from Hotwire.com where he served as VPE. At Hotwire, Ed oversaw all development and engineering functions of the company's e-commerce site, the business intelligence and data warehouse as well as the back office corporate financial system. His major accomplishments include a complete rebuilding of the Hotwire e-commerce application platform and all related structure and processes to radically increase the scalability and stability of Hotwire e-commerce site.

Prior to Hotwire, Ed served as Chief Architect for 2Logix Corp. Also, at several firms, he held senior engineering and management positions. These include AllBusiness.com, Context Integration, Oracle Corporation, and Honeywell Bull. Ed earned his MBA from the Haas School of Business at UC Berkeley. He also holds a B.S. in Electrical Engineering from the University of Texas at Austin.

Byron S. Lee

Byron is currently Vice President of Engineering at LogLogic Inc, the leader in log management, compliance management and security management solutions, where he leads Development, including the LogLogic Applications, Platform and LogLabs teams. Prior to LogLogic, Byron was Vice President of Engineering at AlphaDetail Inc, where he helped to grow an early stage startup to over $10 million in revenue. Byron has over 25 years of experience, from applied research at the IBM Almaden Research Center, to biotechnology lab automation, internet infrastructures, embedded systems, hardware & virtual appliances and software as a service..

Byron has built, coached, and managed diverse technical professionals into effective multi-disciplinary teams, including Software, Hardware and Firmware Engineers, Web and Flash developers, Usability and

Graphic Artists, Middleware technologists, System & Network Admins, DBAs, Corporate IT, as well as QA, Manufacturing & Technical Operations.

Byron has a bachelor's degree in Electrical Engineering and Computer Science from the University of California at Berkeley and a master's degree in Electrical Engineering from Stanford University. He is happily married and is fortunate they enjoy golf, despite the fact he plays horribly, even on the Nintendo Wii.

Mike Moody

Michael "Mike" Moody is currently VP of Engineering and Support for Jaspersoft, a commercial open source BI company. Prior to JasperSoft, Mike headed CenterBoard's EII product engineering development, QA, and operations. He has built a career around managing complex engineering teams and delivering quality products on time. He brings with him more than 25 years of management experience in the software engineering field.

Prior to CenterBoard, Mike was VP of Engineering Operations at Portal Software. He was responsible for all the company's mainstream product and feature releases, overseeing performance engineering/benchmarking, program management, release engineering, QA, documentation, and custom engineering for strategic accounts. He enjoys hiking and plans to summit all of California's 14k summits.

Jacob A. Taylor

Jacob A. Taylor recently created SugarCRM, one of the world's best CRM applications and platforms for application development. Jacob designed, developed, and led the development of SugarCRM for four years in his role as CTO and Co-Founder. This role continued his streak of developing stable, scalable, high performance, parallel processing, fault tolerant, and enterprise grade software. Sun Microsystems Inc. recently published a benchmark where Jacob's architecture achieved "almost linear scalability" between 900 and 3,200 concurrent users. Jacob pioneered a scalable and intuitive CTI system at E.piphany that leveraged real-time CTI controls in a thin-client browser and scaled to over 10,000 concurrent users. Prior to E.piphany, Jacob helped keep the world safe with the Norton AntiVirus team at Symantec, building an enterprise management console scalable to controlling over 250,000 computers.

Jacob specializes in making complicated systems and algorithms fast, efficient, and easy to understand. Jacob is passionate about designing software that people like to use and find easy to understand. He firmly believes that fast, intuitive, and stable programs will get more users than their competition. Jacob believes that programs should be designed and developed to maximize the benefit they provide to the user. Jacob is also a big proponent of letting outside developers expand software with the same capabilities as internal developers. He has seen how this results in the variety of uses and number of ideas expanding exponentially. Jacob currently holds a US software patent for his innovative row level security model. Jacob earned his BS in Computer Science and Engineering from UCLA and an MS in Artificial Intelligence from UCLA. While planning his next activity, Jacob is spending time with his beautiful wife Yousun and two adorable children Aeryn and Austin. Jacob also enjoys interacting with the world through his blog at http://TheJacobTaylor.blogspot.com and twitter http://twitter.com/thejacobtaylor.

Acronym Decoder

A

AMT – Alternative Minimum Tax
API – Application Programming Interface
ASIC – Application Specific Integrated Circuit
ASP – Application Service Provider

B

BSD – Berkeley System Distribution

C

CAB – Customer Advisory Board
CEO – Chief Executive Officer
CFO – Chief Financial Officer
CIO – Chief Information Officer
CMM – Capability Maturity Model
COP – Community of Practice
COGS – Cost of Goods Sold
CPL – Common Public License
CPP – Customer-partner-program
CRM – Customer Relationship Management
CS – Computer Science
CSPA – Chinese Software Professionals Association
CTO – Chief Technology Officer

D

DBA – Database Administrator
DITA – Darwin Information Typing Architecture

E

EBIT – Earnings Before Interest and Taxes
EMI – Electromagnetic Interference
ETL – Extract, Transform, Load
EVP – Executive Vice-President

F

FCC – Federal Communications Commission
FTE – Full-Time Equivalent

G

GA – General Acceptance
GCOV – GNU Coverage Test Tool
GPL – General Public License
GUI – Graphic User Interface

H

HR – Human Resources

I

I/O – Input/Output
IEEE – Institute of Electrical and Electronics Engineers
IP – Intellectual Property
IPO – Initial Placement Offering
ISO – International Standards Organization
ISV – Independent Software Vendor
IT – Information Technology
ITIL – Information Technology Infrastructure Library

K

KB – Knowledge base

L

LAMP – Linux/Apache/MySQL/PHP
LGPL – Lesser General Public License
LOC – Lines of Code

M

MPL – Mozilla Public License
MRD – Marketing Requirements Document
MSCS – Master of Computer Science
M&A – Mergers and Acquisitions

N

NDA – Non-Disclosure Agreement
NIH – National Institute of Health

O

OEM – Original Equipment Manufacturer
OSS – Open Source Software

P

PCI – Peripheral Component Interconnect
PDF – Portable Document Format
PRD – Product Requirements Document
P/L – Profit/Loss

Q

QA - Quality Assurance

R

RAD – Rapid Application Development
RAID – Redundant Array of Independent Disks
RFID – Radio Frequency Identification
RFP – Request for Proposal
ROI – Return On Investment
RMS – Requirements Management System
RUP – Rational Unified Process
R&D – Research and Development

S

SaaS – Software as a Service
SAP – Systems, Applications, and Products
SCM – Source Code Management
SDK – Software Development Kit
SKU – Stock Keeping Unit
SLA – Service Level Agreement
SOA – Service Oriented Architecture
SQA – Software Quality Assurance
SQL – Structured Query Language
STAF – Software Testing Automation Framework
SVP – Senior Vice-President

T

Tech Pub – Technical Publication
TiE – The Indus Entrepreneurs

U

UI – User Interface
UL – Underwriters Laboratories Inc.

V

VC – Venture Capitalist
VOD – Video on Demand
VoIP – Voice over Internet Protocol

VPE – Vice President of Engineering
VPN – Virtual Private Network

W

WAN – Wide Area Network

X

XSL – Extensible Stylesheet Language
XML – Extensible Markup Language
XP - Extreme Programming

Bibliography

Abdel-Hamid, Tarek and Madnick, Stuart. *Software Project Dynamics: An Integrated Approach.* Englewood Cliffs, NJ: Prentice-Hall Inc., 1991.

Adolph, Steve and Bramble, Paul. *Patterns for Effective Use Cases.* Boston, MA: Addison-Wesley Professional, 2003.

Ambler, Scott. *Agile Modeling: Effective Practices for eXtreme Programming and the Unified Process.* New York, NY: John Wiley & Sons, Inc., 2002.

Answers.com, "Board of Directors," http://www.answers.com/topic/board-of-directors (accessed September 18, 2008).

Augustin, Larry. Weblog. http://lmaugustin.typepad.com/.

Beck, Kent. A Seminar to Bay Partners VC Clients. Apr. 6, 2004

Bittner, Creel, Rothman, King. Marasco. *Dr Dobbs - Requirements Development.* CMP Media LLC, 2007. Retrieved from Nxtbook.

Butcher, David R. "King of the Sky: Boeing Dreamliner vs. Airbus A350 XWB." Industrial NewsRoom. http://news.thomasnet.com/IMT/archives/2006/10/aircr aft_design_king_of_sky_boeing_dreamliner_versus_airb us_a350xwb.html (accessed September 18, 2008).

Cantor, Murray R. *Object-Oriented Project Management with UML.* New York, NY: John Wiley & Sons, Inc., 1998.

Carmichael, Andy and Haywood, Dan. *Better Software Faster.* Upper Saddle River, NJ: Prentice-Hall Inc., 2002.

Chandler, Kreta and Hyatt, Karen. *Customer-Centered Design: A New Approach to Web Usability*. Upper Saddle River, NJ: Prentice-Hall Inc., 2003.

Cockburn, Alistair. *Crystal Clear: A Human-Powered Methodology for Small Teams*. Boston, MA: Addison-Wesley Professional, 2005.

———. *Writing Effective Use Cases*. Boston, MA: Addison-Wesley Professional, 2001.

Cohn, Mike. *Agile Estimating and Planning*. Upper Saddle River, NJ: Prentice-Hall Inc., 2006.

Conway, Kieron. *Software Project Management*. Scottsdale, AZ: The Coriolis Group, 2001.

Denne, Mark and Cleland-Huang, Jane. *Software by Numbers: Low-Risk, High-Return Development*. Santa Clara, CA: Prentice-Hall Inc., 2003.

Hohmann, Luke. *Innovation Games: Creating Breakthrough Products Through Collaborative Play*. Boston, MA: Addison-Wesley Professional, 2006.

Hunt, Andrew and Thomas, David. *The Pragmatic Programmer: From Journeyman to Master*. Boston, MA: Addison-Wesley Professional, 1999.

IBM. "Introduction to the Darwin Information Typing Architecture," http://www.ibm.com/developerworks/xml/library/x-dita1/ (accessed September 30, 2008).

IEEE Engineering Management Society. "EMS Mission," IEEE, http://www.ewh.ieee.org/soc/ems/?menu =1&page=3 (accessed September 18, 2008).

Jezequel, Jean Marc, Train, Michael and Mingins, Christine. *Design Patterns and Contracts*. Boston, MA: Addison-Wesley Professional, 2000.

Kawasaki, Guy. Reality Check: *The Irreverent Guide to Outsmarting, Outmanaging, and Outmarketing Your Competition.* New York, NY: Penguin Group Inc., 2008

Leslie, Mark and Holloway, Charles. *"The Sales Learning Curve."* Harvard Business Review, 2006.

Leffingwell, Dean and Widrig, Don. *Managing Software Requirements: A Unified Approach.* Boston, MA: Addison-Wesley Professional, 2000.

"Manifesto for Agile Software Development," http://agilemanifesto.org/ (accessed Septermber 30, 2008).

Marchesi, Michele and others. *Extreme Programming Perspectives.* Boston, MA: Addison-Wesley Professional, 2003.

McConnell, Steve. *After the Gold Rush: Creating a True Profession of Software Engineering.* Redmond, WA: Microsoft Press, 1999.

Moore, Geoffrey. *Crossing the Chasm: Marketing and Selling High-Tech Products to Mainstream Customers.* HarperBusiness, 1999.

Pezzini, Massimo and Holloway, Charles. *"Trends in Platform Middleware: Disruption Is in Sight."* Gartner Inc., 2007.

Pollice, Gary and others. *Software Development for Small Teams: A RUP-Centric Approach.* Boston, MA: Addison-Wesley Professionals, 2003.

Posner, Barry Z., Kouzes, James M. "Credibility How leaders gain and lose it, why people demand it", San Francisco, CA Jossey-Bass business & management series, 2003

"Principles behind the Agile Manifesto," http://agilemanifesto.org/principles.html (accessed September 30, 2008)

Raymond, Eric S. *The Cathedral & The Bazaar: Musings on Linux and Open Source by an Accidental Revolutionary.* Sebastopol, CA: O'Reilly & Associates, Inc., 2001.

Royce, Walker. *Software Project Management: A Unified Framework.* Boston, MA: Addison-Wesley Professionals, 1998.

Ruping, Andreas. *Agile Documentation.* New York, NY: John Wiley & Sons, Inc., 2003.

Sevin Rosen Funds. "Chief Technology Officer Job Description," http://67.208.32.43/openee/upload/CT 0%20job%20descriptiona.pdf (accessed September 18, 2008).

Sourceforge.net. "Software Testing Automation Framework (STAF)," http://staf.sourceforge.net/index.php (accessed September 30, 2008)

Sullivan, Ed. *Under Pressure and On Time.* Microsoft Press, 2001.

Wikipedia contributors. "Business plan," Wikipedia, The Free Encyclopedia, http://en.wikipedia.org/w/index.php?title=Business_plan&oldid=246471454 (accessed October 26, 2008).

———. "Extreme Programming," Wikipedia, The Free Encyclopedia, http://en.wikipedia.org/w/index.php?title=Extreme_Programming&oldid=247150855 (accessed October 26, 2008)

———. "WAMP," Wikipedia, The Free Encyclopedia, http://en.wikipedia.org/w/index.php?title=WAMP&oldid=240874088 (accessed October 26, 2008).

Working Group on Director Accountability and Board Effectiveness, "A Simple Guide to The Basic Responsibilities of VC-Backed Company Directors," www.mohlernixon.com/Documents/Simple.Guide. *Release.pdf* (accessed September 18, 2008).